ungrieving

Copyright © 2024 by Jennifer Stolpa Flatt
All world rights reserved

No part of this book may be reproduced, stored in a retrieval system, or transmitted in any form or by any means electronic, mechanical, photocopying, recording or otherwise, without the prior consent of the publisher.

Readers are encouraged to go to www.MissionPointPress.com to contact the author, or to contact the publisher about how to buy this book in bulk at a discounted rate.

Published by Mission Point Press
2554 Chandler Rd.
Traverse City, MI 49696
(231) 421-9513
www.MissionPointPress.com

ISBN: 978-1-961302-38-9
Library of Congress Control Number: 2024904067

Printed in the United States of America

un grieving

a memoir of emotional abuse, loss, and relief

JENNIFER STOLPA FLATT

MISSION POINT PRESS

Preface

I grew up in a typical small-town midwestern home in the 1970s and 1980s. My parents struggled financially. My older sister and I argued and made up on a daily—sometimes hourly—basis. We went to church. I had to help clean the house every Saturday, keep my room neat, and help with the dishes. I read books year-round, rode my bike in the summer, and watched *Little House on the Prairie* every week. I learned a little bit about my dad's Polish heritage and almost nothing about my mom's mom who moved to the United States from Norway as a child. I played piano and trumpet, did well in school, and graduated as valedictorian from the Catholic high school I attended.

I also spent my childhood pretending that our family didn't have a darkness that ate away at all of us. I didn't have the words to explain to myself or to others that I was growing up with an emotionally and verbally abusive father. Much later I became aware that this experience made my childhood fairly typical too. I realized that beneath the surface of lots of families there is something we resist naming, behaviors we accept as normal that have long-term consequences for the child, the family, and the next generation. I learned that my dad's struggles with mental health, self-loathing, and doubt, while not universal, are not as rare as we thought they were.

After my dad died of cancer, despite the liberation and relief I felt, something kept drawing me back to memories of him. I was grieving a man I called "Daddy" my entire life, although I did not feel the warm fuzzy connected feeling the nickname might imply. I had heard and read a lot about grieving, especially from a Christian standpoint, because of my dad's work with older adults and their families, but within all the advice he had talked about, all the memoirs and books I picked up, I saw no reflection of my experience and my feelings.

I don't miss him and I feel guilty admitting that.

Sometimes I *do* miss him. And that confuses me.

When I couldn't find a book to guide me, I began to write about my own experiences and complex feelings. I wrote about what connected me and my dad and what he taught me—the Catholicism of my youth, our musical abilities, our love of reading, our belief in women's equality. I wrote about the darker aspects we shared—our depression and our self-hatred. And I wrote about what separated us for four years, including that same Catholicism, a separation that meant my parents missed my wedding and the birth of my first child.

To help me I turned to what might contain hints of his thoughts and feelings: his journals—disjointed computer files, printed-out copies in a drawer, handwritten entries in notebooks; notes in books he'd left behind; random slips of paper with poems he'd begun to write; half-completed musical compositions. And I spoke again and again with my sister and my mom, unraveling and then knitting a truer narrative of our lives together.

Writing this memoir allowed me to let go of *not* grieving his death. Still, I came to recognize that the absence of grief includes pain. I came to accept that his death brought both gain and loss. I know now that I am not the only person who wrestles with this cousin of grieving, this *ungrieving*.

My dad left me a strange legacy: an ongoing, fractured relationship with someone who can't contribute to fixing it. My unbroken and eternal tie to my father still exists, tethering me to the relationship I had with him. I keep working on it. I keep trying to understand.

1

1977 (Age 5): Because I Was Fidgeting in Church

My legs are hot in my white tights. I wiggle back on the pew and look at the big box fan at the front of the church, gently blowing the cloth on the table in the front.

Father LeMay is talking again. I pick up my little wicker basket purse with the green frog on the front and I start to open and close the lid over the handle in the center. Inside is a pretty white handkerchief, in case I have to sneeze.

I lean over to Karen and whisper, "How much longer?" I figure she's eight, so she'll know.

"Quiet," she whispers back to me in a tone that scares me. I can see her eyes get big even though she doesn't look at me. She's staring straight ahead and I think she's watching Father LeMay, but I realize when I follow her eyes that she's watching Daddy.

He's sitting on the organ bench, ready to play the next hymn. The organ is turned to the side so he can see us and the front of St. Andrew's.

I look at my basket and play with the top again. I lean over to my mom and whisper, "How much longer until we sing again?" I know we're almost done because all the grown-ups already walked to the front, and that's almost the end.

"Not much longer," she whispers back. "Quiet now. Sit still." She taps my hand and so I set the basket down.

Suddenly, everyone is standing, so I join them. "Faith of our fathers, living still …" The music floats around me.

As the singing stops and my dad starts to play by himself, I hear a voice behind me say to my mom, "Such adorable little girls."

"Thank you," my mom replies, although she barely turns her head, her eyes on my dad. I turn to look at the woman I don't really recognize.

"What lovely dresses they have on too! Did you make those?"

"I made Jennifer's," she points to me, "but my mother-in-law made Karen's."

"Well, you're both talented! So," the woman says and looks my way, "do you already know how to read? I noticed you follow along in the missalette!"

"No," my mom says before I can say anything. "She just likes to follow along. Makes her feel more a part of things, I think."

"That's wonderful," the woman says. "Have a great week, Marie."

"You too." The woman turns and walks away. She knows my mom's name, but I don't think my mom knows hers. I stand and dance a little in the space between the pews. "Stop that," my mom says. I look behind me as people talk with Father and then leave.

My dad has finished playing now and is packing up his music. "Ready to go, Jim?" He doesn't say anything. We follow him, pausing as he stops briefly to talk to a woman I've seen before in church but don't know.

"Be careful," my mom reminds me as we get to the car that has been in the hot sun. I sit on the old towel covering the seats in the back so I don't feel the heat from the black vinyl. The whole car ride home, my parents say almost nothing. "Beautiful music, Jim," my mom says, but he doesn't respond. I figure he must be so hot he just can't wait to get home.

In the bedroom I share with Karen, she helps me take off my tights and find my shorts. "Why couldn't you sit still in church?" she asks me.

"What do you mean?"

"You were fidgeting and whispering. Couldn't you tell that Daddy was upset?"

1977 (age 5)

"I know he told us last week to behave better. I thought I did ..." my voice trails off as I realize Karen is mad at me. "What's wrong?"

"You know he's yelling at Mom right now, right? It's about us. Mainly about you this week I think."

"What?" I hadn't been listening because my only focus had been on getting changed, but now, from the bedroom next door, I can hear my dad's voice.

"Can't you control the kids? Do you have any idea how it looks to the community that as a teacher, I can't get my kids to behave in church?"

"Jim, I thought they were both pretty good today."

"So I guess I just imagined everything! Jennifer was moving around and whispering to you and playing with her purse. If she can't sit still, she can't have anything there. And you need to not respond to her when she whispers to you."

"I was telling her to sit." My mom's voice is quiet. "I will try next week. I'll talk to her this week and get her to understand."

"Well, if it's not too much to ask! I don't want to put you out."

"Jim, I said I will try."

"And you couldn't even be bothered to listen to my music at the end. Too busy talking to the woman behind you."

"She was complimenting me ... on the girls' dresses. I didn't want to seem rude."

"To her maybe. What about me?"

"I'm sorry."

I don't hear anything for a little bit. "I'll go make brunch then," I hear my mom say.

"You need to apologize," Karen hisses at me as we hear Mom walk down the hallway to the kitchen.

"What?" I hate apologizing. I do it a lot so I should be good at it, but sometimes I don't know what to say sorry for. And if I don't have a thing to say sorry for, Daddy gets even more angry.

"Just say you're sorry you were fidgeting at church. Then go say sorry to Mom." Karen is more urgent now, pushing me towards the door.

"But Mom isn't mad. Didn't you hear her?"

"But you're the reason Daddy yelled at her, so you feel bad about that, right?" Karen was right. I did feel icky about that. I always felt icky when Daddy yelled at Mom for what I did.

"So can I go tell Mom I'll try harder next week—instead of just saying I'm sorry?"

"That's fine. Just say it soon to Daddy. He's still in their bedroom I think."

I walk out of our bedroom and turn to the left. Their door is open, and I can see Daddy stretched out on the bed, hands folded across his stomach, eyes closed.

I walk quietly inside, just past the door, and whisper, "Daddy?"

"Hmm?" he says without opening his eyes.

"I'm sorry for fidgeting at church."

"You need to pay attention."

"I'll try harder." I want to explain to him that I already try really hard and that it just feels so hot and so long and so boring, but I don't. I can hear Karen's voice in my head giving me a warning—"just say sorry for fidgeting and that's it."

I wait a moment longer, hoping that he'll say something like "It's OK" or "I forgive you." He doesn't, but I wasn't really expecting it. I turn and walk down the hall to my mom. She's already at the stove, apron on, frying bacon.

"I'm sorry, Mom, for fidgeting in church. I'll try harder next week. I promise."

"Hmm?" she says, turning to look at me, tongs in one hand and the handle of the frying pan in the other. "That's OK, Jennifer. I know it's hard." Her voice isn't as soft as it sometimes is. I think she looks sad.

"Can I help?" I ask.

"Why don't you set the table."

1977 (age 5)

I'm happy to have this thing to do, this way to pay her back, to make up for what I did and how she paid the price. I wonder if Daddy will be happier by the time we eat. If he is, I'm going to talk about the cinnamon rolls my mom made. If not, I will try to be quiet.

2

Flesh and Blood

My dad hated his body. He talked about it with disgust at times and wrote about it in his journals with disdain and disappointment. I don't think he ever felt comfortable in his own skin. I know I never felt comfortable around him. I disliked having to hug or kiss him. I remember having to sit squished in between him and some other adult in the front seat of our car sometimes and I hated being that close to him. It felt like an invasion of my space, of my privacy. His height and weight always intimidated me, and I preferred most times not to be in his presence.

So it made no sense to me that the day after he died, I felt a deep loss as I realized I would never see him again. The loss was more complex than I anticipated. The day after my dad died, people all around me got up and prepared for the day's routine. At tables next to us in the hotel where my husband, Jason, our kids, Anton and Edward, and I were staying, business travelers ate breakfast before heading off to meetings and work. As we drove to my mom and dad's house, people turned into the nearby mall parking lot to go shopping. People waited tables at the dozens of restaurants within a mile or so of where we ate lunch at the brown oval table where I'd eaten so many meals, back when it was in my childhood home. People had conversations about food and work and kids and life.

So did we. My dad's sister, Jo Ann, my mom, Jason, my kids, and I spent the day at my parents' house just outside St. Cloud, Minnesota.

My sister, Karen, and her husband, Mike, were on their way from Wisconsin to join us. Jo Ann, a first-grade teacher, played with five-year-old Anton on the living room floor as the sun shone in on them. She read him books and tossed rolled up balls of paper back and forth, using her talents to create games out of everyday objects. "Watch this, Jo Ann!" I heard over and over again, as Anton proudly demonstrated his ability to play with a toy or read a word. "Wow!" or "Cool!" Jo Ann said in praise.

Jason put Edward, not yet two, down for an afternoon nap in my parents' room and then came to give me a hug. We settled on the beige and gray couch of my teenage years, sunken in spots of consistent use. I put my hand in his and looked over at my mom. She rested in her recliner, exhausted from the months leading up to this moment. "What should we do for dinner?" she asked at one point.

"Apple dippers!" was Anton's enthusiastic reply, which meant he wanted a fast-food meal that included a bag of apples with caramel sauce.

I couldn't bring myself to think about food at that moment as I looked over at my dad's large brown recliner, empty, a visible outline of where his body had molded and shaped it over time. From the table next to it, I picked up one of the pencils with colorful triangular rubber grips added to help my dad's arthritic fingers write. I started to push around the scattered scraps of paper, Christian devotionals, and books that cluttered the small table, but stopped, not knowing how to organize them, not wanting to disturb the way he had left them.

Restless, I got up and wandered to the honey-brown piano I'd heard him play so many times, an instrument he had admitted recently was not worth having fixed up—it wasn't the quality he had wanted but rather what he had been able to afford. I gently played a few keys towards the top. "It's out of tune," my mom said. "Your dad hadn't played it since last summer. His fingers didn't work the way he needed them to anymore … the arthritis and, I don't know, maybe something with the chemotherapy too."

I moved away and began to look over the titles of the dozens of CDs of opera, symphony, and some jazz on bookcase shelves, the dust covering them a reminder of how little attention had been paid to cleaning in the past several months. In my mind, I heard the music of Chopin, Liszt, George Winston, or Bach as I read the names on the spines of the CDs.

As I wandered from room to room, I saw crosses, crucifixes, and religious statues and images. Each one made me feel a twinge of discomfort; they reminded me of sermons my dad had preached at us about being better and more loving people, even as he had put us down, criticized us, or belittled our ideas. The objects' presence felt like hypocrisy or a talisman of some kind, strategically placed to try to overcome the negative energy.

Near the kitchen, I pondered the photo collage he had put together a few years before. My older son Anton appeared as a toddler amid the pictures—no baby picture present since he was born during my four-year estrangement from my parents. No engagement or wedding photos of me or my sister were in the collection either. There was at least one photo of my parents near a waterfall from a day where I thought I remembered all four of us being miserable because my dad was angry about something. In the photo, his smile appears strained, at least to me, and my mom's eyes look preoccupied.

All afternoon, inside and outside of that house, everybody acted almost as if it were a normal day. But I was also looking at every familiar item around me in a new way and I longed to talk about our new reality. There we sat, surrounded by memories of a living being who was no longer living. Surrounded by reminders of his physical presence, I wanted to talk about his sudden and permanent absence. I wanted to point to the objects and say, "These pens and pencils, do you realize he will never write anything again? These albums and CDs of music, do you realize he will never hear anything again? Do you realize that his ears can't hear? His body is useless now. What does that mean? What do we do now?"

My mom talked about heaven. "Maybe your dad is playing a game of cards with Grandma and Grandpa right now," she speculated.

"I don't know," I replied. "I don't know what heaven is like."

"Your grandma would really like that," my mom added. "She used to love playing cards with us when we would come over."

"But I remember Daddy complaining about having to play cards sometimes, right?"

"Well, sure. But we had good times too." My mom looked out the sliding glass doors to her left and retreated to memories.

I didn't share where my mind went next because it contradicted the happy and clear-cut image my mom gave us. Here is my puzzle: Growing up I was told that in heaven everyone could do whatever brought them joy. My grandma really enjoyed playing cards, so if she wants to play cards with my dad in heaven and my dad doesn't want to do it, who "wins"? After all, what's heaven for her might be hell for him. Or would it not be hell anymore because he would know he had all eternity, so why not waste a little time on a game he doesn't love? Or does he now love it because he can see how much joy it brings my grandmother? But wouldn't it bring her less joy if she now knows he doesn't really love it? Couldn't that sort of "knowing-it-all" heaven lead to unresolvable complexities and thus result in a heaven with no happy actions at all?

I didn't know what my dad was doing or if there was anything like "doing" after death, and it wasn't helping me deal with the ache in my gut to picture him happily or even semi-happily playing a game of cards with my grandmother. I wasn't in heaven. I was here, and he wasn't.

As the day went on, people outside kept moving, acting as if nothing momentous had occurred. And of course it hadn't—to them. Inside, people kept moving, acting as if nothing momentous had occurred. And of course it had. Maybe most of us just didn't know it yet.

Inside that house, a yawning ache, a gaping hole inside of me grew and grew. It was as if every few minutes I could briefly feel the total depths of nothingness. I would look over at his empty chair in disbelief.

What did it mean that he would never again sit there? Edward would ask for Grandpa, or Anton would say something about going back to the hospice where he had last seen Grandpa, and I would have to try to explain that he wasn't there any longer.

The ache of loneliness I felt grew and hardened into anger. Had I been able to talk about him, to cry about him, to feel a loss in those moments, perhaps it might have softened. But we didn't talk about him. We didn't cry over him. We didn't talk about our loss. I didn't really know how to start the conversation either, but I would have preferred to sit quietly at least until one of us figured out a way to begin to say something that reflected the complex emotions inside. I wanted to retell what had happened the previous day. I wanted to say that I was relieved he was gone and ask if others felt the same. I wanted to say how angry I was about everything he'd never been for me. All my feelings seemed out of place, so I stayed trapped with my grief alone.

In the early evening, my sister and her husband arrived. My parents' small home grew smaller. The open-concept living room, dining space, and kitchen allowed no space to hide. My parents' bedroom and bathroom were off limits in my mind, in part because they still held so many of his personal items. I would cross that border in the coming months as I helped my mom sort through his things, but I wasn't ready yet. The tiny second bedroom was my dad's office—a cluttered mess of two electronic keyboards, a desktop computer, hundreds of computer disks and CDs, papers and files everywhere, some in drawers, others stacked on top of each other, some on the floor. This room that was barely big enough to be called a bedroom was virtually inaccessible.

There was no room for me. I wandered from person to person, but there was no space for my grief either. Eventually, my husband, the kids, and I went back to our hotel. Alone with Jason in our room, I began to lose my façade of calm. In a shaky voice, I told him, "I need to talk to my sister. I need to *talk*. I know I can talk to you, but it's not the same. I need Karen." Jason understood, and despite the late hour, he told me to go.

Karen understood too. I showed up at her door around 11:00, and she greeted me with a cheerful, surprised "Hey!" I said, "I need to talk to you." She nodded. Her face relaxed into sympathy and understanding. "Let me tell Mike."

Over the next three hours, sitting in the darkened breakfast room downstairs in the hotel, she listened. I told her every detail of his death the day before. I told her how angry I had become that no one wanted to talk about him today. "Why won't anyone acknowledge how awful this feels? How can we grieve if we act like he's not gone—or if we just spend time talking about how happy *he* is in heaven? He stopped breathing, right in front of us. Why doesn't anyone want to talk about that?"

She listened without judgment, helping me begin to mold my anger into something more pliable, something I could shape and consider from multiple angles. "But do you really miss him?" she asked me. "Don't you remember how horrible he was to be around? Don't you remember how mean he was? Don't you remember just a couple of months ago when he pitched a tantrum because he didn't like something we said? Don't you think you miss what you never had?"

"Maybe. But maybe I also miss his presence. How messed up is that?" I expressed my multitude of regrets over what my relationship with him had not been, could not be, and now never would be. I wanted to go back in time and say more of what I needed to say. I wanted to hear him say, "I'm proud of you," or, "I love you," one more time. I wanted to go back in time and erase all the horrible things he had said to me over the years. I wanted a normal relationship, not this legacy of pain and damage.

"How do I go on?" I asked. "How do I deal with this aching sense of loss and this anger over how awful he was too? How is it fair that I have both? How am I supposed to grieve him when I feel like I didn't even know him all that well? Who am I missing?"

That night, I told my sister the story of my dad's last moments. Over the next several weeks, I would tell that story several times, almost eagerly, to people who would listen and whom I trusted. I told it to my husband and a few close friends. I would think about it multiple times each day. I would linger in the moment, as if watching myself in a movie. I replay the scenes in my mind to help distance myself from it, to preserve it, to understand it better.

The camera first shows Jason and my kids out for a drive. They are in search of an antique store Jason wants to visit. The camera returns to Quiet Oaks Hospice. The four of us—my mom, my dad's sister Jo Ann, my parents' friend from Bible study, and I—are seated in a circle at the foot of my dad's bed. The midafternoon sun brightens my dad's room, quiet classical music plays on the CD player next to his bed, and outside my dad's window are signs of spring—green grass, budding flowers, birds returning.

In a moment, my parents' friend and I turn towards my dad's bed, and I say, "That seemed like a different sort of breath, yes?" She nods. She is the first to move to my dad's side, but I quickly follow.

The camera zooms in. There, the grieving daughter stands by his bedside, grasps his now limp, impossibly soft hand, and calls to her mother. The camera pans to show the other loved ones gathering around his bed. The wife asks for the nurse to be called. The daughter reminds her of the do-not-resuscitate choice made months earlier. Everyone gathers closer, waiting for another breath that never comes. The daughter, believing his spirit may still be on the verge of leaving his body, says, "I love you, Daddy," one last time through tears streaming down her face.

She stands. Her mother sobs a few times. Arms extend for hugs around the bed as the dead man's sister receives and gives solace to the dead man's wife and daughter and friend. The daughter offers to say a prayer of thanksgiving for the life that has now ended. Her spoken words echo those she has heard her father say over other deaths, even over the deathbed of his own mother. The scene ends. The mourners slowly pull away from the bed, no one keeping them there any longer.

Even after the nurses came and spoke soothing words to us, I didn't want to leave. We had things to do at the beautiful hospice there. My husband was going to finish the puzzle in the basement, a puzzle some other grieving family had started and left undone because their reason for being there had gone away too. I was going to savor another delicious meal prepared by the staff there. I was going to wander through the corridors and look at the gentle artwork on the walls. I was going to shush my children. I had already, in just a few days, settled into a routine. But that day we had to leave, at least physically.

My spiritual self said that Daddy had left already, but it didn't feel that way. We walked out the front door saying goodbye to the staff and volunteers. They were allowed to stay behind. I felt as if I were deserting my father. He was still in there, lying on the bed. Part of me was still standing there next to him. Part of me was hearing our shoes crunch the gravel of the driveway. The stands of trees surrounding the building, the sky above us, the fresh air filling our lungs beckoned—"Stay here, where it's beautiful and peaceful." We got in our cars. We slammed the doors, closing off the natural world outside, and left.

But somehow, even years later, I am still there. My mom is still holding my dad's hand and sitting in a chair by the bed. I am still holding my dad's other hand. I am still saying, "I love you, Daddy." He is still hearing me. I stand there waiting for the next breath, and there is nothing.

※

A few days before he died, I noticed my dad's toenails were incredibly long. "Why isn't the staff caring for him?" I thought. "He's going to scratch his legs! Those scratches will only get worse and lead to other problems." Thankfully, before I opened my mouth to voice these thoughts, I realized that his body was soon not going to matter.

In a single moment, in the absence of a next breath, it all ended—his body's ability to form and express ideas, to think new thoughts, to fulfill new dreams, to add new knowledge, to function and move, to breathe and digest food, and yes, even to grow toenails. I held the box that held my dad's ashes, so I know where his body went after his death. I know how light that box felt, how little physical effort it took to lift and carry my father, a task made impossible in life by the six inches and hundred pounds he had on me. My sister and I both carried him at his funeral. In movies sometimes people throw themselves on caskets as they leave the church, not wanting to let go of the person inside whom they loved so much, whom they knew so well. Part of me didn't want to give up the box with the ashes, but inside there wasn't the body I had known. The dust inside was beyond my comprehension.

Sometimes I picture my dad's body entering a fiery cavern to be burned. I watch the flames tickle the arms I had seen lift, carry, write, and play music, which were now lying still at his sides. I see the fire surround him and then, inevitably, consume his flesh. I see his face still and stern. The thought of my own body being burned after death, my remaining bones pulverized into dust, fills me with horror. I can hear him now telling me, "That's as it should be. You are younger and alive and want to continue to live. You *should* be filled with horror at the thought of losing your body. I was dying. I had come to see my body differently."

I'm not entirely sure why I picture his cremation. It's awful and I hate it. I hold on tightly to memories of his dying breath as well, how his lips fell open after death, as if air would now come and go without the efforts of his body. As much as I was mystified by where his spirit went, I was just as fascinated by the loss of his physical body, the often-foreboding presence that dominated my life. I tell myself to focus on the spirit, to remember that the physical is just a shell, not worth my further consideration. I don't know if I'm right or not.

For a long time, I thought I was grieving wrong, focused not on what a true Christian ought to focus on—the afterlife of the spirit with the divine—but instead on the loss of his physical presence on earth. And why would I mourn the loss of a voice that had yelled and hurled insults, feet that had stomped at me in anger, a petulant smile set in mockery of me?

But it is the physical manifestation of my father that I interacted with my entire life. It was the face he gave to the world, the outer essence that people came to associate with the inner self that was Jim. It was the body he battled with over weight issues, the toes whose bumps made him embarrassed to ever be seen without socks, the five-foot-eleven-inch frame that hadn't shrunk much when he died at age 70, the form that aged and ached and creaked, the incarnation of self that he hated for its inability to play the sports and use the hammers and saws his father believed made you a man.

Perhaps because of these experiences, I think my dad knew how much a part of the self the body truly is. I know he looked for confirmation of that theory in his religious studies. I remember him talking about the biblical story of Jesus and the hemorrhaging woman, who has been cast out from society because her body didn't conform to strict Jewish law. She is stuck in a state of being ceremonially unclean because of her constant menstruation. When she touches Jesus's cloak, believing she'll be healed (which she is), what does she imagine that healing will look like? My dad reminded me that it's a parable about *spiritual* wholeness, but he also said that Jesus the feminist knew that women who were marginalized by his society couldn't be brought more fully into society unless their physical bodies were viewed differently.

The parable contains this hidden truth: the body matters. It is a part of who we are. Healing her hemorrhaging was not a denial of the physical. It was a recognition of the integrated value of the physical. It's also a recognition that like our own society, the one in which Jesus lived and worked valued a purity and perfection of the (masculine) body over all else. My dad knew full well that state of purity and perfection isn't possible, but I think he spent far too much time in his life hating the shell he had been given, seeing it as weak and wrong, seeing his use of it as wrong as well. Part of me wishes Jesus hadn't healed the woman but instead had turned and healed the society by making them see that her bleeding wasn't something to be corrected, but something that simply was. "Stop treating her differently because her body acts differently!" he could have yelled. He could have become angry, as he does elsewhere, and told people that yes, the body matters, but not in the way you think it does.

As I linger at my dad's bedside in my mind, as I remember how he looked as he ate the last meal I had with him, or as I ponder his body entering the cremation chamber, I consider again and again the part of my dad's essence that was not just contained within but *was* his physical body. What was it like to spend a lifetime feeling as if your body didn't match what others wanted it to be? If he could have touched Jesus's cloak and been healed, what would that have meant for him? Instead of actual physical change, would it have meant instead internal and societal acceptance of his softness, his weakness, the ways he wasn't the manly man I think he thought he should have been? I wonder what that sense of wholeness would have meant for him—for all of us around him. I wonder if I can learn from him in time to value my own wrinkles, my strange birthmarks, my aging body. What could it mean for those around me if I could touch Jesus's cloak and be healed—not transformed to be young, but healed, complete, full, and united in a way that surpasses concepts of the mind-body duality, that embraces the value and importance of our physical essence as much as it calls upon us to focus on our spiritual essence?

After my dad died, I looked for him in his books and found only fragments of his ideas. I looked for him in his music collections and found only his interests and a limited history. I looked for him in his journals and found tantalizing tendrils of emotion but not a full person. I looked for him on his computer and found papers he wrote for school that show a narrow slice of his mind. All the ephemera he left behind are like wispy smoke rising from his cremated remains—not tangible, not long for this world, not enough. To more fully comprehend him, I return to pictures, images, sounds, and my experience with who he was as an embodied spirit.

I strive to hold on to a sense of a vital part of him: his walk, the way he sat, the way he shook hands with people. I remember laughter, a product of the physical body. When my dad was really enjoying a moment, which wasn't often, he would throw back his head, and his laugh would start loud, almost an eruption of sound, then go soft, with surprising barks of loud noise again and again.

I listen. I look at pictures. I watch videos. My kids both have recordable storybooks that my parents made about a year before my dad died. They don't remember my dad, so when they were young enough for storybooks, they didn't often ask for the books. I wanted them to create memories of him—to have a sense of his self—so occasionally I was the one who said, "Let's listen to Grandma and Grandpa's book." As I sat with one child on either side of me, I heard my dad's voice say lines like "I love you more and more," and part of me was transported back in time, hearing those words said to me. My dad is gone. I held the box with his ashes. Yet his voice still speaks. It sounds like him. It *is* him.

If I hope to understand the inner self that was my dad, I must try to come to terms with the shell that lived, grew, changed, died, and was destroyed. I must try to come to terms with the physical self that repulsed him and that kept me away. As I replay the movie of his last moments, I search for a way to understand what I left behind in Quiet Oaks Hospice, what was put into the cremation fires, and what is no longer here.

I have gone with my mom and my kids to visit the spot where my dad's ashes are. Part of that choice is the tradition in which I was raised—you visit burial sites of family members. I also love cemeteries; they're peaceful, reflective reminders to cherish the days we have together. They tell a story of unity even when I know that the lived experience of their inhabitants was not always united or pretty. I remind myself that under those tombstones and behind those plaques are families flawed like my own, fathers who couldn't accept themselves and daughters who suffered the collateral damage of that self-directed anger.

I go to visit my dad's ashes because I still believe a part of my dad is in that box. And I don't think that makes me a bad Christian. Those fragments and ashes were once his bones and flesh that created the voice I hear in recordings. Those cremains were once his skin and muscle that I see reflected in photos. That physical presence was a part of him. In going to visit his ashes, I pay my respects to the importance of the physical body as a part of our individual essence.

I look out over the lake below the cemetery, surrounded by tall, strong trees. I feel the breeze and the warmth of the sun. I hear the call of cicadas, June bugs, and birds. In the peaceful calm, in my children running around or sleeping in the car, in my mom's tears and my own, in my awareness that someday her ashes will be there too, in the breeze and birdsong, I find a wisp and an echo of my dad.

3

1978 (Age 6): Because We Didn't Practice

Daddy's at church practicing organ, so Mom, Karen, and I roam the house freely. Karen and I have set up a fort in the living room with some help from my mom, stretching blankets over and across our TV trays, the ones with the nature scenes on them, two with bright green trees and two with autumn oranges. We use the heavy tan volumes of our encyclopedia set to hold the blankets and big towels in place.

Inside the winding tunnel, Karen and I are busy setting up house, putting in pillows and a few favorite stuffed animals, some scratch paper my dad brought home from work, the purple mimeographed side leaking through but still leaving some blank space for us. The heavy out-of-commission black rotary telephone we play with sits in the center of our tunnel house. "That's the hallway phone," Karen declares.

A blanket slips down, and Karen blames me: "You pulled it down! You have to be more careful!"

"No, you did it!"

"Girls." My mom conveys irritation and a warning in one word. Karen glowers at me but retreats to the other end of the tent tunnel. A while later, I ask if she wants to play school inside.

"No," she says, bored with our construction. Another blanket has fallen, blocking the hallway phone from the end.

"Let's ask Mom to put on the stereo!" I suggest, and I know Karen knows exactly which record I mean. "Mom!" I holler through the blankets. "Mom! Can you put on the horse music?"

I exit the tunnel and watch my mom move to the huge stereo on the far wall of the living room. I'm taller than the stereo, but it stretches forever across the wall, its two speakers hidden behind wood lattice and soft, fuzzy fabric I get yelled at if I touch. In the middle on the top is the wooden cover she has to lift in order to get at the record player inside. She pulls out one of the albums from the cavernous storage inside the stereo box, and I try to sound out the words on the cover.

"Aaron Copland's *Rodeo*," she says, helping me.

"Put on the dancing one, Mom."

"You mean 'Hoe Down,' I think." She looks at the back to find the right spot, then gently places the needle among all the mysterious black grooves to find the music we want.

As the first notes sound, Karen and I cry, "Yes! This one!" My mom returns to her work in the kitchen, and Karen and I mount our imaginary horses to dance around the room. I gallop and trot around our TV tray tent structure, not caring anymore as I bump blankets and they fall. I stop abruptly at the other end of the living room in front of the open glass door that leads into my dad's study with its book-lined shelves behind his desk. I don't enter. I turn around and hop and skip back down to the other end of the room. The floor shakes as Karen and I ride around the living room.

"Your dad's coming," my mom calls. She has been on the lookout as usual, trying to make sure she sees his car coming down the street so we have time to fix things. The music stops—first inside of me and then outside, as my mom comes in to stop the record. Karen and I turn to the tent tunnel and begin to pull off blankets, put away encyclopedia volumes, and fold up TV trays. In a series of well-rehearsed, rapid motions, we restore order to the living room, erasing signs of play.

As the front door opens and we hear my dad greet my mom, Karen rushes to sit at the piano, open her book, and begin to play. Lessons!

My stomach tightens. We should have been practicing instead of playing, I know.

I slip off down the hallway to our bedroom, unnoticed for now. I hear my dad and mom talking briefly in the kitchen and hear my dad's voice get louder as he talks about some man at church and his comments about the music. I also hear Karen running through her song, and I know the one note she keeps hitting is wrong. I know she's supposed to hit a black key instead of a white one. The whole song sounds off the way she plays it—not the way Daddy played it for her last week at the end of her lesson.

"Karen, I don't think you practiced this week, did you?" my dad says. I can hear him from where I sit on the floor with my doll Jennie. Her dark brown hair looks beautiful with her navy-blue dress. I lean her against the leg of my bed. I take a small brush and pretend to fix her hair. Jennie smiles at me.

"Yes, I did! I practiced every day!" I can hear the tears in my sister's voice.

"Here, let me play it for you again, so you can hear how it's supposed to sound."

"That won't help. I know how it's supposed to go, but I can't get it to sound like that no matter how much I practice."

"Well, you're obviously not practicing the right way," my dad says to her. My stomach churns again. I think back to hearing Karen practice the night before while my dad mowed the lawn. She played the song over and over, hitting the white key instead of the black key. She would start fast and then slow down when it got hard. I remember she smashed the keys once in frustration.

"Play the left hand alone, then the right hand alone, then the two hands together," I hear my dad say. He's told us that so many times. It makes sense to me to start slowly and learn from there, like how I'm learning to ride my bike with the training wheels on first, but on the piano there's nothing to stop me from falling, nothing to hide my errors. I play the left hand alone perfectly. I play the right hand alone perfectly. But when I come to play them together, my mind whirls.

At one point, my right hand is supposed to move down while my left hand moves up. How can I tell my right hand to go in one direction while my left hand goes in the other?

I hear Karen's piece in parts now, the lower notes first as my dad says, "Steady tempo! Don't rush when it gets easy." Then I hear the melody alone. "OK, now try putting them together, but go slowly."

The first few measures go well, but then Karen hits that same wrong note again, and I hear her smash a bunch of keys at once. "I can't do it," she says through tears. "I'm sorry."

"You need to practice more! And don't hit the piano keys that way!"

"I don't care!" Karen yells. "I'll never learn this stupid piece! I hate it! I want to learn one of the songs at the end of the book. They're more fun."

"You must learn the basics before you jump ahead. But I suppose I don't know anything, do I? I'm just the music teacher. What would I know?"

"I hate piano! I'll never learn it. I'll never be able to play like you can!"

"Not with that attitude you won't! You have to practice exactly the way I tell you. This is pointless. It's pointless to have a lesson on Saturday when you don't practice during the week. This is a waste of my time."

"I'm sorry, Daddy," Karen says with a sob. "I'll try harder. I'll practice more often. I promise." I hear her sniff several times, and then I hear the left hand start slowly again by itself.

I hum the tune to myself as I brush Jennie's hair. I know I haven't practiced enough either. Maybe I can get him to skip my lesson today. Maybe I can tell him I didn't practice, even though I did. I know I'm not ready. Otherwise, I know what will happen when it's my turn. I'll settle on the dark blue towel that covers the bench to protect its wood from the sweat on our legs. I will close Karen's piano book and open my own. My legs will swing beneath me. "Keep your legs still," my dad will say.

1978 (age 6)

I will put my fingers on the keys. "Bend your fingers," my dad will say. I will look at the numbers written to match the fingers I am to move. Which finger is number two on my left hand again? Does the numbering start from my pinkie or my thumb? I will hang my head and let my hands fall in my lap. My legs will start to swing again beneath the bench. "Sit still," my dad will say.

I imagine what it would be like to play perfectly at my lessons every Saturday. When I do, the sticker that adorns the page looks so beautiful. I want more of them. I want my dad to say, "Good! Now you're ready for …" and play for me a real piece of music, not just exercises. I want to hear him say, "You're ready for this much more difficult piece, one I've played before." I want him to smile at me, to tell my mom at dinner afterwards what a good student I'm becoming, how well I play the piano.

"Your turn," Karen's voice interrupts my fantasy. Her head hangs low, her shoulders slumped, and I can see the tears still in her eyes and on her cheeks. I hop up and head down the hallway.

"Daddy," I say quietly as I walk into the living room. "I'm sorry. I didn't practice enough. I'm not ready for my lesson."

He's sitting at the piano, his head turned to face me. His lips twitch in and out like they do when he's angry. His fingers drum a steady beat along the small wood rail that holds up the music. "Fine," he says, with his face already turned back to the piano. "Next week." I turn and walk back to the bedroom I share with Karen. She's lying on the floor between our beds, and she looks up at me as I come in.

"Figures. You don't have to have one, do you?"

"No." I know she's angry, and I don't blame her. "I'm sorry."

"It doesn't matter." She picks up Audrey, her doll with the red hair, and begins to fiddle with her dress. Then she drops her and closes her eyes, squeezing out the remaining tears of anger, frustration, disappointment at the interruption of our morning dance.

From down the hall, I hear my dad playing the piano now. In my mind I can see he has opened one of the tall, dark green books. I've looked inside at all the notes he plays at once, the overwhelming mystery of it. I hear the fluid motion up and down the keys punctuated by crashing chords. It makes me think of waves crashing on the shore, going in and out, smashing against rocks. I danced to that image once as he played, but he told me it was wrong to do that—to make the music seem less important and serious. Now he pauses to repeat a section. He must have heard a mistake. All I hear is perfection.

4

Music Lessons

When we began to plan my dad's funeral, I decided I wanted to play something on the pipe organ as a prelude. My dad had taught me how to play organ when I was a teenager, and I had played off and on for church services ever since. I wanted to honor that part of our connection.

I chose two pieces to play before the funeral Mass began. First, I played a miniature my dad had composed and given to me while he was still alive. I also chose to play a piece by Jean Langlais. Like much nineteenth- and twentieth-century French organ music, the Langlais piece is "weird" by many people's standards, but my dad taught me that while people in the pews want to hear Bach, Handel, and hymn tunes, it's our job as musicians to push their boundaries and let their spirits explore some atonal, decentered music sometimes.

The day of his funeral, we arrived in the downstairs chapel at the Cathedral in St. Cloud before anyone else. I saw the pipe organ for the first time, set against one side of the pleasant well-lit center area that held pews and the altar, marking one border of the shadowy dark aisles along the sides. It was an instrument I'd never played before and one so old it's on the national historic register. I tried to turn it on to run through the prelude pieces, but although I've played on numerous pipe and electric organs in my lifetime, I couldn't figure out how to turn it on, to let the air flow through the pipes. We waited until the church's regular organist arrived.

That meant I sat down at the organ for the first time just moments before the funeral service. The shadows surrounding the worship space, the strangeness of the pedal board and keyboard before me, the realization that I was playing for my dad's funeral, and the nerves I always feel when I play overwhelmed me. I didn't know if I wanted to do this after all. When I play, I focus far too much on the people listening. I find my mind flitting to one or another of them to imagine how they might notice mistakes or critique my performance. Almost overcome by nerves, I lowered my head and thought of my dad, of his performance anxiety late in life, of our shared nervousness. I whispered, "OK, Daddy, here we go."

The miniature from my dad begins in a simple and straightforward way, a mournful melodic phrase played alone as single notes. My fingers lingered over each note, and I felt the echo in the emptiness of my chest. Then the left hand enters and overlaps at times with the melody. The notes meander almost aimlessly as they explore a theme rather than stating one directly. He seems to be considering some of the musical paths we might take as listeners, and as I played, I thought about the strange journey his life had taken. Dissonance arises from time to time in the music, and there isn't much resolution, which made me realize what an apt analogy it was for our complex relationship. I communed briefly with my dad's spirit in his composition.

Then I set aside the taped-together sheets of paper on which my dad's music is printed and opened the orange cover of the Langlais book. The slow chords at the beginning slowed my own breathing. I rested in the sadness of the discord, allowing the minor resolutions to save me from the collapse of tears. Amidst the complex harmonies and moments of deep mystery, the tiny resolutions felt like a deep sigh of relief. I lingered on the second-to-last chord the way my dad had taught me. The suspense built, and the final resolution absolved me.

I slid off the wooden bench and became aware again of the people milling about. The Mass began. A violinist played the hymns we had selected. I tried to sing the words that meant so much to me but cried so hard I couldn't. My children, two and five years old, played and colored at my feet.

A few months later, I was helping my mom sort through my dad's extensive collection of organ and piano music. I would open each piece, look at it briefly, and if I thought there was ever a prayer I'd be able to play it, I'd take it. Otherwise, my mom was giving it to the organist from their church, a man who had practiced his scales more as a youngster than I did and far surpassed my abilities.

After numerous days working at it, I thought we were just about done going through all his music. Then my mom mentioned that my dad's briefcase contained the music he'd been using in the last few months he had played organ at a few local churches. I brought the briefcase back to where my mom sat in her living room. At first, I struggled to open the familiar hard-covered black briefcase, and the two of us worked together to figure out the locking mechanism. When it finally popped open, I saw my dad's copy of the orange Langlais book.

I felt as if I were existing in two moments at once. I was with him as he put this book inside his briefcase in some small church somewhere. I remembered the care with which he always treated his music. I heard the snaps of the briefcase I'd always known him to use as he closed it, the scrape as its hard surface slid across the wooden organ bench to be held at his side. I sensed his mixed emotions—frustration at mistakes he'd made, the peace of spiritual connection, sadness over his cancer.

Back in his living room I held some of the last music he ever performed. I looked up at the ceiling and breathed deeply, trying to make the tears roll back inside my eyes. How had I known to select that book, that piece for my dad's funeral? I shook my head in disbelief and tried to explain to my mom what felt like so much more than a coincidence, what felt like the kind of connection that transcends time. In the final year of his life, this piece of music had spoken to his emotions—to his sense of impending loss. In the first moments of my grief for him, I had thought of this same piece of music. Its haunting complexities and final resolution encapsulated not just my emotions, but his. Music was a language through which I understood my father.

※

On one of my childhood birthdays, I remember awakening to hear music floating down the hallway—my dad playing variations on "Happy Birthday" on the piano, complete with grand flourishes and complex chords. It was a magnificent rendition worthy of an audience larger than just our family. Like that improvisation, most of his playing seemed glorious to me. My dad never seemed perplexed by any composer, be it Beethoven, Bach, Bartok, Debussy, Rachmaninoff, or Shostakovich. He never slammed the keys in frustration, ran away in tears, threw the pages of music on the floor, or screamed out loud, all techniques my sister and I tried over the years.

As a child, I envied my dad's proficiency on the keyboard. What I didn't realize at the time, of course, was that his own youth included more hours of practice than I would ever tackle. He started to learn the piano when he was around five and added the pipe organ at his church as soon as his feet could reach the pedals.

I grew up hearing that he had taught music at Incarnation Catholic School in Minneapolis and Loras College and Wahlert High School in Dubuque. When I was young, he taught choir and directed musicals at the public high school in Granite Falls, Minnesota. Throughout my childhood and adolescence, he directed church choirs. In my life, my dad's opinion on all things music was important to me.

He taught my sister how to sing properly, having her lie on the floor with a book on her belly, holding notes and breathing just so. He accompanied my trumpet solos and my sister's flute solos, coaching us carefully to stand properly and to express the music appropriate to the composer and style. At a young age, younger than most, I learned words like "mordent," "fermata," and "fugue."

When I was a teenager and I first started to play pipe organ, my dad taught me that the best way to play the pedals is not to look down at your feet, but to put your knees together and get a feeling for what an octave or a third or any standard separation is between your feet. Once both your hands are busy jumping around on multiple keyboards up top and your eyes are following three lines of music, there isn't time for a glance down to see where your feet are. I had to keep my knees together so I could learn to feel the right degree of separation.

I learned from my dad how to breathe with a congregation on hymns, short breaks between phrases in case they're easily winded, and longer breaks at the end of a line or verse, so they can gear up for the next one. He taught me that congregations love the *idea* of slowing down a hymn, and they'll try hard to do so, but they hate the *reality* of singing slowly because then they get out of breath. The typical response is to blame the organist. I learned how to use a light staccato in the pedal, properly placed, to keep the tempo moving. To this day, when I get compliments on my organ playing, it's usually on how easy it is to sing with me.

My dad was, with us at least, not a patient teacher, but he built an amazing foundation for us. He was an excellent professional pianist and organist. After he died, my sister and I found a company that would take the records and tapes we had of recordings of his performances, digitize them, and preserve them. My dad had never liked to listen to his performances, so it was the first time we heard certain recordings, especially the only full-length piano performance we have, the Haydn Piano Concerto in D Major. My dad was 25 when it was recorded in 1964 and I can picture him as a young man playing it. I listen past the intonation problems of the orchestra accompanying him and marvel at his technical prowess, at the fluidity and beauty of the phrasing.

I know he never felt satisfied with his musical abilities. I imagine that as life carried him forward and as work, home, and life took up more and more time, he simply didn't have the space to practice as much as would have been necessary to maintain or deepen his skills. I remember he said once about his own journey as a musician, "There comes a day when you realize the record company won't call. You'll never be that level of a professional musician." I realize he had that dream once upon a time.

For my dad, music was essential, uplifting, and illuminating, yet there are parts of my dad's journals where he seems apologetic for his love of music. He writes about how much he enjoys sitting and listening to a great symphony or part of an opera, but then he writes his regret at spending time on it and says he should have been more productive—trimming the bushes or cleaning up his papers.

It was also the case that he only found certain types of music uplifting. When my sister first discovered popular music, my dad dismissed it as not worth one's time. For a while, I "sided" with my dad, playing the 1812 Overture loudly on my small green and white record player whenever Karen would put her headphones on to listen to something contemporary. Eventually, I grew tired of annoying her in this way, and I came to like styles of music my dad rejected as not truly musical, or worse, as nonsense or drivel. After he died, my mom shared that the albums of The Beatles and Simon and Garfunkel in their collection had been hers from before she met him. I remember seeing them a couple of times growing up, but I didn't hear music like that until I chose to listen to it in my room, headphones on so he wouldn't be bothered by it. I remember once I shared an album with him, hoping he might like a couple of pieces that used cello in them. He said it was "kind of interesting" but he didn't respond emotionally to it the way I did.

I know he felt classical music deeply, but I think he was almost embarrassed by the emotions he experienced. Years after I left home, he and my mom went to hear a live performance of Beethoven's Ninth Symphony. My dad told me that he sat in the concert hall, tears streaming down his face during the finale, unashamed. "I surprised myself that I could let myself feel it so freely," he told me. I was surprised as well.

I was only rarely in the room when he played piano and didn't watch him closely as he played organ—we knew to keep our distance to avoid being accused of breaking his concentration. But when I did see him play, it was a strange experience. His face was impassive, immobile. He didn't move as he played; in fact, he hated it when pianists moved with the emotions of a piece of music. Perhaps the movement of the music itself was enough for him. He sat still as his fingers took his mind into another dimension.

Despite what I knew was my dad's musical brilliance, a toxic combination of perfectionism, nerves, anxiety, and depression often overtook him, deafening him to what the rest of us heard. Every Sunday that we heard my dad play, my mom, sister, and I would add our compliments to those of others. "The Widor Toccata sounded wonderful, Daddy!" "Oh, I slopped through the last bit," he would reply. "That Bach Fugue is one of my favorites, Daddy—so complicated!" "I messed up the ending. It went better in practice."

I understand nerves. I once had such shaky hands that when I tried to turn a page of music, I flipped the entire book off the piano. The young man I was accompanying at a solo contest did not find this any more amusing than I did. Thankfully, the judge understood and allowed us to begin again.

Even today, nerves are sometimes my enemy, but these nerves are completely absent when I practice. With no one else there, I can fully lose myself in the piece of music. Like that day at my father's funeral, I don't think about how the music is being received, just how it's being created. In those moments, I don't make many mistakes, or at least I don't hear them. Alone in the church when I practice, I sense an indescribable stirring within myself. On one keyboard, I play a high, sweet, haunting melody—a soprano melody my vocal cords can't replicate. On the pedals, my feet produce a bass so deep it touches a chord within my body I didn't know was there; it resonates through me as much as through the church building itself. I wonder if my dad experienced moments like that. I hope he did.

After he died, I found more music he wrote himself than I expected among his files and on his computer, some compositions completed but most half-done. I don't have enough music theory background to truly assess his works, but part of me knows they are limited. I can sometimes hear why he gave up on certain pieces. I also can imagine that he wasn't willing to go back to them and work through a revision process. Some completed pieces he had obviously performed because there were registration notes at the top, notes to himself about what stops on the organ he used to create different sounds.

During his lifetime he gave me two such pieces: the miniature and a set of variations on the Quaker melody "Simple Gifts." He took the simple melody of "tis a gift to be simple, tis a gift to be free" and created intricate movements around it, playing with the theme and producing different moods. One mood is darker and one quite bright, light, and carefree. As I play these pieces, I see the many aspects of my father—from the tragically comfortable depression that enveloped us both at different times to the silly, playful side of him.

When I play a piece of music that my dad used to play, I hear in my mind his interpretation of it, the way he might have subtly changed a tempo or held a chord a bit longer for effect. When I play the music he composed himself, the experience feels much richer. I seek to find him behind it, at least to understand his emotions and thoughts at the time of its creation.

My dad believed that music, whether sung or performed on the organ, was a deep form of prayer, a reaching out to the divine. He used to quote St. Augustine that "to sing is to pray twice." That may not be the exact translation of what Augustine said, but I think my dad was trying to teach me, to teach everyone who would listen, that music has the power to stir within us something fundamental, a need to connect. Whether we are on pitch or not, whether we make mistakes or not, we reach out in prayer to the divine. And since all of us are a part of the divine, connected to it through love, then when we make music, we reach out to each other as well. We reach out to our loved ones, living and dead. I reach out to my dad at the same time as I reach out to my creator and to all others, perhaps hoping in the encounter to know them better, perhaps ultimately settling for being a part of something greater than myself that I can never understand.

And so it is true that I catch a glimpse of my dad in his musical compositions, or in following his registrations on music I inherited, in thinking through the lessons he taught me, or in considering the ways in which music infused our lives together as I grew up. The feeling of connectedness is fleeting, but perhaps it is enough.

The gifts granted to me by my father's love of music abound. Music has helped me earn money. I've made music with wonderful people in churches, pavilions, concert halls, and parks. I've performed an organ recital of classical music to a church full of people who clearly loved me enough to come out on a Sunday afternoon and listen to my efforts. I've performed two recitals of '80s rock songs adapted to the organ to help raise money for our local LGBTQ Center, hearing people sing and clap along, seeing them dance in the aisles with joy. I've gifted my younger son renditions of his favorite video game music performed on organ as a birthday treat. I've sung solos with a community-university chorus that were praised by a director I respect. I've accompanied my sister's flute playing on the same pieces my dad did. I've accompanied my older son's trombone solos and learned pieces I thought were beyond me because I wanted to be a part of his musical journey. I've been transported away from my daily worries and stresses. I've used music to motivate me, to help me find and release my tears, to celebrate life's victories, and to explore my inner spirit's voice. Even now my much fuller self-esteem bucket gets a donation of compliments quite regularly.

By surrounding me with a variety of music from a very young age, my dad helped me learn to inhabit it. I regularly danced with my own young children to all sorts of music, exaggerating the melodrama of the piece for fun. When he was young and I took Anton to orchestra concerts, I enjoyed seeing him tap his fingers in time with the music. When I took a teenage Anton to see his favorite trombonist play with the New York Philharmonic, we turned and smiled at each other at amazing musical moments, reveling in the secret that is appreciation of a particular flourish. Although my dad couldn't or wouldn't allow himself or us to experience music in these ways, my ability to do so is in part because of the gift of musical appreciation he gave me.

Perhaps even more importantly, in the struggles and arguments with my dad, in the practicing and performing moments of my life, in the discussions of technique and motivation, I forged some sort of connection with my dad that means more to me now than it did when he was alive. It's a connection I'm allowed to have even after his death.

Now I talk to my dad regularly when I perform or practice a particular piece. When I play a piece of music I remember hearing him play, I linger in the experience a bit longer, knowing he is in it with me somehow. Sometimes I get nervous or sloppy in my technique, and I start to make more mistakes than usual. Then I remember his lessons. I draw my knees together to feel the distance between an octave or a third on the pedal board; I breathe with the singers by lifting my hands from the keys; I think about the meaning of the music and not about the people who are listening. On good days, the pedal part seems less like something extra to worry about and becomes instead the completion of the chord. I let go of my mistakes. And when a piece ends, sometimes I hold the final chord a second longer. I encounter my dad in that second, and I think, "Amen, Daddy"—so it is and so it will be.

5

1980 (Age 8): Because I Didn't Want to Play Scrabble

It's a Sunday afternoon in October, and I'm dreading school the next day. I imagine sitting in math class, my fellow third graders mixed in with fourth graders, all of us independently working at various levels, all the others somehow knowing that I'm advancing beyond them in math and hating me for it. I will stand in line by the teacher's desk when I have a question. When math class ends, I will go to spelling, and I will win the class spelling bee, and everyone will hate me more. Recess will come, and I will retreat to a rocky area away from all the playground equipment where the other kids congregate. Sometimes I will be visited by a fourth-grade girl who also has few friends. My best friend and neighbor, Leah, is only in second grade, so I never get to see her at recess. I do see her in the evenings and on Saturdays. I go to her house or we play in my front yard.

Today is Sunday, and I am free from school. Technically, I am free to see Leah. But today is Sunday, so I'm not.

"Can I go see Janelle later?" Karen asks at lunch after church. Janelle is her best friend and lives in a beautiful white house up on the hill. She has an all-white grand piano in her sunken living room, and outside her house there's a tiny bridge that connects two parts of the garden but no water flows underneath. I've never seen the piano or the living room, but Karen described it for us once after she got to visit her.

"No. Not this afternoon," my dad says. "It's Sunday! You see your friends at school during the week. Sundays are family time."

"But maybe after we play games …"

"There won't be time. It'll be dinner, and it gets dark early. You don't *need* to go see your friend today. You need to spend time with your family."

My mom washes the dishes. Karen sits on her twin bed in our room looking angry. I sit at my desk and try to write in my journal. Normally I write about what I did that day, but I don't know what to say about today yet. I write that we went to church and ate and are about to play games.

My dad calls us to the living room and says, "Let's play Risk first." Karen is to my right at the card table, sitting down carefully so as not to bump its folding legs. My dad puts a record on the stereo, a symphony I don't recognize. I face the wide expanse of windows looking out over the backyard. The sun shines on the forest of twenty-some pine trees. The two blue-green swings and attached seesaw sit idle, and the sandbox is empty with only the birds to enjoy it. The windows are open to let in the gentle fall breeze.

"I'll be yellow," my dad says. I'm happy because that's one of my least favorite colors. I choose blue instead, my favorite. We begin the game by placing little plastic armies on the various countries on the game board. My mom goes to Australia, a corner of the board that is fairly easy to protect from invaders, a good place to defend but a difficult place from which to attack because all of Asia stretches out in front of you, one of the most difficult regions on the board to manage. I often aim for South America, another defensible position. My dad takes on North America. My sister heads to Africa. We place army after army on the board.

I shift in my chair, and my knee bumps the table leg. "Don't bump the table!" my dad yells. "All the armies jump, and how will we know who was where?" I resolve to sit still.

We begin attacking and defending, throwing the dice and facing the whims of chance. I launch out from South America and think

I may have a chance to conquer the board, only to find I don't get the right cards or the right numbers or I stretch myself too thin. The record on the stereo ends, and I find myself humming.

"Can you stop that?" my dad says. "I'm thinking and it's distracting." I resolve to be quieter.

I attack Karen and she attacks me back on her turn. We're desperate to conquer countries, get cards, develop a set, and get more armies to stay alive, so we turn on each other as easy targets.

I sigh. "Why can't you attack somebody else?" I ask her. "Go after Mom or Daddy."

"You're right there!" she yells. "Mom's way over in southern Asia, and Daddy's nowhere near me. I have to attack you."

So when it's my turn, even though I do have a choice, I attack her back.

Karen is eliminated first, not by me, but by my dad. "You have to be careful," he says as he rolls the dice and defeats her, "not to spread yourself so thin."

"Yes," she agrees quickly. "Can I go?" she asks when all the armies of her color are gone from the board. I know she wants to retreat to our room and read or listen to music. I know because it's what I want too. Part of me is jealous that she's already lost.

"You're not going to Janelle's," my dad says firmly.

"I know. I meant to my room."

"No. You will stay and watch the game. We're here to have fun as a family, so stay until the game is done."

We look at my mom to see if she'll intervene. She gives us a small smile and prepares herself to be eliminated from the board next. Karen sighs and resigns herself to helping people count out armies as the battles unfold in front of her.

My dad wins about two hours after we started. We all help clean up.

"Let's play Scrabble," my dad says.

"I hate Scrabble," I admit with a sigh. "It's so long, and I never think of words with my letters."

"It's good for you," he says. I'm sure it is, but all I can think of are the long stretches of time where we sit there staring at our letters, trying to make sense of them. I'll look up and see the backyard and want to grab my book and go outside and read. My dad will catch me staring out the window and say I should be looking for words, but I never see a word in the out-of-context letters, nothing more than "it" or "in" if I'm lucky enough to grab those tiles.

"What about Sorry?" my mom suggests. "Or Parcheesi?" At that point, she's named almost all the games we own that aren't designed just for kids, like Candy Land or Chutes and Ladders. My dad doesn't play those with us. He used to a little bit but not anymore.

"What's wrong with Scrabble?" my dad asks my mom.

"Nothing. I just thought maybe we could play a game Jennifer enjoys more."

I tense up. I don't want to be the reason we play a specific game. I wish I hadn't said that I don't like Scrabble. I don't want to have a fight. We've made it through an entire game without fighting.

"You always take their side. What about what I want to play?"

"Fine. Let's play Scrabble," my mom says.

"Fine," my dad says mockingly. "Let's play Scrabble," he parrots.

"Jim," she says, "I'm just trying to have a conversation about which game to play."

I hold my breath. How can I stop this? How can I go back and not say that I hate that game? Why do I never learn? If I had just said, "How about Parcheesi?" would he have become angry?

Karen glares at me. "Why didn't you just agree to play Scrabble?" she mutters through clenched teeth.

I feel tears in my eyes. "Let's play Scrabble," I say, but I am ignored. The fight has begun.

"I suppose you think that the kids should just go off on Sunday afternoons and play with their friends! I suppose you think I'm wrong, Marie."

1980 (age 8)

"No, Jim, I agree it's important to spend time together as a family. We've talked about this. But we played Risk and now I wonder if maybe we should all do something else."

My mom's voice is calm and even. My dad's voice is not. "Like what, Marie? Like go to Janelle's? Is that what you want for Karen? For this family?"

"Well, Jim, I'm not sure I see the harm—"

"So I'm wrong. I see now. I'm just stupid. Stupid Jim trying to have fun with his family. Trying to hold the family together."

"Jim, please. We do things as a family. We just did."

"But no, I see clearly now," my dad gestures wildly with his right arm. "My idea of helping the family—playing a game together, listening to music, spending time together, it's just crap. I'm just crap. It's all stupid. That's what you mean, isn't it, Marie? Isn't it?"

"No, Daddy, that's not what we mean," Karen says. My dad pivots on his foot to turn towards her. I cower inside. Why did she say anything? "I just think that maybe we played a game and now we all go do something else."

"Like go to Janelle's, huh?"

"Like go to my room or go outside and play with Jennifer." Karen's tone is exasperated. "We played a game. We had our family fun. Now maybe we do something else."

My dad's eyes narrow, and his finger jabs the air between them as he says slowly, separating each word, "You don't tell me what our family does. You are not in charge here."

"Jim ..." my mom's voice trails off.

"And you," he turns to me. "What do you have to say for yourself now? Now you're all quiet, huh? Now you don't have an opinion?"

I feel the tears on my cheeks. The sunshine outside seems cruel now. It feels so dark in the living room. It doesn't feel like Sunday. It doesn't feel happy.

"Let's play Scrabble," I say quietly. But it's far too late now. He whirls and accuses and yells, then pivots to the next person and repeats. I cry, and Karen attacks him. My mom cries, and Karen attacks him. Then Karen cries.

Time passes, my mind growing weary trying to follow his logic and counter it. "I'm so sorry, Daddy," I say at last. "I want to spend time as a family. I want to play games. I shouldn't have said anything else."

"I'm sorry too, Daddy," Karen says. My mom's crying turns to a sob at one point, and Karen and I reach out to her. She is still sitting at the card table. My dad, Karen, and I have been standing for almost an hour.

My dad beckons us to come to him. "Marie, you too," he says and gestures for her to stand. "It's time for a group hug." We all fall in together and hold on. "I believe," he says, "the family that fights together stays together. So this too was a blessed event. This too was an afternoon blessed by God's presence because we are all together."

I lean on Karen's shoulder and cry. I don't understand what my dad's saying. I don't get why God would be OK with what happened. I don't feel blessed. I just feel exhausted and sad. I just wish the day were over.

We pull apart, wiping our tears, my mom half-chuckling over needing more Kleenex in the living room, and then she says she needs to start dinner if we're to eat soon.

"I'll want to watch *60 Minutes* tonight," my dad says. I picture him sitting in the basement on the bristly brown couch we inherited from the former owners of the house, watching our small black and white TV. I know enough not to complain about missing *Wide World of Disney* again.

"Of course," my mom says. "I'll go start the oven."

Karen and I go back to our room. She lies on her bed looking sad. I go to my journal and begin to write. "We played Risk today. Daddy won. We had fried chicken for dinner." I don't write the rest.

6

Conversations

A few months before he died, my dad was done with the chemotherapy that had stopped fighting his cancer, so he temporarily regained some of his appetite and energy. It was the strange period when you know the person is going to die but they almost seem to be getting better. My sister, dad, and I were sitting in their living room. He was in his chair with my sister on the couch and me on the floor, near the sliding glass doors that led out to the concrete patio slab outside. I didn't want to sit in my mom's chair in case she wanted to wander in from the kitchen table, and I sometimes prefer the floor anyway—more room and more options to sit the way I want to.

Abruptly, my dad said, "Do you have anything you want to ask me?" I was instantly confused. Did he mean about life? About his impending death? About our plans for that evening's dinner? About *anything*?

If anything was fair game, a thousand questions swirled in my mind: Have you ever been truly happy? When? What made you happy? Are you satisfied with life? What was your relationship with your dad really like? Why did you used to yell and rant at me for no reason when I was a kid? What was it like to be depressed and try to function for so long with no medication or counseling? Do you love me? Do you ever feel like life was just a waste of time? Do you worry about the future still, or do worries end when you get this close to death? Do you feel angry and ripped off that life is ending while you still had plans? Do you have regrets? What are they? Are you glad you had kids? What would you redo if you could?

In an alternate universe, the ensuing conversation was a fabulous opportunity for me to learn more about who my dad truly was, to heal old wounds, and to find peace before his death. In this universe, I think I asked something like, "Are you scared of dying?" I already knew what he'd say: "Of course. But I also have faith that I'll see my creator." I suspect he did say something like that. I cried and wished I hadn't. It felt awkward to cry since I wasn't sure if I was crying over his coming death or something else entirely. And then the moment evaporated, the opportunity to ask all the unasked questions lost forever.

For *some* of the questions swirling in my mind I already knew the answers: "Of course I've been happy, too many times to count. I yelled because I was depressed, overwhelmed, and scared. I love you. It was hell to live through depression with no medication or counseling. Thank God your mother was there to help me. I wouldn't have made it without her. Of course I have regrets. You probably don't want to know them."

In that moment, I wanted to learn about my dad, but I'm not sure his answers would have helped me understand him as an individual any better than I already did. I'm not sure an opportunity was ever there in the first place. Maybe there are some questions that we can't ask our parents. Maybe there are some answers our loved ones can't give, or won't.

Any time my dad briefly opened a window into who he was, I tried to listen, to learn more about the person he was before I came along. A couple of years before he died, we were walking around the St. John's University campus in Collegeville, Minnesota, the place where my dad earned his bachelor's degree as a young man and then his master's in divinity just before he was diagnosed with cancer the second, and last, time. It was a beautiful day and the campus was at its best, with the kinds of views colleges use in marketing materials to sell themselves to students and their parents. It was a rare occasion because he was telling stories about places there and what they meant to him at different times in his life.

When we saw my son Anton running ahead with my sister, my dad said, "I just wish I could believe he'd remember this day someday. I wish he could keep this memory." I said something like, "Maybe you'll be around to bring him here again later," but I think we both knew that wasn't likely.

My dad was right. Anton was too young and he doesn't remember it. I wonder sometimes if my dad had lived longer, would Anton and Edward have asked him questions about his life, his depression, his choices? Would they have tried to trace down through history their own environment and identities? Because of the distance of a generation, would they have had the courage to ask him questions I couldn't? If my dad had lived longer, would he have had the courage to answer?

One of my talents is post-conversational paranoia. I've met others who are also exceptionally talented at reconsidering comments they've made and extrapolating from them all the horrible assumptions those who heard them are now making. I have done this overthinking after social situations, meetings, classes, emails, phone conversations, and all manner of moments in which I opened my mouth and words came out. I can remember random comments I made months ago that I *guarantee* the listener does not remember, and I still wonder, "Did I do more harm than good there?"

Actually, I can't *guarantee* the listener doesn't remember the comments. They might not only remember the comments but judge me based on them. They may have put me in a different box or labeled me as an undesirable companion solely because of that comment. That comment may be the one story they tell other people about me when they find out we have a mutual acquaintance. "Oh yes, I know Jennifer. One time she said to me …" and then that will ruin that other relationship too. Post-conversational paranoia is truly a gift I have.

When my spiral into this kind of illogical thinking starts, I try to remember what a friend once told me: people who know you know lots of things about you and are willing to forgive one or two stupid comments from time to time, chalking them up to the bad days we all have. And people who don't know you probably don't think about you much after just a brief conversation. Another way to help myself through moments like this is to remind myself what former Israeli prime minister Shimon Peres once said: "When a friend makes a mistake, the friend remains a friend, and the mistake remains a mistake."

The ultimate in post-conversational paranoia is after someone's dead. There's no next encounter to confirm that all is OK between the two of you. There's no follow-up to reestablish normalcy. There are no further opportunities to ask questions or to clarify comments. There's just that last conversation.

After someone I know dies, I think back to the last time I saw them. I consider carefully what I said, whether I was kind and generous with my time, and for a moment, sometimes, I wish I could unsay things or restate them in a more humane and life-giving way.

People I know who are of strong faith have told me to pause and realize that in an afterlife united fully with the divine, anything left unsaid is understood. People told me I could have a follow-up conversation any time with those who had joined God. Perhaps because of disbelief, I still get stuck on the last conversation I had with them, the last moment of earthly communication.

The day before my dad died, my mom was still at her house getting ready when Jason, our kids, and I arrived at the hospice. Anton and I had been over to visit my dad earlier in the week. Jason brought Edward, then not yet two years old, to the bed, and we let him see Grandpa and touch his hand. My dad wasn't very responsive. I think morphine and death's imminence were taking care of that. Then Jason took the kids downstairs to the family room.

Alone in this hospice room that had become somewhat familiar, I sat on the side of my dad's bed. I took his hand with more ease and familiarity than I ever had before. He was suddenly more approachable because I knew he didn't have the strength or the capacity to lash out at me if I did something he didn't like or said something of which he didn't approve. Suddenly, as I looked back over a million memories, I only wanted to linger in certain ones. The memories of belittling comments or controlling behaviors faded to the background. After all, it seemed best and appropriate not to try to resolve anything in our relationship. Those opportunities were gone.

I started to talk to him. "It's a beautiful spring day today, Daddy." I cried at the thought that he'd never walk in the sun on another spring day like this again, but my words didn't catch in my throat as tears slid down my face.

"A day like today makes me think about a lot of different days in our lives together." I opened my good memories to share with him. "It's not as warm yet, but I was thinking as I drove over from the hotel this morning about those days you picked me up for lunch when I was in college and working my summer job. Those days you swung by the Job Service in Winona and we drove the few blocks to the Mississippi River, do you remember that?" I didn't pause for a response. I wasn't even sure he could hear me.

"I remember we would sit in the sunshine, eat our bag lunches for 20 minutes, and then you would take me back to work. You know, I appreciate more now the sacrifice you made during those lunches. I get it now that I'm a parent. You had lots of stress from work, I'm sure, but you just listened to my problems and my worries. My boredom or frustration or whatever must have seemed so trivial to you as you worried about money and mortgages and life and death. But you didn't say anything to me. I try to remember that now with Anton and Edward."

As I thanked him for those times I felt the warmth of the day, the breezes off the river, and the calm of the moment. I hoped he could too. "Anyway, those half-hour lunches were sometimes the only thing that kept me going. Thank you."

I paused and looked up and out the window. I hadn't thought about those summer lunches in years. I was grateful the positive memory had come to me at what felt like just the right moment. I was glad to be able to thank him with authenticity for something he had done that mattered to me. My hand squeezed his a little and I looked back at his face, relaxed and without pain.

"So, I know it's near the end." My voice caught briefly but I was able to continue. I took a tissue from his bedside table and wiped the tears that had slid down to my neck. "If I were you, I'd be wondering about Mom. You've been her constant companion for so long and you've helped take care of her. I want you to know that Karen and I will do all we can for her. I want you to know it's OK." I remembered him telling me years earlier how important it can be to tell those who are dying that it is OK to let go. I didn't say those words, but I hoped I was close enough.

I sniffed and chuckled a little. "I have to tell you, speaking of Mom, she tried to tell the 'holy smokes' joke to Joe here at Quiet Oaks Hospice." The "holy smokes" joke was the one my dad used to ask my mom out the first time. They were teachers in the same Catholic school, and in my mom's classroom was an old phone that didn't work anymore. My dad went in one day after classes were done and picked up the receiver. He said, "What's that you say? The church burned down?! Holy smokes!" It's not that funny, but every time my mom heard it, *every time* my dad told it, she would laugh—genuinely laugh. That laugh wasn't about the joke really, but about that moment and the beginning of their relationship.

"You know how Mom struggles to tell jokes, getting the punchlines or the parts mixed up. I was there and I can't even tell you what order she used telling it to Joe, but it didn't make any sense." I laughed again. His face shifted into what looked simultaneously like a grimace and a smile. I wondered how much control he had over his expression at this point. I was heartened to know he could hear me and was understanding me.

I took a deep breath. I looked at the birds fluttering around the feeders outside his window, at the flowers beginning to emerge and blossom near the landscaped rocks. "I want you to know I love you, Daddy."

He said quietly, almost in a croak, "I love you too," and pulled his hand away from mine. Those were the last words I ever heard him say.

My post-conversation paranoia makes me wonder if I should have said, "You were the best dad in the world," but he wasn't and I think he knew that. I don't think those words would have comforted him or me.

Still, I recognize what a tremendous gift my last conversation with my dad was for me. I hope it was for my dad too—a parting gift, as it were. In case he can't read my heart now, I hope he knew in that moment what was in it. I know I won't get that gift with every loved one. That's too much to ask for in this universe of randomness. Maybe my last conversations with other loved ones will be about the weather or a baseball game score. I wonder if afterwards I'll talk to them as if they were still around, just to try to have a more poetic final chat. I wonder if that will help.

❧

One morning, my six-year-old son and I had a few moments alone together in the kitchen before his brother and dad were awake. I love these moments. Being alone with one of my children offers me the best opportunity to try to see them as individuals. When they're together there's so much competition for attention, for position, for space that they often become just a tangle of emotions and body parts wrestling physically or metaphorically in front of me.

I was interested in Edward's development at that moment because in the weeks leading up to that morning, he had become more keenly aware of death and mortality in what I have come to understand can be a normal and healthy way for his age. For example, after losing his second tooth a few nights before, he sobbed. He wanted it back in. When he turned six, during his birthday celebration at a nearby pizza place, he started to cry. I asked him why. He said, "I don't want to turn six."

"Why not?"

"Six is one year closer to death."

That was not the answer I had anticipated. "But life is very, very, very long, Edward. We've told you that. You will have so many more birthdays to come. You've just begun!" With a sniff and some ice cream, he reconciled himself to continuing on life's journey.

During this early morning summer conversation, the light shining in through the sheer white curtains next to the kitchen table, Edward's eyes suddenly filled with tears. "Mama," he began, "in your last breath, I will love you. I will *say* I love you." My heart ached, and my tears almost spilled over in response. I reminded him that my death is years and years into the future. He said, "I know." Then he paused and looked me in the eye. "I will love you even after you die," he said with sincerity and gravity.

Upon hearing this story, my pastor recommended burning that memory into my brain so that no matter what happens, my son's love will be with me in my final moments. I like that idea a lot. Not having the perfectly scripted last conversation with those we love is incredibly difficult. But at one point in our relationships hopefully we had a good conversation, one where we saw into each other's hearts and knew love. Why can't remembering that one stand in as our last conversation?

Still, my mom and I try to end every conversation with "I love you." That's a safe way to make sure that our final *words* to each other will be ones of love, but words aren't a conversation. My husband and I say "love ya, bye" at the end of every conversation. My sister and I end every phone conversation with me saying "talk to you later" and her saying "yep" or some variation of affirmation and then we both say "bye." Years ago we tried ending our phone calls a different way once we realized we were in a decades-old rut, but I called her back to end it the "right way" instead. We laughed at ourselves, but she was grateful I'd called back. So if we continue that tradition, that will likely be the last thing I'll ever say to her—"talk to you later." And maybe I will.

I can't control what my last conversation is like with every human being with whom I come into contact. I can't be sure to end every conversation with kindness and show kindness to all strangers and always smile. I have bad days and bad moods. I yell at my kids. I'm cranky to my sister, my mom, and my husband. Maybe my pastor is right, and I can choose a "last" conversation from among my many memories of those closest to me. If I let go of the notion of time as linear, of last and first as fixed points in time, I can have it all. I can declare the loving moments, the best moments, the clearest conversations to be my last and defining conversations.

When both my boys were born, I held them in my arms, brought their faces near mine, nuzzled our noses together, and said, "Welcome to the world … I'm your mom." Granted, it was a one-sided and brief conversation, but maybe in my final moment, I will try to remember it.

7

1985 (Age 13): Because He Was Unemployed

Our house doesn't come alive when my mom comes home from work, but it feels better. My dad is just as likely to explode with her home as he is when she's gone, but I also know there's one more person who might bear the brunt of his anger. I feel guilty at the relief of sharing this burden.

She sighs as she comes in from the garage and there's pain on her face. "How was work?" I ask.

"OK," she says. I'm in the kitchen trying to help by starting dinner. I have the heavy cast iron skillet on the stove, and I'm browning hamburger for three-soup hot dish. The hamburger has been frozen, bought at a sale price and saved for a dinner later. I added a little water the way my mom taught me, so it won't stick or burn right away, but I'm still nervous as it sizzles and spits. When I flip the big chunk of frozen meat over to help it break apart or brown on another side, I worry that the splash of burning hot water will hit my hand. I worry that I will touch the skillet in the wrong spot and burn my finger. Part of my relief is that my mom is home to take over.

She moves to the freezer to put away the ice pack that helped keep her sandwich and carrots cold until lunchtime. "Where's Karen?"

"In her room."

My mom doesn't ask where my dad is. She knows he's in the basement, where he's spent most of his days during the past year.

I return to carefully turning the defrosting meat, pulling away the sections that have browned and pushing them into other parts of the pan. When my mom takes the spatula from me, I make toast and set the table. When my dad wanders upstairs a little later, my mom's cheery tone seems forced: "How was your day?"

"Like yesterday," he replies. He doesn't ask about her day.

Dinner is mostly a conversation between my mom and Karen and then my mom and me.

"How was marching band?" my mom asks Karen.

"All right, but really hot! Some of the kids just won't listen so it takes forever to practice anything."

"How was your day?" My mom turns her attention to me. "Did you practice trumpet yet today?"

"This morning. I practiced piano a bit too," I reply. "I read *Pride and Prejudice* most of the afternoon."

"Such a good book," my mom says, her tone drifting off in memories.

My dad eats in silence and I try not to notice, wondering if he's angry with me, worried he'll yell at me for not having a more productive afternoon. But I think he's not even listening to us.

Later, my mom, Karen, and I do the dishes as he watches the news in the living room.

"I need to talk to you downstairs after you clean up, Marie," my dad says to my mom.

When my mom goes downstairs, Karen and I don't turn on the TV. We listen. This is our ritual on such nights—stay quiet and see what we can hear and learn. We hear raised voices sometimes and we catch bits of conversation. We sneak to the top of the stairs, quietly open the door, and even sometimes step down two or three steps, hoping to catch more. The stairs are dark, but I can still see the rough brown carpeting on them. At the bottom of the stairs, the fluorescent lights of the basement illuminate the dingy brown, green, and orange carpeting that covers the concrete floor.

I hate and fear our basement. When I have to go downstairs to do laundry or get a can of pop from the downstairs refrigerator, I always make Karen or my mom stand at the top of the stairs and talk to me the whole time. The downstairs is full of possible dangers—spiders or the sudden realization that the drain has backed up if the washing machine isn't working right again. Beyond all those dangers, it's my dad's territory. Most days I avoid the basement.

Tonight Karen and I can't hear much from the stairs because they're talking so quietly, so we tiptoe to my bedroom. There's a vent in the floor that's right above the basement couch, so we can often hear better there. Karen sits on the edge of my bed, and I sit on the floor by her feet, feeling safe because of her company.

"So it's OK to ask *my* parents for money, but not your mother, is that it, Marie?" my dad's voice is raised in irritation.

"No, it's just that my mother doesn't have a lot—"

"And my parents do?"

"Well, they seem to have enough. They said to ask again if we needed more."

"You're just ashamed to ask your mother. You're afraid your sisters will hear that we're struggling. Especially Oney. You're afraid that your precious favorite sister will hear that your husband can't provide for you like hers can. She already looks down on us—"

"That's not true."

"Don't tell me they don't! We go up there for family reunions, and we see their beautiful new house and hear about their amazing businesses. Don't tell me they don't look down on me! They do! I know it!"

I hear a bar stool squeak, and I picture my mom on one of the two black vinyl stools we inherited from the previous owners. They sit next to the fully upholstered bar that's never been used by us for anything except as a place to set unpacked boxes or stacks of books that don't fit on the shelves. I picture my dad where he always sits, in the old orange chair we brought from Granite Falls. We hadn't moved our basement couch, planning to buy a new one, because we thought that our financial situation was improving. That was back when he was still optimistic about his new sales territory. That was when he thought that the problem had been the customers in the area around

Granite Falls—that they didn't want to buy life insurance, that there weren't enough of them. Here in Winona, where he had grown up and where people knew his last name, he was convinced he could sell more.

He was wrong. He hated calling people he didn't know. He would put it off all week and then not have appointments, no chance to sit with people to try to sell them the product he believed in so much. On other nights, voices had drifted up through the vent, my dad explaining to my mom that he owed money to his employer because he wasn't selling enough to pay even his base salary. One night, his voice said they had ended his contract, leaving him unemployed.

"I'm just wondering if maybe my next check will cover what we need it to cover," my mom says.

"You don't make enough, Marie! I've told you that before."

"I just wonder if maybe you'll be able to find work soon …"

"I can't take just *any* job, Marie. I can't take a demeaning job or people won't hire me for professional work again." There is a pause and I hold my breath. Are they suspicious of the silence upstairs? Karen and I look at each other in fear. If he discovers we've been listening, what will he say?

But it has nothing to do with us. "So did you talk to them about your need to sit, Marie?" my dad asks. My mom has apparently been rubbing her leg the way she does now every night after work.

"I mentioned something about a stool to the line supervisor," my mom replies. "She seemed to suggest that if I can't do the work that may be a problem, so I'm thinking it's best not to rock the boat right now."

"That's ridiculous! If they expect you to stand there for eight hours each day on the line, they need to give you a stool! You need to stand up for yourself. Don't be such a pushover!"

I picture my mom on the bar stool, listening. I think about how tired she must be. I wonder when my dad will let her come back upstairs. I could offer to rub her shoulders and neck for her. I know how she loves that. I don't do it often enough. I should take better care of her.

I don't hear her reply to his suggestions because she's too quiet now, but I hear his response, loud and clear: "I'm sorry to keep you then! Go upstairs! Sorry that I wanted to spend time with you—my wife. Imagine that. Imagine how I've been at home alone all day today. Down here all day looking at the budget and the finances and trying to see how we'll make this work. Then I want to spend time problem solving with you and talk about you asking your mother for a loan and you don't want to spend time with me. I understand. I'm not worth spending time with, so why would you want to."

"That's not true, Jim," my mom says loudly enough that I can hear it. But then her voice lowers again. I don't hear how she tries to coax him back into a better mood. I don't hear much of the next hour of conversation. Karen and I drift into her bedroom where we play a game of Life on the floor. We know the game so well that we can play it without talking and finish in 20 minutes. Then she turns on the Twins game on her radio, puts on her headphones, and retreats into a Harlequin romance. I know better than to interrupt or she'll yell at me.

I return to my room and sit on the floor, my back against the twin bed that sits tucked against two walls in order to fit in the small space. I move my hands along the carpeting, the strangest I've ever seen anywhere. It's made up of long bumpy rolls of colors that you would never expect to put together—orange, red, yellow, green, white, blue. Upon seeing it for the first time, my family declared it the ugliest carpeting they'd ever seen. Since moving in, I've lost myself in it, listening to music and dreaming of escapes. It's the carpet in my private space, my room, so my love for it overcomes my shame at its ugliness. It doesn't matter anyway as no one outside the family ever sees it since we don't have friends over.

I hear only indistinct murmurs from down below now, so I decide to read for a while. I lose myself in Jane Austen's world again. I read more about a father who struggles to know how to deal with family problems, how to support his five daughters. In Austen's world the mother is far from capable. I think of my mom downstairs, sewing my dad's spirit back together just as she used to sew clothes for us back in Granite Falls, back before we moved to Winona and she took whatever job she could find, working in a university chemistry lab where she washed dishes and mixed chemicals, in a library preparing books for a new digital system, and now in a factory as a line worker.

I worry about what I've heard and what I haven't heard. I worry about the future. I put down my book, listen to the music, and pick away at the peeling skin on the insides of my palms, the eczema I hide from my mom because I know we can't afford a trip to the doctor. When she finally comes upstairs a couple of hours later, she sits in her chair and my dad in his in the living room. My dad has a bowl of ice cream, then a bowl of chips, and then another bowl of ice cream. He offers my mom ice cream too and she takes it. He finds the 10:00 news and then a rerun of *The Bob Newhart Show*. He laughs loudly a few times, and I picture him, his head thrown back and his mouth open wide.

I go out later to say goodnight to them both. My mom has her book open as the TV blares. She's reading a mystery, lost in it so completely despite the noise that I have to bump her arm to get her attention to say goodnight.

She smiles at me instantly. I lean over and give her a kiss. "Good night, Mom."

"Good night, sweetheart." Her voice is warm and loving and quiet.

I kiss my dad too, as I have been trained to do every night. "Good night, Daddy."

"Good night." He doesn't smile at me, distracted by the television.

Later that week, I hear my mom on the phone with my grandmother. I hear my mom saying thank you to her. I know this means that a check will come later, a loan that will likely become a gift.

8

Meeting Marie

My dad used to steer conversations about himself away from the topic by saying, "That's enough about me. What do *you* think about me?" His lighthearted approach hid the truth—that he didn't like to talk about himself. Conversations with him on that topic were fairly rare and always short. He didn't talk much about his own childhood—"that's in the past"—and only occasionally would he allude to a life before having children, a life full of dreams and hopes.

After his death, I attacked the problem of not really knowing who my father was as a person in the only way I was trained to do so: research. Since my primary resource, my dad, was gone, I would turn to secondary sources like his journals and conversations with my sister and my mom. It finally dawned on me one day, however, that I was making at *least* one terrible mistake. I was living out my dad's joke in almost every conversation with my mom. Essentially, I was saying to her, "Enough talk about Daddy. What do *you* think about Daddy?" My mom was right there, but I wasn't asking her about her. I was letting her stay in the shadow of my father's memory.

In part, I didn't think I needed to ask her questions about herself because my mom didn't feel like a mystery to me. Growing up, I was closer to my mom and spent more time around her. When my dad, overcome with stress and depression, would bark at me and my sister for little to no reason, we would scurry to our rooms and later venture out only to talk with my mom. She was always the comforter, the supporter, the shoulder, the hugger. In pain or exhaustion, I could put my arms around her and hang on for dear life, willing her to support my body weight even as I got older. Her gentle spirit and smooth skin were home to me.

When my dad was selling insurance, he had to travel in the evenings to people's houses. My sister and I would look forward to dinner and books with just my mom. Then we could have what we all three really wanted for dinner—mac and cheese and hot dogs. The house felt cozy and complete on those nights. I would come and go from room to room without thinking about who might be where, being completely myself. My mom was all about unconditional love, warm hugs, homemade sugar cutout cookies after school, stories, answers to any question, help with homework, unending patience, and all things soft and fuzzy.

I knew my mom's labels and character description: former librarian and schoolteacher, wife and mother, loving, self-sacrificing, lovably a little nutty. She gets things laughably wrong like calling the 1980s TV show *Prescription: Murder* instead of *Diagnosis: Murder*. Yes, Mom, we've all wanted to prescribe murder for someone, but they probably couldn't make a long-running TV show on that premise. She loves reading mysteries, putting together jigsaw puzzles, and watching British comedies from the 1970s. I knew my mom, so instead of asking my mom about herself, I could concentrate on just using her as a source to help me better understand the man she'd been married to for so many years.

But then a funny thing happened. I asked my mom a question—I forget now what it even was—and she told me a story from when she was dating my dad. And another man. At the same time.

I did a double take and she noticed.

"I was quite a flirt," she said. She started telling me about guys she met on a trip she and a female friend took to New York, a couple of years before she met my dad. Flirting? My mom? The woman with low self-esteem? My family's official collective narrative did not include these events or labels for my mom.

I started to ask more questions, and suddenly the answers were different from before. She would retell a story, adding more depth about the decisions she made, the feelings she had. My dad hadn't wanted to hear much about her family or childhood (his "it's in the past" mantra took care of that), and she hadn't wanted to talk about men she'd dated before him. I can understand those choices, knowing my dad. I can understand why she kept large parts of herself safely hidden away from all three of us. But after his death I began to hear her stories.

When I called to ask her what she'd been doing lately, she told me about day-long marathons of watching sci-fi and crime stories—shows that hadn't been my dad's interests. It turns out she didn't like British comedies from the 1970s as much as I had thought. Instead, with excitement, she would tell me about weird shows of giant man-eating snakes and dinosaur mutants that still roam the earth. She laughed and said she wanted to "catch up" on 40 years of bad TV.

Karen and I began to help her redecorate her house, and I discovered that my mom loves to be inspired by artwork on her walls. We framed drawings her mother had made years earlier that she had always meant to get around to framing. We framed a painted bag I'd purchased in Costa Rica over a decade earlier and sketches of flowers made by a friend she'd known when working as the director at the Arcadia Public Library years before. Down came the pieces that had meant more to my dad than to her. Up went works that meant something to her.

The new images of flowers, butterflies, and paths through beautiful nature joined a gift we'd given her years earlier, a small, framed print of *The Herring Net* by Winslow Homer, one of my mom's favorite paintings. In it two figures, one much larger than the other, both shrouded in slickers and rain hats, battle to get a net full of fish into a small boat while the seas roil around them. They fight to stay afloat and provide food amidst rough waters and cloudy weather threatening worse. The pieces we selected signaled a new era for my mom. Homer's beautiful but dark painting seemed now a fitting image of how my mom had fought to survive and protect us for so long. It was time for a new metaphor.

※

In the early years after my dad died, whenever I drove from Marinette, Wisconsin, to my parents' home in Minnesota for a visit, I observed my mom more as I would a friend. I noticed that she's nice to total strangers and rather chatty, a quality that maybe she had when I was a teenager and at that point would simply have embarrassed me. But maybe she didn't. Maybe when we were in public she was afraid to be that chatty person, afraid that she'd hear about it in the car on the ride home afterwards from my dad—"Why did you say that?" I don't remember her being friendly to waiters and waitresses, cashiers and clerks, not the way she is now.

Now I see how she brightens people's days. A young man at the bank holds a door open for her, and she smiles and chats with him about what a lovely car he has. His sincere smile back to her as he engages in *further* conversation with her about the weather takes me by surprise. The waitress she talks to about *her* day relaxes a little bit more and checks on my mom more than she probably would on other customers. My mom makes a self-deprecating comment at the grocery store about her cane, and the bagger and check-out clerk rush to remind her she's still doing great.

These are all total strangers until my mom invites them into a moment of civility and kindness with her, a moment when she shows her true self, a self at which I marvel. My mom is so much more than the kind and gentle person I thought she was. She is aware of others and reaches out to them to help them through whatever is happening in their moment as they help her through hers.

I saw her one day in a café, the sun shining in through a window illuminating her beautiful silver hair, her soft, wrinkle-laden face resting in a smile of contentment, her light blue-green spring jacket complementing her light-pink lipstick. I saw her as if for the first time, not as an elderly woman with a cane who struggles to assert herself, but as a beautiful woman, one whose spirit is reaching out tentatively to the world, asking if she has a place in it after all these years. In that private moment, one she's not even aware of, I felt deeply connected to her as a person. I told her later that day how beautiful she looked in the café, how it struck me, and it seemed to come as a surprise to her that I would label her that way. I resolved to tell her more often how beautiful she is.

As the years after my dad's death passed, when I called her, I would hear about conversations with her neighbors. She talked about baseball a lot with one neighbor, and increasingly my mom watched every Minnesota Twins game, learning the players' names, stats, and tendencies, and offering opinions about pitching changes or best plays of the week. When I ask her about what seems to me to be a newfound love of the sport, she tells me about enjoying watching the Twins before she met my dad. Karen and I talk about what it's like to have our mom explore possible friendships and her personal interests. In the novelty of it we see a deeper problem, one we always knew but never really processed: our mom never had lunches or chats on the phone with friends. She never had friendships the way we've been able to have.

Then one day on the phone she tells me about going to a widow and widower luncheon to meet people. At every table with an empty chair, she was rebuffed. I picture her moving with difficulty around tables, using her cane with one hand and balancing a plate full of food with the other. I hear the cavalier tone with which people say, "Sorry, this seat is saved." I feel the pain of rejection that she describes to me later.

So I tell her not to go there again. "Try the senior center and go do a puzzle or play cards with someone. Those are things you like to do that you know they like to do too."

"That's true ..." and in her voice drifting off I hear the fear of trying to meet people.

I ask more questions, now about life with Daddy as his wife. When I examine her past, I find the root of that fear in the stinging rejection she'd felt so many years at home. My sister and I recall consistent belittling of my mom by my dad. I remember numerous times sitting in the back seat of the car and hearing him critique how she had behaved at an event. "You should talk more to so-and-so," or "You shouldn't have laughed at that joke so hard," or "You need to stop saying anything about your private life in public." I can remember on Mother's Day driving home from church and hearing him criticize her for our behavior. Unable to defend her, I sank into the back seat of the car, vowing to behave perfectly the next time so she would not pay for my choices. I tell my mom these faint memories, and she tells me others, stories that are hers alone to tell.

Hearing her, I remember more. During deep and sometimes contested conversations in the living room or kitchen between my dad and me or my dad and Karen, my mom would try to contribute. I can remember on a few occasions my dad saying with genuine surprise in his voice, "Marie, you make a good point." A lot of times I remember him dismissing what she had to say, sometimes before she even finished saying it, with phrases like, "Marie, that's just simplistic thinking," or "Marie, that's not going to get us anywhere," or "Marie, you're not listening to what I'm saying" (translation: "you're not agreeing with me").

Sometimes she would try to defend us in a fight, tell him that what we had done or said wasn't unreasonable, try to get him to back down or ease off his temper tantrum. I remember a few times hearing her voice with an exasperated tone: "Jim!" He would mock her back, saying "Marie! Marie! What?! What?!" his face contorted as he mocked her. "Every time you take their side. You always stick up for them and never for me. You're supposed to be my support and my partner. You should take my side and not the kids' side."

Sometimes our fights would escalate because we would then try to defend her. Karen and I wanted to protect her. We wanted to build her up somehow. I think we were hoping somehow she'd stand up to him and successfully make him back down. I know there were times I hoped she would take us and leave.

Now in talking to her I find out she thought about that too.

She stayed, partially out of fear of the unknown. "How would I have taken care of you both?" she asked me. I reassured her that there were few, if any, options available to her. My mom's mom told her after two of my mom's sisters got divorced, "I think if you and Jim get divorced, I'll move to Canada." I'm sure my grandmother was exaggerating, but it put doubt in my mom's mind as to whether there would be any emotional or financial support for such a choice. It made her feel even more isolated and stuck.

She stayed because it's hard to identify controlling behaviors as abuse, because one just didn't talk about such things then. And she stayed because she loved him.

I know in his way my dad loved my mom. He wrote in his journals about her as a gift from God, someone who kept him sane, someone who was a foundation for the family. He valued and appreciated her. He gave her Valentine's Day cards most years, cards she treasured. But I stop and contrast those cards with the ones I get from my husband, full of inside jokes and cute comments, references to his love for my mind, my appearance, my sense of humor.

My sister and I recall no displays of affection between my mom and dad. I remember perfunctory kisses at leave-taking sometimes. I vaguely remember as an adult seeing my mom and dad hold hands once or twice. They would hug each other, but rarely. There was no cuddling on the couch. There were no passionate embraces interrupted by our walking into the room. I think of how in my pain, in my sorrow, and in my daily malaise, I turn to my husband and collapse into his arms, finding there all the support I need to get me to the next moment. I never saw my dad protecting my mom from the world and its pains through a spontaneous embrace. My mom attests now to the fact that we didn't just "miss" it—these demonstrations of affection weren't there for us to see.

I wonder now what that must have been like for her. As I think about my husband's affectionate nature, I wonder what the absence of such snuggling and hugging and kissing would do to me over time, over decades of cohabitation. I wonder how the emotional abuse and neglect and withholding of affection that were a part of my mom's life, a life lived right next to mine but also so far away, created the person she is today.

It should not surprise me that after my dad's death, my mom struggled to find out who she was. It wasn't just that I didn't know her. I'm not sure she knew herself anymore. I'm sure every widow or widower faces a similar challenge upon the death of a spouse, finding one's self again. For someone like my mom, who had been emotionally abused for five decades, there are added layers of complexity. Her rediscovery process is still ongoing years afterwards, and I suspect it may continue until her death.

❧

I quickly became intrigued by the mystery of Marie once I realized I didn't know her as well as I thought I did. I wanted to know more. My husband explained to me that we enter our parents' lives *in medias res*, in the middle of things. As children, we don't even get the Spark notes to the backstory. We're inclined to accept that who they are to us is who they have always been. But increasingly I want to understand how she became who she is.

I go through pictures with my mom now, hungry for more stories, even to hear stories I heard when I was a kid but interpret differently now with these bits of newfound knowledge in the background. I look at pictures of her as a small child and listen to her describe the layout of the house in which she grew up, trying to memorize the images her descriptions suggest. I try to imagine her with her friends, with her sisters, happy and unhappy, dreaming of a future that was probably much rosier than what came to find her. I hear about her dad's own dark side, his temper, his frustrating inability to communicate clearly.

She and I return one summer with my kids to the neighborhood where she grew up. We see her childhood home, but no one answers my knock so we can't beg a peek inside. A few months later I see it is for sale again, and we get to see pictures of the inside, much changed of course from my mom's time. On the trip to her neighborhood, we visit the library down the hill where she had her first job. We talk to a librarian who remembers the woman my mom worked for. My mom describes the prior landscape of the library room in which we stand. I see her transported by memories, every corner reminding her of something or someone. I want more, so I eagerly ask her questions about the view out the window of the breakroom, now a children's reading room. Now there are buildings, probably apartments, a parking lot, a few trees. "Was the view the same? Did you sit here for lunch? What did you think about? Where did you think life would take you then?" She tries her best to answer my questions. Unlike my dad, my mom doesn't want to leave the past buried. She seems as eager as I am to uncover it, to dust it off, to examine it, to relive it.

We drive by the grade school where she worked shortly after that. I think of her work as an elementary school teacher just starting out, and I think of the stories of when she met my dad at her second teaching job. And now I know there was that other guy too. I ask her about what might have happened if she'd taken different paths, but she doesn't speculate much. Maybe there's no point anymore, or maybe for her there never was.

And when we talk in these ways, she repeats at the end of the conversation, and sometimes in the middle too, that she is so glad to have us, that she wouldn't trade me and Karen for anything, that we are so precious to her. In those moments, the enormity of just how much Karen and I mean to her hits me. How is it possible that we eclipse all the belittling, meanness, lack of affection, and shattered hopes?

When I was a child, I had a set narrative for my mom and my dad. I realized after my dad died that not only were there prequels to read, but the authorized version of her life was quite a different story than the one I had read. As I hear her tell stories of her life, I want to see how her character's interactions with every other character shaped her. I want to see how having me as a child changed her. To some extent, my wonder is self-centered: "Enough about you, Mom. Let's talk about how knowing you can tell me more about *me!*" Maybe that's a reasonable motivation. Maybe it's what drives us to try to make sense of anyone else—a fictional character or a real person in our lives—to see them in relation to ourselves.

My mom doesn't keep a journal and never has, so after my mom dies, there won't be diaries and journals for me to read to unravel further the mystery of who she is and was and wanted to be. She told me she kept a diary once when she was a kid, but she didn't know what the purpose was. She wrote the first day, "It was sunny so I played outside." The next day she dutifully wrote again, "It was sunny so I played outside." On day three it rained, so at least she could change her message to "I didn't play outside." She stopped keeping the diary shortly after that and never got back to it. If I convinced her now to start a personal journal, I suspect it would tell me more about the weather she lived through than her thoughts on those sunny or gloomy days.

So now is my opportunity, and I try not to waste it by talking with my mom too much about my dad. Yes, he was her husband. She maybe knew him better than anyone. Maybe. I know now he didn't let her in completely. When I talk to my mom, I try to ask why she made a particular choice or what *she* thought of a decision we made as a family. I try to see her vulnerabilities, choices, flaws, and strength. I avoid bringing up my dad sometimes because I don't want to bring up pain and hurt. If she's enjoying a day where she doesn't think about how he treated her—and I wonder if she ever has such a day, if his voice and criticisms are as embedded in her mind as I suspect they are—I try to avoid bringing him up. And if we're talking about him, I try to remember to shift the conversation. "Enough about Daddy, Mom. What do you think about *you?*" Then I pray for the courage and wisdom to hear her reply.

9

1987 (Age 15): Because I Saw How People Hurt Him

Some of the elderly residents perk up the moment my dad and I enter the dining room of St. Anne Hospice. I wonder if they're happy to see a teenage face for a change, but I know it's really my dad they're eager to see.

"Hello, Bernice," he says to one woman in a wheelchair as he gently squeezes her shoulder. "Good morning, Tom," he says to another resident whose arthritic hand he gently shakes. "How are you, Eloise?" he says to yet another.

They are all eager for a smile, a touch, a word from my dad. He visits them regularly as a part of his job ministering to older adults through the Cathedral of the Sacred Heart in Winona, Minnesota. Today, I have come with him to play trumpet as he holds a prayer service.

"Jimmy," says one woman he approaches. Her head shakes slightly, and her hand struggles to reach up from her lap. "It's so good to see you." He doesn't cringe at being called "Jimmy," a name he detests, so I know this is someone who knew him as a child, back when the nickname that never stuck was still used by some in his parents' inner circle.

"It's good to see you too, Alice," he says as he takes a seat next to her in a chair he pulls up from a circular dining table. "How are you today?"

"Better now! You're here!" she says with more energy than I would have thought possible based on her physical appearance. He has taken her hand gently between his, and her shaking stops temporarily.

He chuckles softly. "Thank you for that. That makes my day. *You* make my day brighter."

"You're a blessing to me, Jimmy. May God bless you too. Is this your daughter?"

"Yes," he says and motions me over. "This is my younger daughter, Jennifer. She's going to play trumpet with me today on a couple of the hymns we'll sing. What do you think of that?"

I hold my breath. What does she think of that? What do any of these people think of my presence here?

"How wonderful. Thank you for being here too," she says as she looks up at me with beautiful blue eyes surrounded by soft wrinkles. "Your father is such a blessing to us. You must be very proud of him."

"Yes," I say, wondering if I am and what that feels like.

As we place a music stand near the piano, hard-of-hearing residents shout directions at staff who patiently reply in loud but calm voices. I warm up tentatively, not wanting the brash noise of my trumpet to overpower their voices. Wheelchairs circle around and are placed near the rows of chairs that fill in as well. There are about 30 people there when my dad stands up to begin the prayer service.

His voice is different in this place. He speaks clearly and loudly, in long and arching phrases that rise and fall like melodies. He welcomes them and reads opening prayers. As he speaks in front of them, I notice how carefully he moves his mouth and lips to obscure his teeth inside. He's sensitive about the large gap between his two front teeth, and it's been a decade since he's been able to afford to go to a dentist, so his teeth are stained and dingy, all out of place. Like my father, I often smile with my lips closed, even though my teeth are whiter, because I try to hide my underbite and the large gap between my two front teeth.

He invites them to sing along if they know the first hymn, "Now Thank We All Our God," and directs them to a handout with the words on it. "I am proud to have my daughter Jennifer with me today. She will join me in leading the music." He sits down at the piano and I silently blow warm air through my trumpet to keep it ready. My dad plays an introduction flawlessly, and I join him on verses one and three. The sound of the trumpet echoes in the cafeteria that has no fabric—no carpet, no wall coverings, nothing that would be difficult to clean. I play more softly so as not to disturb anyone. I pull back into myself and struggle to hit a few of the high notes on the descant on verse three as a result.

I settle back into my seat up front as my dad begins to read three scripture passages, something from Acts, a Psalm, and a Gospel message about the Apostle Thomas. Thomas doubts that Jesus is who he says he is, questions whether Jesus has truly risen from the dead, and only believes when Jesus invites him to touch his wounds.

"I'd like to offer a few words of reflection on that reading from the Gospels," my dad begins after closing the book from which he had read. "It's a wonderful reading for all of us to hear because it helps us see how normal doubt is. Even when faced with the physical presence of Jesus, Thomas doubted."

My attention drifts in and out as I hear him say what I've heard him say before at home, that "without doubt, faith is meaningless. It's not faith, just blind trust. It's OK to question."

It was essentially the same message Father Rolstad gave me the Wednesday before during my pre-confirmation meeting with him; I had worked up my nerve to tell him what I knew my dad already knew, that I didn't believe everything the Catholic Church teaches.

"I'm not sure I do either," was Father Rolstad's surprising reply. "What do you question?"

"Lots of things. Hell. Eternal damnation. Why would God talk about forgiveness so much, send his only son to die for us, and then say that 'if you make me angry enough, I'll reject you forever'?"

"That's a great question. What do you think is the answer?"

"I don't think he would. I don't think that's what God is like. But in religion class, Mrs. J-B said that I'm wrong. She asked me, 'What about Hitler? Is he in heaven?'"

Father Rolstad smiled and asked me, "What did you say in reply?"

"I didn't really know what to think. I just said, 'I don't know. I'm not God.'"

"Did that end the conversation?"

"Pretty much."

"I imagine so."

Father Rolstad had reassured me that I was probably "more ready than most" to be confirmed. But was it OK to say "I do" to all the statements the bishop would make if my heart was really saying "I think so" or "some days I do"?

In this cafeteria serving as a sacred space, my dad is saying that we find God in the questions we ask, in the doubts that we have, in the moments when we fear that God doesn't even exist. Some days I'm not sure there is a God, especially when the darkness seeps into my soul and I wish I were dead. Some days I believe there's a God and that he's mad at me for not being a better person, for talking in church or for being disrespectful to my parents or for being fascinated by my own body. Some weeks at church, I lose myself in the mystery and the ritual—the incense, the music, the bells, the kneeling, the Latin "Agnus Dei" we sing sometimes instead of "Lamb of God."

My dad's voice pulls me back. He asks these older residents for their blessings and concerns. Many provide names of relatives who are ill, resident friends who are dying or unable to come to the cafeteria any longer.

They mention blessings too. "For my daughter-in-law, Bev, who comes to see me every Sunday."

"For you, Jimmy," says Alice, "and your daughter, and your care of us."

"For the staff here."

"For my new hearing aids, so I can hear the word of God."

After the concerns and blessings, my dad prays with them again. He tells them, "I have brought holy Eucharist, sanctified at Mass just this past Sunday. For those of you who are baptized Catholics, I will be honored to help you share in this sacrament." He says a few other prayers, and I begin the process by taking communion. He seems to know almost everyone, and so it is that he says "the body of Christ, Ralph" and "the body of Christ, Helen" to each of those who come forward or who he approaches.

Then he and I play another hymn, one of my favorites, "Joyful, Joyful, We Adore Thee." I hear a little less singing, and some residents are dozing in their wheelchairs. I listen to the melody and harmonies that the trumpet and piano make together. I play with more volume this time, hoping they will feel the transcendent spirit of the music whether they can sing along or not.

Afterwards, as I pack up my trumpet, I hum to myself, happy to hear snippets of the residents' conversations with my dad, with each other, and with the staff members who have come to help some of them back to their rooms.

"So good to have you here, Jim. Thank you."

"Beautiful service, Jim. Please come visit me again soon."

"Awfully loud music, didn't you think?" I try not to look at the resident who said it, but I suddenly feel very awkward.

Another voice grabs my attention: "I wish I could get to Mass, but at least we have this." I turn to look at my dad to see if he heard it.

Then another voice follows: "When do you think Father can come to visit me? I so wish to have a visit from Father …" I see my dad's chest and shoulders rise and then fall in a sigh that seems to deflate him.

I look at the person who made the last comment. It's Alice. I wonder, does the priest she longs to see even know her name?

As my dad and I walk out, he greets the nurses at the central nursing station, but his voice has an edge to it now. I suspect he's already thinking of all the other work he must do today, of returning to the office at church, of seeing Father and conveying Alice's wishes. "Thank you for coming!" the nurses call out to us. We walk outside to the summer morning light. The sky is blue and infinite. Cars full of busy people move past St. Anne's.

I'm angry at Alice and the others for tearing him down. My dad is here every week, sometimes more than once a week. He knows her aches and pains. He listens and consoles. He prays with her. He brought her communion. Why isn't that enough?

As we get in the car, I ask my dad, "Why do they want a priest to come? What else could they need?"

My dad watches traffic and at first I think he hasn't heard me. He turns onto the road and heads towards home to drop me off.

"The Church and its leaders," he begins finally, "would tell you that the priest, as an ordained person, brings a special power, a special connection to the divine. They can consecrate the Eucharist. They can absolve sins. They can perform the sacraments."

"I know all that from religion class. But …" I look out the window, wondering if I dare say what I want to say. "But I just doubt all that matters as much as the love and concern you bring. Don't they see that?"

My dad is silent and I worry. He said all that about doubts, but did he mean it?

"I don't think they do see it. They are products of a different time. And they believe the Church is right. That Father is ultimately right."

We have made the short trip home and we are in the driveway. I open the car door but before I step out, I get brave. "Well, I think they're wrong. I think what you did today—what you do—is important and powerful. Thanks for inviting me to play." I wait to see if he has a reply, hoping he won't be angry.

"Thanks for playing." I look over at him and he gives me a little smile. I grab my trumpet from the back seat and head inside. He will return to work. I will wonder if what I said was OK, if it mattered to him.

10

Role Playing

When I was a little kid, my sister and I played church. We also played house, school, *Little House on the Prairie*, bank, store, art gallery, *Wizard of Oz*, and a variety of other pretend games. I have fond memories of all of them, including playing church on Sundays after the official service ended, after we had brunch, and before we played family board games in the afternoon.

Karen and I would head to our shared bedroom—a long room that housed our twin beds, a small desk and dresser, a toy chest, and a closet that filled an entire side wall. The closet had one of those 1970s-era folding, rubbery doors. We would open part of it, set our little green table just inside of it, and cover it with the pink blanket with the silky edges. Karen played the role of the priest, of course, since she was the older sister, just as she was the teacher in school and the mom in games of house.

My dad played organ for the local Catholic church, so we had extra missalettes at home. These paperback volumes came out every church season and included readings, music, and prayers for that time of year. Karen would begin our play Mass with a song, read some prayers from the missalette, and then give a brief sermon. "Do good things. God and Jesus will love you for it. Be nice, especially to your family."

I don't remember what we did for communion, but I do remember taking up the collection was a big part of this reenactment. We had good props for this part—a small plastic basket and play money. I think we may have done two collections in the same service sometimes. That part perhaps seemed the most grown-up of the Mass from our perspective.

One week, my dad walked by as we played church. "Do you think he heard us?" Karen asked me as she froze in the middle of passing me the collection basket.

"I don't know …"

Apparently, he had because later that day my mom told us, "You can't play Mass again. It's not respectful. It's not right. God wouldn't want that."

"Why?" Karen asked.

"Communion is sacred and special and you can't play at it," she replied.

Years later, when Karen and I ask my mom about this, she remembers, "I didn't care one way or the other, but your dad was really upset about things like that."

"Do you think it was that Karen was pretending to be a priest?" I asked. "He always believed women had the right to be priests so I don't get it."

"I think, in his eyes, you were taking a sacred act and making it trivial."

I know my dad felt Holy Communion was a very special sacrament, but I know he came to disagree with the Catholic Church's stance on denying access to communion as a way to condemn certain actions like divorce and remarriage, marrying outside Catholicism, or even not going to confession. My dad once came home from playing organ for a wedding incensed at a priest who refused someone communion as they had approached, hands outstretched. "He knew she was divorced and had remarried. So he just let her stand there, embarrassed. Eventually she walked away, hands at her sides. It's all about power and control, not about the sacrament!" He vented to my mom. "Where was Jesus's love in that moment of public humiliation and rejection?"

Years later, Anton started playing church when he was about four or five. He would make paper bulletins, just like we use at the Lutheran (ELCA) church we attend each week, but his were just stapled sheets of paper with scribbles on them. He didn't know how to write many words and didn't want to take too much time on that element. His favorite part was standing up on a footstool in the living room and welcoming everyone. The welcome would be repeated several times. Then Anton would announce what was coming next, and if it was a reading, we would just skip that part (since he couldn't read). Then we'd sing a song (he had me and Edward participate once his brother was able), there'd be a children's sermon (complete with a candy treat for his brother just like at our church), and another song or two. It was mostly about the music.

Anton's church services didn't have communion. He talked about that part a few times when we ate tomato soup with oyster crackers. He would go through the motions and say the words. I wasn't sure how to respond and I don't think my reaction was the best one. I tried to explain the difference between play and a special act, all the while wondering if I knew the difference myself or if the difference even mattered. Later, I wondered what harm Karen and I had been doing by acting out communion as children. My worry that my son would never understand the act at church as sacred just because he made a game of it at home seems silly in retrospect.

Long before I expected, Anton wanted to start taking communion at church. I figured he was too young, but our pastor said he would meet with him. At one point he asked Anton, "What is communion? What does it mean?" Anton answered, "I'm not sure." At that moment I felt embarrassed, as if I should have taught my son better than that. But Pastor Scott liked Anton's sincerity, and while he did teach him about the meaning of communion, he also acknowledged that none of us really understands communion in the fullest sense. Anton started taking communion shortly thereafter and doing so made him much more engaged in the service each week. At the age of seven he started singing with the adult choir, and a congregation member kindly hemmed a special robe for him to wear. Even hemmed, the robe draped his small frame in yards of extra fabric, his hands sticking out as if trying to escape.

As I observed him on Sundays, part of me knew that on some level he was still "rehearsing" rather than truly engaged with the service, but I also think that most of us are still playing church. Perhaps the ritualistic repetition that is akin to a child's play, the repetition with only half understanding, is not only normal, but healthy. At least that's what I tell myself some Sundays if I'm not paying strict attention.

※

When I was almost 10 years old, I was given a very special "grown-up" Bible, my first without illustrations. At the front of it was a checklist that listed every book and every chapter in order. When I open it now, I remember that I approached it as I would any new book: start at the beginning and move through chapter by chapter. I left off on Leviticus 12. Then you can see that I jumped around, looking for a sense of completion by reading all the shorter books—Haggai's two chapters, 2 John and 3 John's single chapters and the like.

Now I look at Leviticus 12 and try to see it from my 10-year-old perspective. It's about how the rules for babies are different if you have a girl rather than if you have a boy, that if a woman gives birth to a girl, she must stay away from people longer. Reading such texts undoubtedly would have helped me rehearse my role as lesser than men, not fit to be a priest. I'm glad I stopped on Leviticus 12, but I'm confident that in the chapters in Deuteronomy that I later sampled and in the parts I had read before it, I read similar messages. Even as I was acting my way into religion, I was learning a limiting role, a bit part.

"You don't need to read the Bible in order," I remember my mom telling me one Saturday as she cleaned the bathroom and I complained about the boring parts.

"What am I supposed to do then?" I asked.

"Read the parts that speak to you. Read the Psalms and the Gospels and then sample the rest."

I'm glad she let me know it was OK to skip around. Perhaps it's important for someone in the world to read and understand what an ancient civilization believed about a baby girl being born, but I don't think it will help me lead a better life. I can remind myself as an adult of the cultural norms that surrounded the writing of those passages, but I also can't help asking why we still value them—why we still build churches and religions that lift these kinds of passages up as sacred.

The first Bible I bought my son was a picture Bible adapted by Archbishop Desmond Tutu. On the cover, Jesus has the brown skin he wore in life, and inside there's nothing from Leviticus. I liked it from the start because of the beautiful language, the simple ideas, the way in which it selected stories that are not just easier for children to digest, but important. The Ten Commandments include things such as "do not hurt anyone" and "be thankful for what you have." These were lessons I wanted my children to learn. And when I placed a grown-up Bible in their hands, I was sure to explain that you don't start at the beginning and read straight through.

During the pandemic, when our church closed, we spent some Sundays around the table, each browsing our own chosen section of the Bible, seeking ideas and insights about how to be better people. We would share those excerpts and have conversations about the history, the imagery, the ideas, the language—anything that caught our attention. I was trying once again to shape their view of a divine, hoping to get them to focus on love, compassion, equality, and grace. Later, as Edward grew impatient with our practice, I encouraged him to spend this time learning about other religions and was happy as he brought forward insights about Taoism or Buddhism, with peace and harmony as values.

Still, I can't control what they hear at church or what they hear outside of church related to religion. I can't control what messages they hear in the name of the Bible, a book that many people revere and see as an authority in its entirety. I can't control which passages they might encounter from the Bible, and there are certainly some that I don't ever want to hear again or want them to ever read. Our pastor preaches from a foundation of historical criticism, cultural context, and translation complications, and I have tried to teach those concepts in little bits to my boys, but I was always aware of the intellectual limits a child has, and now as they grow up, I am aware of the waning power of voices of faith in their worlds.

I have always said I just want my kids to grow up to be good people, regardless of whether they believe in a particular faith or a certain image of a divine. Sometimes a voice inside me expresses worry over their possible futures, perhaps with no organized religion at all in their lives. I am never sure if that voice is mine or my dad's. I wonder about my own journey and question whether I believe because my dad believed—and whether the genesis of belief matters.

※

As children, once we were forbidden to play Mass, Karen and I would play "nun" sometimes before bed by using my blankie. It was a light-blue knit blanket with a sateen edge all around it. The center knit part had long ago begun to fall apart. By the time I was around eight or nine, there was a hole large enough in the center for me to stick my head through. The blanket would drape across my shoulders, the sateen edge shimmering in the dim night-light of our room. For some reason, this was the beginning of playing nun.

Playing nun was nowhere near as satisfying as playing church had been. In fact, it was not even a fully developed game. I had no idea what nuns did. Priests had active roles in the Mass and in the daily lives of Catholics everywhere. I'd have several nuns as teachers later when we moved to Winona, Minnesota, and I attended a Catholic school from fifth grade through high school graduation. But aside from teaching and praying, I wasn't really sure what they did.

Very importantly, despite my respect for nuns and their right to choose that path, I didn't want to be a nun. At one point my mom intended to become a Maryknoll sister, travel, and help others. She was a postulant and then a novice in the novitiate. My dad was in the seminary for a year too. They met years after they both left those paths, so there was no dramatic story of how they tore each other from their divine callings for an earthly love.

Just as my dad had contemplated at some point, I wanted to be a priest. I wanted to be the one who got to talk, in part because I like to talk, but in part because early on I realized that while each week some people were going through the motions at church, each week many people were listening intently and following what Father said to do. To be a priest, to speak each week, was to have the power to create change, to affect people's lives and thoughts.

I once started writing a novel about the first woman Roman Catholic priest. It began with a dramatic scene of women and men storming the Vatican, demanding reform and overthrowing the papacy and all the hierarchy. Then the reader turned the page, and I admitted that "this isn't how it happened." I began another depiction of a semi-dramatic scene of men and women picketing outside the Vatican for months, demanding reform. Then the reader turned the page, and I admitted that "this isn't how it happened either." Then the story of the realities of being the first woman leading a Roman Catholic parish began.

The intro parts are easy enough to analyze—I was trying to work through how this change could occur. What could lead to this type of revolutionary redesign of that church's structure and dogma? After a few chapters I stopped writing. At the time I didn't know why, but now I think I do.

I didn't understand why it wasn't possible in the first place for women to be priests, so imagining how people might react negatively mystified me. What would the objections be? Would characters object to a woman consecrating the Eucharist while she was menstruating? Jesus was pretty clear on the hemorrhaging woman not being seen as unclean. Would they object to a woman taking care of parishioners? Why? Women are often cast in the role of caretaker in our society's literature, film, and daily lives. They certainly are in the Bible. Would they object to women preaching? To women living off the church's income? To women making decisions about how the Mass should go? To women wearing a robe? Would they simply stop coming? Would they selectively quote Scripture, ignoring the cultural and historical context and ignoring passages that contradict what they want to believe about women and the priesthood?

Growing up, as I became aware of injustices within the Catholic organization and what seemed like hypocrisies to me, I would go home after church and complain to my mom or to Karen. "Did you hear what Father said about women today? How we're to be treasured and protected? I don't need to be treasured! I need to be valued! There's a huge difference."

Karen would agree, and our anger would feed on each other's memories. "It's like how they constantly blame women for original sin and say that women can't be priests because we're not as good as men, or not as much like Jesus, or not pure enough. How pure are they?"

I dreaded certain weeks in the church year because not only would we have to hear certain biblical passages about women staying quiet or being submissive to their husbands, but because the priest would invariably choose to highlight that message and explain it to us, reminding us that Jesus's message was one of love and forgiveness for women (oh, we are so hopelessly flawed because we are not men). Then he would acknowledge that everyone has their own "special" role: women to serve, men to lead.

My role was to sit and be quiet and learn that my role was to sit and be quiet. The priest's role was to talk and be in charge. I could sing words others had written or play my trumpet, but I could not have a voice of my own.

"How do you stand it?" I asked my mom one week after a particularly upsetting sermon, something about Mary and how she was a perfect role model for women because she just did whatever God said and didn't expect any explanations.

"I often just tune them out and think about God or something else entirely," my mom responded. "They can't control what you're thinking about."

That was true, but they did seem to have a lot of control over what was happening before Mass, during Mass, and after Mass.

When I was a teenager, feminist voices within the church, including some women my dad admired greatly, fought for girls to be allowed to be altar servers. I was angry that we had to fight for the right to serve—weren't we cast as servants in sermons repeatedly? I heard voices say that girls couldn't be too close to the Eucharist as it was consecrated.

My church made me feel unclean. We were somehow trapped in Leviticus as much as we read and talked about the New Testament.

I brought up these same issues around my dad. He echoed my frustrations. Like me, he believed that women should be ordained priests in the Catholic Church. My dad admitted more than once to me that he felt tremendous sadness having to tell me that the church institution he had devoted so much of his life to and in which we worshiped put limits on me because of my biological sex. The Catholic Church teaches (at least officially since 1870) that the Pope is infallible; my dad taught me something different.

But despite his disbelief in certain church practices, we stayed.

His struggles with the Catholic Church are as present in his journals as they were in our conversations. He wrote about his frustrations with a hierarchy that was all male, a hierarchy that didn't value those like him who aren't ordained but still serve the Church. When I was a teenager and my dad became a lay minister in the Catholic Church, I learned firsthand that someone could be just as educated and do similar work but be seen as much less important than the ordained. Like the ordained priests and nuns surrounding him, my dad worked with older adults in our congregation, visiting people in their toughest moments and helping them through. Yet I saw firsthand how my dad's ministry to parishioners failed to fulfill their wishes. The more training my dad received, the more his prayer and ministry became priest-like. But to parishioners, he wasn't the real deal. To them, he was acting. They wanted what they perceived to be the authentic representative of God.

I was surprised to read in my dad's journals, more than once, that he believed his "talents in the priesthood would have been a disaster." He seems to have come to a sense of peace that the priesthood was not his vocation, but he was still haunted by the reality that without that title, parishioners and priests alike didn't respect him as much. His journals talk about how he felt privileged to be allowed into people's lives and most vulnerable moments, and yet he was aware that the priests and bishops didn't value the work he was doing: "This church really offers no support to people like me as I see it. The priests have requirements to make retreats, pray certain prayers. With lay people it is simply presumed. And then I feel that often what they do offer us is not spiritually filling and even misses the point a good deal of the time."

I know the way he felt neglected and even abused by authority within his church fueled his doubts in both the institution and in God. How could his faith remain unshaken when he felt called again and again to serve an institution that insisted he—and all women—were "less special" than a select group of men? The Church's use of God to justify the status quo ate away at him. His resulting doubts and disharmony affected me, my sister, and my mom.

My dad always said we had to fight for change from within, but we never figured out how to do that. Meanwhile, my church made me feel like less than a full human being. My dad kept saying I was equal and that those in charge were wrong. Not knowing what else to do, for years I played along.

11

1988 (Age 16): Because I Confessed the Truth

My back and knees ache, begging me to lean back on the wooden pew. Instead, I move from one knee to the other on the cushioned kneeler, trying to alleviate my discomfort. My folded hands rest on the back of the pew in front of me in the prayer-ready position. The only light coming into the cavernous cathedral is what comes through the multicolored stained glass windows. The cathedral two blocks from Winona Cotter, the Catholic high school I attend, is quiet, except for occasional whispers by my classmates, quickly shushed by a word or glare from a teacher.

I am meant to be preparing for the sacrament of confession, a time to reflect on my sinfulness. I laugh inside. When *don't* I think about my sinfulness, my unworthiness, my lack of value? Every night in my room, every day in class, every time I'm walking between classes or to the lunchroom aware of others' judgment of me, I think about what a pile of crap I am.

I think back to how many times in the past five years I've sat here and in St. Stan's Church before that, going to Mass or waiting for the sacrament of confession. I confess the same sins every time, and yet I still go off and screw up again and again.

I picture my journals at home, the pages I have torn into tiny pieces out of fear that someone will find them. I see the articulation of my desire to die, my feeling of absolute worthlessness in a pile of tiny scraps on the floor next to me in my room. My mind tapes the pieces back together again.

In this quiet, reflective atmosphere of church, I venture deeper inside myself to examine the darkness more closely, to greet it with intimacy. It seeps into my heart and my soul at an almost imperceptible rate, like a dank, mushy sludge. I envision my funeral in this cathedral space and find peace in the end to the struggle.

But I am nagged by guilt. I remember my dad saying that "the greatest sin of all is to give up hope. God is hope, so to despair is to deny the existence of God." Is that true? Is God so angry with me for these thoughts that I am truly alone? Is that why even sitting here praying I feel so empty? Has God abandoned me?

It makes me mad, though, that my dad preaches to me about hope and despair. What is he doing in the basement and what has he been doing for so many months now if not despairing? Those long talks he and my mom have that are getting longer and longer can't be about giving each other hope. I heard her sobbing in the bathroom last weekend, sobbing again in their bedroom the other night. She was alone, the closed door telling Karen and me not to check on her. And the crying didn't sound like other times. Her sobs sounded like I feel when I want to end it all.

I see our teacher move to the back of the church, no doubt in response to the loud "uh-oh!" I heard from Brian seconds earlier. I'm convinced he said it not because something went wrong, but to hear the echo and to see if he could get away with it. I look at classmates in front of me and see two girls take advantage of her absence, starting to whisper and laugh behind their folded hands.

None of them seem to be taking this experience very seriously. Maybe they don't have any darkness to explore. Maybe behind closed doors at home their lives aren't like mine. I know they think my life is perfect. Everyone at school and church and in the community thinks that. I get straight As, Karen is a successful college student, my dad is this amazing organist, my mom always has a smile, my grandparents are respected members of the community.

I wonder what would happen if they knew the truth. I wonder if things could get better. I wonder if help could lead to genuine hope.

When it is my turn, I walk to the chair across from which my teacher, one of our priests, is seated. I've never said confession in the boxes I see in the movies and on TV. Maybe it would be easier to tell the truth in one of those. Even sitting across from Father, I don't look at him. He begins the ritual with the usual words, as do I. "Bless me, Father, for I have sinned. It's been one month since my last confession." Then for some reason I decide not to tell my usual sins of yelling at my sister or disrespecting my mom. I go off script.

"Sometimes I fantasize about killing myself." I'm surprised there are tears trickling down my face because what I feel isn't sadness. I feel empty, detached, as if I'm not really living anymore, so why am I still breathing?

I begin to feel fear, however, when he says to me, "How long have you had these feelings?" and "Have you told your parents?" What comes next? How will my dad react? This suddenly seems not like a good way to get help, but a way of airing our dirty laundry—something I've been told repeatedly not to do.

"No, I haven't told them."

"God loves you very much, Jennifer. He would be very sad if you killed yourself."

"I'm not sure about that. And that's probably a sin, right?"

"God forgives you these sins, but would not forgive you if you killed yourself. You need to get help for these feelings." He pauses, during which I glance up to meet his eyes. "I'd like you to come to my classroom later today, to tell me this same thing outside of the confessional. That would be best."

I notice the lingering scent of incense, of candles both extinguished and still burning. Thoughts of my dad slip away, and I wonder what it would be like to confess these fantasies for the first time in the daylight.

He seems to be holding up my absolution until I agree to do so, playing a kind of spiritual game with me. I don't know what will happen next, but I agree to it. I slip back into the pew, allowing myself to sit after I kneel for the two "Our Fathers" and the three "Hail Marys" he's told me to say as a penance.

Later, I do as Father asked and tell him my secret outside the confessional. I stand in front of his desk after his class ends and repeat, "Sometimes I fantasize about killing myself." With the empty desks behind me, it feels like I am watching myself, a character in a movie.

His line is delivered clearly and slowly: "I am so glad you let me know this, Jennifer. I am going to let your dad know so he can make sure you get some help with these thoughts and feelings."

I spend the rest of the day mostly out of touch with the world around me, wondering and worrying, and in the car after school, my dad brings up the topic immediately.

"What's this I hear about you thinking of killing yourself? Is that true?" He sounds, I don't know, maybe angry, maybe confused.

I don't know what he's thinking or how he'll react. I'm scared. I look down at my lap and fiddle with the metal spiral of a notebook. "I don't know," I say quietly. "I … yeah, I think about it sometimes."

My dad pauses. "You know that suicide is a sin, yes?"

"I know," I say quietly. I feel embarrassed. I wish I hadn't said anything.

"I had no idea you felt this way sometimes," he says. We sit in silence, staring through the windshield at kids laughing, walking, talking to each other. I want to go back in time and not tell Father so that I can be like them.

"Do you think this is just normal sadness and stress about life? Being a teenager is difficult. Is this more than that?"

I don't know what to say. I have no idea what's normal for other people, but for me, this feeling of being worth nothing has been seeping into my thoughts gradually over time, so gradually that it now feels like normal. I wonder if there is another way to feel.

I shrug and start to cry. "I don't know, Daddy. I just … I just don't want to do anything sometimes. I just don't want to be here sometimes, be alive."

We are still not looking at each other. I close my eyes. I don't know what else to say.

He shifts the car into drive. "I'll talk to your mom about it tonight. We'll see about taking you to a doctor."

My mom. I hadn't thought about her reaction. I know that when he tells my mom, she'll cry. That will be my fault. I cry a little harder and sink into my seat. I feel the darkness coming, welcoming me, offering me a place of escape.

12

Huddled in the Dark

It was a few years after I confessed my suicidal thoughts that a doctor finally diagnosed me with clinical depression and I started down a long path towards something better. At first, doctors convinced me and my parents it was PMS. I read a book my dad bought about it, and was told to eat protein for breakfast, limit my sugar intake, and exercise daily. My mom quietly supported all these efforts, finding a quick and easy breakfast I could stomach with my morning before-school nerves (bologna and cheese—no bread). I even tried jogging for a short time, something that was probably not a good idea since I had mild asthma and no inhaler plus knees that ached after running. Under the OB-GYN's direction, I took birth control pills until I passed out one morning in the bathroom and my dad said "no more" to that. As I started college, I was put on over-the-counter anti-inflammatories. I'm still not sure how they were supposed to help.

Not surprisingly, none of these treatments worked. In the meantime, my dad and I had several awkward conversations about it all. I remember crying and nodding a lot. I don't remember what he said. No one at school ever mentioned it to me, and the priest never spoke to me again about my feelings or what I had told him.

When I returned from college my freshman year and went for a checkup, a general practitioner asked me what part of my cycle I had the depressive symptoms. "The week before your period?" I nodded. "The week of your period?" I nodded. "The week after your period?" I nodded. "Is there any time you don't have any of these symptoms?" I shook my head.

Then came the diagnosis that eventually made so much more sense to me. Then came a winding, uphill path down which I slid several times. Eventually, the path led to a place where I could say, "I suffered from clinical depression and wanted to end my life. Now I don't."

As far as I know, it was several years after my diagnosis that my dad's doctor suggested to him that he might have depression or anxiety. I don't know when my dad's battle with mental illness began. I don't know what other mental illnesses he suffered from that went undiagnosed and untreated. Maybe it all started when he was an adult, facing the stresses of being a new father. If so, then he was a man living in America in the mid-1970s, and it wasn't easy to go to a counselor for depression, and personality disorders as we now understand them weren't even defined. Maybe it started earlier, when he was a teenager and facing the stresses of not living up to his dad's expectations. If so, then he was a teenage male living in America in the late 1950s or early 1960s. That person definitely did not easily get access to counseling or accurate diagnoses of mental illnesses. That young man would have been told in innumerable ways by society to live with it, to buck up, to "be a man." As a result, for decades my dad struggled with untreated depression and possibly other mental illness *while* dealing with financial worries, job troubles, several household moves, two small children, unfulfilled dreams, and daily aches and pains.

His journals make it clear that for all those years, my dad moved through time, wasted time, spent time lamenting time's passing, and then realized he didn't have enough time. My dad's journal entries have not just dates, but times—very specific times: 12:12 a.m., 12:55 a.m., 1:15 a.m. He writes about how desperately he needs to and wants to go to bed earlier so that he can get up and start his day at a normal time and with more energy, but he doesn't. And then he criticizes himself for staying up to play computer games just like he used to stay up to watch reruns on TV. He pleads with God in his journal, "Please help me to make a break. I must read more." I learned by observing him to hate sleeping in. If I woke up at 9:00, I had already lost the day.

His restlessness started young: "I still remember an occasion when I was a kid where one night I became so frustrated because I wanted to do a number of things, but by the end of the night had done none of them and had to go to bed feeling like I had lost the battle of time."

He writes of his guilt over not caring for the yard more: "I just don't feel like doing it. I would rather spend my time in here with this [computer]." He starts projects but loses interest or energy: "I brought the file cabinet into this room with Marie's help. Now if I could get to working on my papers lying about I would certainly make some progress, wouldn't you say?" But "the days come and go. So many things I want to do but they sit here. Piles of stuff that needs sorting. I don't know why I avoid it. Other stuff I want to do, but don't do."

When his depression started for him or which came first, the feelings of inadequacy or the lack of initiative, doesn't really matter, I suppose. By the time I knew him, it permeated his perspectives. My depression began in childhood with the feeling that I couldn't get enough done, which in my adolescence became a conviction of my incompetence. I achieved at school and at home and at church and convinced myself it was all a sham. As an adult, I learned it's called imposter syndrome. As a child, I just knew that if I were truly as amazing as people seemed to believe, I wouldn't feel so wrong inside.

So many voices saying "Great job!" surrounded me and my dad, but our own voices whispered constantly, "They'll find out the truth soon enough. They'll find out how awful you are on the inside. Just wait."

I worry that the pattern continues down to another generation. After making a mistake or being reprimanded for some behavior, my older son would sometimes start a shame spiral. It began with "I'm just a stupid kid" and, on occasion, ended with "It'd be better if I were dead." I first heard him say that when he was eight years old. I heard my voice in his and I saw my dad's depression. Terrified, I rushed to tell Anton that it isn't true, to let him know how devastated we would be without him in our lives, that mistakes are a normal part of life, and we can't hold ourselves to a standard of perfection, but I worry that it's too late. It's either a messed-up gene inside him that I got from my dad and passed along to him, or I've already screwed up in raising him, or both.

My husband and I talked with his teacher, who expressed shock that this happy-go-lucky and friendly kid could harbor such darkness inside, and I am reminded that no one at my high school, aside from the priest, ever knew about my depression. I'm reminded that very few people, if any, knew how consistently depressed and ill my dad was. We started to work with my son on worrying, on perfectionism, on checking his thoughts and stopping them from becoming obsessions. I was happy to see a workbook come home from school that taught him about self-esteem. My husband has told him many times to remember that suicide is a permanent solution to a temporary problem. Now a teenager, my son has told others that same message. My husband and I won't rest easy, however. We'll continue to watch for warning signs in him and his brother as they grow. I'll live in fear that I won't see the signs in time, that my beautiful, fragile boys won't find a teacher to whom they can confess their true feelings, that depression will finally more fully claim a member of my family.

※

Those who have struggled with depression know that it acts slowly, turning out the lights one by one so that even moments of joy are shadowed. A heightened sense of paranoia, a diminished sense of self-worth, a decreased belief in self-efficacy creep in. The world around you, even your immediate surroundings, can be full of flowers, praise, and sunshine, or mud, criticism, and rain, and the feeling inside is the same. The disconnect between what happens and what you feel is complete.

Depression manifests itself in seemingly innocuous ways sometimes. After all, everyone has negative thoughts or moments of self-doubt. When people who suffer from depression make self-deprecating comments to others, it's easy for others to see their emotions as normal. The danger in depression is that what is expressed on the outside is often just a hint of the uncontested message that is constantly repeated inside. My dad's journals, early entries that are written in smooth, beautiful cursive and later entries that are typed on his typewriter or computer, are full of self-loathing statements, many of them about his weight, lack of exercise, or self-image. "Lately, again, I am slipping into depression I think. I do not exercise. I sleep a lot more than I want to admit. I must sleep on average 10 hours a day." He completes an exercise one day, an introspective sentence completion form for Christians. Several of the answers sprinkled throughout point to his own darkness. Hidden away for decades, these pages shout self-hatred at me:

> I would do anything to ... be my appropriate weight.
> I wish I could change ... my lifestyle.
> It's embarrassing for me ... these days when I know I am so overweight.
> I'm very sensitive about ... my weight.
> I really need to ... exercise.

In a different entry in a different year he writes, "Once again I am lost and feeling like I am in the darkness. I sleep and nap regularly. I eat—too much. I don't exercise. I do little that gives me a feeling of accomplishment."

My dad beats himself up over bowls of ice cream. He ties it to his health. He did have high blood pressure, and he knew losing weight would have helped. He did have cholesterol issues and later diabetes; he admits that watching what he ate would have helped with that. Even his depression might have been lessened had he exercised more regularly.

But what troubles me now, looking back, is the tone of his journals. He talks to God and seems to think that God will think less of him for eating ice cream or being overweight—for not caring for his creation more. As if any loving God could look upon this suffering creature and think, "Gee man—lose some weight already!"

I want to criticize myself less than my dad did. I don't want to waste time on silly things like that. Yet taking away those thoughts doesn't cure depression. His self-loathing (like my own) was a sign of something deeper. It wasn't just about how people saw him. It was about eating because he was sad and then about being sad that he was sad and eating more and then becoming aware of it all and feeling frustrated and out of control. It was about living with untreated mental illness.

One day in church, years after his death, I heard the oft-said directive to "love thy neighbor as thyself." I didn't hear the rest of the sermon, and I went through the motions of the rest of the service. I thought of my dad and wondered what he made of the phrase.

My dad was well loved by many people. Outside our family, he often regularly expressed love in profound and consistent ways to others. Granted, he also had some *huge* long-standing battles with people, usually those who got closest to him, including a couple of bosses and at least one instructor who he believed had said something so deeply cutting that they could never be forgiven. By comparison, he was much kinder to clients and strangers, much more forgiving of older adults or prisoners to whom he ministered, than he was to himself.

I wish Jesus had talked more about that second half of the phrase, about the need to love thyself. Maybe he did. The Gospel writers, after all, were working long after his death to record what people remembered and had passed down orally. Maybe those writers all had good self-esteem and assumed that everyone had that part down pat.

Maybe that's not what Jesus said or meant. I've read and heard theologians and pastors draw attention to the fact that while "love thy neighbor as thyself" is the wording in lots of places in the Bible, John's Gospel records it differently: "As I have loved you, so you must love one another." Here Jesus is telling us to love each other unconditionally, but the text remains silent on how much we should love ourselves.

I wish the Gospel writers had provided a footnote or a glossary or that somehow Jesus had done a better job of explaining how we are to love ourselves as he spoke. The writing teacher in me takes over as I read these passages, and I mentally write a marginal note saying, "What do you mean by 'loving thyself?' What if you don't love yourself? Consider adding in a definition or clarification here."

Maybe I ought not to criticize Jesus or the Gospel writers. Still, I think it's important to linger on the idea that implied within the biblical directive is the assumption or the understanding, the *fact* that before we can do anything else, we must love ourselves. The foundation to following Jesus, the pre-activity that must occur, is that we love ourselves. And we can't do that fully when we suffer from depression. If that's true, then perhaps depression is the most important illness we could combat as Christians. Teaching and learning to value the self may be the very foundation of all that we are meant to do in this world.

My dad's life proves that it's possible for someone to *not* love themselves and still do good in the world. However, his lack of self-love also led to the existence of destructive relationships with a handful of coworkers and supervisors, with his wife, with his daughters, and with himself. I wonder how much good he could have done in the world and in our family had he been able to say on a semi-regular basis, "I have value. I am a good person. I love myself."

Instead, my dad suffered. The society that surrounded him didn't do much to pave a path towards healing for him. Bosses, insurance companies, television, his parents—nobody normalized the idea of seeking help through counseling and medication. Nobody normalized for him the need to express his emotions.

All the years I struggled with depression, I worried that God was angry, that my mom was anxious, and that my sister was sad. I realized recently that I never felt guilty about the worry and anguish I caused my dad with my thoughts of suicide. Maybe I intuitively knew he understood the type of self-loathing that leads a person to consider suicide a viable option. Still, the illness we shared is not one that easily allows people to come together and help each other climb out of the darkness. Instead, we huddled in our darkness alone.

13

1989 (Age 17): Because He Didn't Like to Talk about the Past

"I don't want to hear that story," my dad says. The white tablecloth on the dining room table at my grandparents' house has a small reddish-brown stain in front of me where I dropped some casserole on it. The dinner plates have been replaced with dessert plates, and my grandmother is reminiscing about my dad's childhood. Since this almost never happens, Karen and I are eager to hear more.

My grandmother chuckles. "It's a good story, Jim."

"What is it, Grandma? Tell it," Karen pleads.

"Yeah, please tell it, Grandma," I add as I turn to face her.

Across the table from me, my dad takes a bite of his cheesecake and says nothing.

"Well," my grandmother begins, "your dad was about five or six years old, and I needed some bread for dinner. I sent him to Bambenek's Grocery on the corner." I think of the small store a block away, the one where we get that delicious roast beef sandwich meat.

"Bambenek's was the only grocery store we needed then. And I trusted Jim to go down there and get a loaf of white bread for dinner."

I look briefly at my dad and try to picture him as a six-year-old with the same serious expression he usually wears now. When he walked down the street, did he kick stones? Did he pause and look at a caterpillar crawling at his feet? Or was going to the store an important errand, one he took seriously? I know better than to ask. He's indicating his displeasure that we're even hearing the story by ignoring it and us while he takes his plate to the kitchen.

"So," my grandmother continues, "about 15 minutes later he came back in, carrying a loaf of bread and crying. I asked him what was wrong. He said, 'They gave me the wrong kind of bread.' 'What do you mean?' I asked him. 'I asked for why bwead and they gave me this, not what you wanted.' And he held out to me a loaf of rye bread." My grandmother stops telling the story to chuckle again. "I couldn't help it. I laughed out loud right then. I don't think your dad understood what had happened, but I did. It was an honest mistake on their part. He couldn't say 'white bread' and so they gave him what they thought he'd asked for—rye bread."

"Finished?" my dad says in an irritated tone as he reenters the room. I can't quite figure out why my dad is upset. There was nothing embarrassing about this story about him as a cute little boy.

"That reminds me of you, Jennifer," my mom says from across the table. "Do you remember when you couldn't say certain letters? Your dad would sit you on his knee in the big brown rocking chair and say to you 'say house' and you would say 'houf.' Then he would slow it down and say 'say hou-sa' and you would say 'how-fa.'" My mom laughs.

"Well, yeah, I sort of remember that," I reply. "I was five."

"No, you were thive," Karen adds.

"What?"

"You couldn't say your beginning f's either. It was hilarious. Why you could say an 'f' when it was supposed to be an 's' but not when it was there for real, I don't know."

I lightly smack Karen on her upper arm, a reminder that I'm not five anymore.

By this point, we've all begun to collect our plates and carry them into the kitchen. My dad's tired tonight, since he played for 5:15 Mass and will play again tomorrow for two Masses, so we're going straight home, no card playing this Saturday night. My grandma's health hasn't been the greatest lately anyway. Her heart condition seems to be getting worse. So it's good for everyone if we call it a night and let her rest. We call out our thanks as we leave.

"I hate that story," my dad says to my mom when we get in the car to head home. "You know that. You should have stopped it."

"Sorry, Jim, I forgot. It's a cute story."

Karen and I steal a glance at each other in the back seat. Our raised eyebrows say it all. We've seen this strange shift before, where something that was clearly not my mom's fault becomes my mom's fault. My grandmother brought up the story and told the story, but my dad blames his wife instead.

It's probably not possible to avoid what Karen and I know is coming, but Karen tries. "I think it's fun to think of you as a little boy. It's interesting to hear about that time in your life."

"Yet somehow you don't like it when I tease you about your flaws or foibles," he replies.

"I like it when you talk about how I used to say 'chick-a-jars' for chocolate chip cookies or 'fees of puzz' for piece of fuzz."

I smile at Karen. I like those stories too, even though there are more of them that they remember for Karen than for me, the curse of being the second child.

"Well, I don't like it. And the whole dinnertime conversation tonight was my mother talking about people I don't know but she assumes I remember. Why do I care about the Przybilskis or the Czechowskis? I don't remember them, and I don't care what's happened to their cousins."

"Well maybe, Jim, we should skip a Saturday dinner with them. Just have one together as a family—the four of us."

"I'm so sorry, Marie, that I have to trouble you to spend time with my parents once a week." Karen's fingers repeatedly tap the seat between us, her irritation rising. "My mother may not even be alive much longer. We never know. And Karen will be looking for a job soon, Jennifer off to college. I'm sorry it's too much to ask for my family to appreciate my mother while she's still with us."

"Jim, that's not it. You know I am happy to spend time with your parents. It's just that you were saying how annoyed you were with your mother's—"

"I was *not* saying how annoyed I was with my mother! No, it's obviously just too much trouble to spend a Saturday evening meal with my parents."

"Jim!"

Karen's fingers are practically drilling a hole through the seat cushion. We're over halfway home, and I'm hoping we can get inside before Karen explodes. For now, this appears to be between my mom and dad only, and much as I'd like to help my mom, I can't do that without being sucked into an hours-long fight. It's each one of us on our own in these situations. If you can avoid the blowup, do it. Escape.

My dad's silent now. I breathe more quietly, hoping not to make a noise, not to draw attention to myself. When we get to the driveway, I get out quickly and shut the door behind me as quietly as I can so I won't get yelled at for slamming the door. I let him go in the house first, and he heads to the living room. I go to my room and put on my headphones so I can't hear what follows.

14

Inheritance

In our upstairs hallway, Jason and I hang family photos—of our parents when they were kids, grandparents and great-grandparents at different ages, of ourselves and our children from different times. A few months before my dad died, I began to notice a picture of him as a baby every night as I would leave Edward's room. My dad had always hated the picture, and I had inherited it from him about a year earlier, taking it from the closet floor where it had been stored. In the picture, my dad is sitting up and smiling, clearly delighted by something off camera. He is wearing a dress, a common enough occurrence for the time with male babies, but a detail that had always bothered him.

Every night as I closed Edward's bedroom door behind me, I saw my dad's face as a baby, and I thought about him as an infant, full of promise. Then I thought about the end of his mental growth and the end of his body's decline. I thought about Edward as a toddler, his future stretching out beyond my own time. I studied other pictures on the wall of my parents as children and my grandparents as parents themselves, fuzzy black-and-white shots that seem so old as to be part of a legend or fairy tale.

I lose track of myself, of my historical moment. The photos we have of our ancestors, even our parents, are history and not lived reality. History can seem unreal to those who didn't live through it.

To see my grandparents as parents means to peel away the layers I knew. I can't simply recall the smell of a Saturday dinner—a cherry pie made from scratch, popover biscuits from my grandmother's own recipe, and vegetables folded into a casserole, green peas somehow kept carefully separate from the rest of the mix since I didn't like those. I can't simply picture my grandmother sitting with us on the green swing on their screened-in front porch, enjoying an ice cream treat from Zesty's. I can't simply hear her praising me for my good grades. I must do more than admire the roughly made manger my grandfather gave me, with the dried hot glue in globs among the pinecone pieces for the roof. I must do more than remember the checks he sent me when I was away at college, his signature inside the card shaky from arthritic fingers and a stroke-damaged mind. I must recall more than the jolt I received every time those same fingers would poke me in the sides when I was a little girl, my grandfather's way of saying he noticed me.

These images don't explain the fractured relationship my father had with them. To inhabit the life my father led as a child, to see what influenced and shaped him, and to consider my grandparents as parents seems impossible. How can I know why my grandmother put her son Jimmy, as they called him then, in a dress for this baby picture? Did she wish he had been a girl, as my dad believed? Or was it just the fashion and maybe easier? What did she say to Jimmy when he was a boy? What advice did she give him? For what did he get punished and what kind of punishment did he receive? What parenting mistakes did my dad witness and try to avoid with me and my sister?

I learned from my mom, not my dad, that my grandmother was seen as a country bumpkin by her husband's family. My grandfather's family was from "the city of Winona," and she was from a farm out by Pine Creek, Wisconsin. My grandmother completed the eighth grade, while her husband graduated from high school. My dad bravely wrote part of his truth in his journal, that "my mother cared a lot about her kids, did the best she could, but had her own baggage that sometimes destroyed what she was trying to love." Her baggage probably created some of the mantras that guided my own life: Hide your problems.

Don't air your dirty laundry. Smiles greet the outside world. Nothing bad to see here behind the scenes.

On different days, my dad writes cryptically in his journals about his parents, saying there are things he doesn't have the courage to put down on paper. I'm not sure what is more haunting to me, wondering what he couldn't say or reading what he had the courage to write. In one entry he more fully inhabits his childhood. He may have been reliving moments and recalling the feelings they inspired:

> Never worked hard enough. Work meant physical labor. Reading was wasting time. Playing piano was an achievement she could take some pride in. Always had to prove something in order to get attention.
>
> Hurtful remarks about my physical appearance. No male presence in my life of a positive kind.
>
> What seemed to matter the most was what others thought. They were the test. They were the standard by which one judged oneself.
>
> Disappointment. Feelings of inadequacy and no one was there to give support.
>
> A need to talk, to share, to gain approval, to receive approval for my pain.
>
> A love based—it seemed—on appearance, that is, what one could show and what one could do to please. To be loved for who one was—didn't seem to ever occur—after a certain point.
>
> Not being what she wanted—a girl.
>
> Feelings of being inadequate and then needing to be on top in order to feel secure. Unable to recognize accomplishments of others as legitimate and not threatening to me personally.
>
> Feeling a need to be humiliated as if it was my due, what I deserved. Projecting that onto another.
>
> Am I able to live now without the need to judge myself against another? Do I still need approval of what I can do?

In this passage, I can be a child with my father, be the same age he was remembering and consider what it felt like to have one's passions for music and a life of the mind dismissed. I hear the voices he heard that stayed with him through adulthood, calling him to be something he was not, to appear happier and better and more successful than he was.

"My mother seldom took an interest in what was important to me," he typed. The voices he took from his childhood forward are different from mine. I consider how my mother indulged my imaginative play by writing down by dictation my first ever story when I was too young to write it out myself—a story that bore a striking resemblance to *Frosty the Snowman*, but which she praised, nonetheless. I think about the time and attention my parents gave to helping me hone my passions and interests. My dad read my essay drafts for school and almost always asked me, "Are you sure you want to start that way?"—an annoying question for any writer, but an important lesson about audience awareness. My parents were present at every concert, recital, competition, and event.

My dad was far from perfect in this respect; he dismissed my love of watching sports as a waste of time and baseball as particularly dull. He found my sister's and my passion for science fiction to be mystifying and "crazy." If he asked a question about one of our interests that he didn't share, or if we offered information, he took the opportunity to tell us he didn't understand it and then rudely to tune out what we said about it. I remember on more than one occasion a toss of his head, a huge sigh, fingers in his ears, a toddler-like expression of his boredom with our interests. I wonder how much of this was learned behavior.

My dad used to say that he learned how to express affection or love only from my mom, not from his parents. He didn't learn it very well, I know, or the lessons came too late in life to stick. But I laugh when I consider the word "affection" in relation to my grandfather, Stan. My grandfather used to argue with my grandmother at the dinner table, drink beer, sleep in his chair, yell "Play!" when conversation threatened to derail a card game, and watch TV. He was probably an undiagnosed alcoholic. Maybe he showed affection when I wasn't around, but I suspect he simply believed it was an extravagance.

In an effort to better understand my dad and the way he was when I grew up, I move back a generation, and I try to imagine my grandfather, Stan, as a young dad. From what I know, he liked bowling, hanging out with the guys, drinking beer, and listening to music. I'm sure he had dreams for himself and his family. I look at him in his high school graduation picture or his wedding photo. The firm set of his mouth, the twinkle in his eyes—is that happiness? Is that a sense of satisfaction and accomplishment?

Stan came back from World War II changed, as the family story goes. He was a master sergeant in the Pacific theater and was part of the force that went into Japan after the bombs were dropped. He sent home beautiful, delicate china to my grandmother but brought back no stories. When someone asked him once at dinner what it was like to go into Japan, he said a few words, nothing very clear, and then left the table. I look at photos of Japan after the war and imagine what my grandfather saw. Then he came home, and the world expected him to be fine. I don't think he was.

And shortly before his service in World War II had begun, when he was just 27 years old, Stan was with his own dad in the hospital room when he died after a tragic fall from the scaffolding where he had been working. My grandfather wrote to his brother, my great-uncle, a long letter about the events that transpired between the accident and his death, reliving the horrors of it because he wanted to help his brother, who was thousands of miles away preparing for the war, understand what had happened to their "beloved dad." I wonder what my grandfather was like before his dad's death. How did the war and the sudden loss of his father change him? What would my own dad's childhood have been like had those events not shaped *his* dad? Had his grandfather been alive when his dad returned from the war, what healing conversations might have occurred? What work together might have helped ease the pain?

When my grandfather died, my dad wrote in his journal with honesty and directness: "It's over. Dad is dead." I linger on the phrase "It's over." What exactly was "it"? He wrote later that "I believe in my heart that I did what I could do for him. I know I did not do anything extraordinary, but I did do those things that helped him stay in his house where he said he wanted to stay."

My dad and grandfather had nothing to talk about, even if my grandfather had been able to talk much after strokes robbed him of some of his ability to speak. Still, almost every Saturday, my dad made sure my grandfather was at our house for dinner, picking him up and dropping him off afterwards. He'd offer him a beer the minute he walked in the door. Before and after, my dad would complain about the obligation. My mom would join in and my dad would yell at her. I think hearing her complain exposed his own guilt over not wanting to spend time with his father.

My dad wasn't there the moment his dad died. He didn't later have to wonder or marvel or struggle to process the mysterious nature of the moment of his passing, though he did have to deal with finding his dad some hours after his death. My grandfather probably died at night of a massive stroke. When my dad found him the next morning at around 10:30, he had one shoe and sock off, "perhaps getting ready for bed." His face was "covered in blood from the mouth to the forehead and there was a pool of it on the floor." My father describes the details clinically at first in his journal. When he entered his house that morning the first clue he had that something was amiss was that he saw his legs, I presume up in the air. My grandfather had been sitting on a bench by the dresser and had fallen over backwards. It was likely a quick end. My dad's journal later says, "I am sorry it was this way, but at the same time, I am glad for him that it is over and that he was able to leave this world without a period of lingering illness in a rest home."

I am struck by the ease with which he expresses compassion for this man who so troubled him his entire lifetime. My grandfather was not a father by most definitions: "He was a provider, but not a very involved or effective father." And yet my dad sees his father as a human being first and foremost: "I wonder what went through his mind these last years. Perhaps not much, except the sadness and loneliness that he experienced."

And then my dad surprises me with his honesty. He writes in the weeks after his dad's death:

> I know I am relieved that he is gone. That probably doesn't make me sound very good, but I guess I don't care. I just don't say it very much. But I know in my heart that it is true, nevertheless. Even though I feel guilty thinking that way, I also am reminded that I did do as much for him as I felt I could. No, it wasn't enough. I could have done more, but even so, I believe I did enough for him. And so did my family. He was a hard man to like.

I feel close to my dad as I read these words, closer than I usually do. He and I are at the same point on a wheel, different moments in time. I can't help but think how alike we are, how similar our paths. I understand this ungrieving of a parent. He understands mine for him. My inheritance includes this understanding of grief that isn't.

15

1992 (Age 20): Because I Wouldn't Perform

I'm sitting in the soft light of the group counseling room in the now-familiar circle of fellow college students looking for answers and help. There's the cute guy in a wheelchair, paralyzed from the waist down, whose eyes I dread meeting because I'm convinced he'll read my attraction there and laugh at me for hoping he would reciprocate the interest. There's the young girl with lots of tattoos and piercings who looked so tough that I couldn't relate to her until last week's session, when she fell apart in tears over her sister's terminal illness. There's the therapist leading the group, maybe 30 years old, a young guy who also makes me feel uncomfortable because he's good looking. Right now, I study everyone's shoes around the circle as the leader asks us to consider what we might share from our week.

"For example, did you have any incidents that really upset you or a dream you find interesting?" My ears perk up at the word "dream," and I'm back three nights ago in my dorm room bed. The group leader has seen my head move. "Jennifer, do you have something?"

All eyes turn to me. I haven't spoken much in group yet. I told them about my family on the first night and a little bit about my depression and thoughts of suicide. I talk more in my individual counseling sessions where my counselor, a blind woman in her 50s, sits in a comfy chair, her guide dog at her feet. In this circle, everyone can see me and I feel exposed.

Besides, I don't really know what to share most weeks. "Do you blame everything on us?" my dad asked me recently. "Is it all my fault and your mom's fault, this depression of yours?"

"Yes!" I wanted to scream. But that wasn't the whole truth. I just wanted to hurt him. "No, of course not," I replied.

"What do you talk about then?"

"I don't know. My feelings, how I view myself, why I think an A- is a sign of my failure as a human being."

But here in group counseling, I don't want to talk about my perfectionism or my depression. All my problems seem so silly and small compared to theirs. But this dream I'd had—that was interesting enough perhaps.

"Sure," I say. The group leader leans forward and puts his hand up by his ear to encourage me to speak up.

"Sure," I repeat. "I had a dream the other night that troubled me." I pause to gather courage and take a deep breath to speak loud enough to be heard. "In the dream, I'm at home. I'm down in my parents' bedroom, which is at the opposite end of a hallway that starts in our kitchen." I pick up speed as I imagine myself back in the dream. "Their bedroom is in between mine and my sister's. In this dream, my sister is lying on the floor, and I'm sitting astride her. I have this huge knife in my hands, and I'm stabbing it into her chest over and over." My voice trembles a bit, and I look at everyone's shoes again so I can't see how they might be reacting. The horror I felt when I woke up after the dream returns. "I hear the door to the garage open at the other end of the hallway, and I know my dad's home. I look at my sister's dead body and the blood all around it, and I think to myself, 'My dad's going to be so mad at me for this mess.'" Tears come to my eyes as I feel an overwhelming sense of fear.

Most of the people in the circle chuckle, and I look at the group leader, who has a smile on his face too. "Seems like a strange reaction you imagine your dad having, yes?"

I think about it and smile a little. "I guess. What I don't understand," I start to cry, "is why I would hurt my sister in my dream. I love her. She's always there for me. I would never hurt her on purpose." The guilt I've felt since I woke up from the dream washes over me again.

It's quiet for a moment. I should have kept this to myself. Maybe it wasn't as relevant or interesting as I thought.

"Wait a second," says the girl with the tattoos and piercings. "Didn't you say once that you and your sister look a lot alike?" I nod. "So how do you know the girl you're killing is your sister?"

"Huh?" My tears stop and my brain engages.

"What if the girl you're killing is you, and you actually think that if you were to kill yourself your dad would mostly be angry about the mess it would leave behind?"

I look up to meet the girl's eyes. I can see the group leader nodding his head. "What do you think, Jennifer?" he asks.

"Wow, I mean, I guess that fits how I feel. When I'm feeling like ending it all, I usually figure my dad wouldn't care."

"Do you really think that's true?" the girl asks. "Do you really think he wouldn't even miss you?"

Sitting here in the dim light in this circle with people who are looking at me with concern, I know that many people would miss me. But when the darkness consumes me, when I'm convinced I don't contribute to the well-being of anyone or anything, when I know in my soul that I am hideous inside and out, it's not that obvious.

"I'm so glad I don't have to deal with what you have to deal with," the young man in the wheelchair says to break my silence.

"What?" I say with incredulity, meeting his eyes before I think about it.

"I mean, sure, I had the accident that put me here." He taps the armrests of his chair. "But I don't ever remember hesitating on whether my dad would miss me if I were dead. I always knew he would. Always. It must suck to sometimes question whether your own dad values you or not."

I look around the circle at the other students nodding their heads.

"I mean, part of me knows he'd miss me if I killed myself," I say. "But part of me also thinks he'd be angry with me for the mess I'd leave behind—how people would talk about it, about him, see it as his failure. And I also know he once told me that part of him regretted having kids—that we changed what was possible in his life."

"Whoa," one girl responds.

"I guess that's not normal?" I say with a small smile.

Now almost everyone is shaking their heads no.

"So Jennifer," the leader says in a wrap-up voice, "what does all that say to you?"

I think for a minute and then dare to meet his eyes too. "Maybe I need to think more about my relationship with my dad if I want to feel better."

"Sounds like something to follow up on in your individual sessions, yes?"

I nod. I smile weakly at everyone around the circle, feeling supported by their presence even though I know I'll do the rest of the thinking alone, after I leave them.

Just three days later, my parents are visiting me in Eau Claire, eager to take me out for dinner. As always, Karen has driven down to join us. She leaves her car in my dorm parking lot and we all climb in my parents' car, my sister and I in the back seat like old times.

"Where to?" my dad asks.

"How about pizza?" I suggest.

"Your mom and I just had pizza last night." I think back to my dinner last night—my usual bowl of salted rice in the on-campus cafeteria, one of the few foods there I can tolerate.

I name another restaurant nearby, hoping he'll say yes. I think of sitting in the restaurant booth and someone taking my order, bringing me a diet soda, a roast beef dip sandwich, and maybe a piece of pie afterwards, the luxury of being waited on.

"How about the buffet?" my dad asks. I know it's what he's wanted all along. The question wasn't sincere. He and my mom have driven an hour and a half up to see me to help break the loneliness of my sophomore year away at college, so I know I should go with their choice. And Karen's driven an hour down to see us all, so I would rather avoid a fight if possible.

"Sure!" I say. "Sounds great." My parents ask about classes, and I tell them what I'm studying, what papers are due when, what exams are coming up. I worry that my dad will ask about my counseling sessions, so I chatter on about subjects that feel safer to me even as I know I'm giving far more detail than anyone wants to hear. I glance awkwardly across at Karen and remind myself of the dream interpretation that took away the awful feeling I had. She begins to talk about her teaching, teachers she's becoming friends with now in her second year on the job, her late nights advising the school newspaper.

When we get to the buffet, I head for the salad bar first and add lettuce, shredded cheese, chunks of hard-boiled egg, bacon bits, and croutons to a plate. I don't like dressing so I leave that off. I grab a small glass of lemonade and set the plate and glass on the table. I head over to the other sections and grab a dinner plate. I put ham, corn, potatoes, a chicken drumstick, and a roll on that plate. Back at the table, I dig into the salad and am halfway through before my parents are settled in.

"It'd be nice if you waited for us to begin," my dad says.

"Sorry," I say, and swallow the mouthful I have. "I was hungry."

"Well, if you could wait, I wanted to go get a salad before I started eating."

"No problem," I say, and he heads back to the salad bar. My mom, Karen, and I make small talk, looking at our plates full of food.

When my dad sits down again with a salad plate, we pick up our forks, but he pauses us again: "Let's all say grace together before we eat."

I look up at Karen in confusion. This is new. We've said grace at home before every meal except breakfast for my entire life, but my dad has never suggested we do so in public. In fact, he's always talked about how important it is not to make a show of your faith in public places, not to make it seem like you think you're better than others because of being a practicing Christian.

"What?" Karen asks.

"Let's say grace," he says, slowly enunciating each word. "What? Have you forgotten it already?"

"Of course not, Daddy. We just don't normally do that in restaurants."

"Well, I'm going to say grace. And I suspect your mother is going to join me, right Marie?"

"Sure," my mom says, folding her hands together, but she doesn't meet our eyes.

"And if you don't want to join me, then that's between you and God." The way he says it makes it clear it's also between us and him, so my sister and I quietly mutter along with them the prayer of blessing we've recited thousands of times before. My dad then makes a very large sign of the cross, much larger than I've ever seen him make before, to end the prayer. I omit the sign of the cross, as does Karen, and my mom does a small and hasty one. I've become aware of the people at the table to our right who have now noticed us.

"So, living on your own seems to have weakened your faith a bit, yes?"

"What?" Karen responds in shock.

"How strong can your faith be if you're not willing to show it in public?"

"My faith is just fine," Karen says. "I just don't feel the need to display it like that. Doesn't Jesus say not to make a big showing of your faith?"

"I'm sorry if being a follower of Jesus is embarrassing to you."

"Jim—let's just enjoy dinner."

"Fine, Marie." I steal a glance at Karen to try to let her know that I feel the same way she does.

"It's hardly worth bringing you here, Jennifer," my dad says, bringing up a new topic.

"What do you mean?"

"Look at your plates. There's no food on them! It's a *buffet*. You can eat all you want. It's hardly worth bringing you to a buffet if you're not going to eat more."

"Maybe she's going back for more later, Jim."

"I'll have some dessert later, for sure."

My dad gestures with his fork to his plate heaped higher than mine with food. "Well then, I guess I'm just a pig for eating so much, huh. It must be so embarrassing to eat with me—I practice my faith in public, and then I eat too much."

"Daddy, I never said any of that. Can we please just enjoy our dinner? I love their ham. Maybe I'll go back for some more."

"Well, don't change your dainty eating habits for me," my dad jabs.

"Yes, they do have good ham," my mom agrees, and Karen chimes in too. After my plate is cleared, I'm full, but I decide to go back and get more ham and another roll.

Then I grab dessert. "I see you're off your diet then after all, yes?" My dad seems displeased no matter what I do, so I give up. I leave half my dessert uneaten. I feel sick anyway. But it's always been easier to just say "yes" and eat with him, even if I felt sick afterwards. I find myself truly looking at him for a moment as he eats. His face is set in anger or disappointment or something.

I hastily glance away as my dad looks up at me. He's not the kind of dad who will offer me a goofy grin if he catches me looking at him. It'll start a bigger fight, so I pray he hasn't sensed my eyes on him. I try to remember my feelings at this moment so I can explore them later with my counselor, try to make some sense of the scars I'm discovering.

An hour later, my parents drop me off at my dorm. I hug my mom tightly, kiss her goodbye, and I see her fighting tears. "You know me," she says, waving away my look. "I could be a professional crier!"

My eyes fill with tears too and my heart hurts. "I'll miss you," I say to her. I wish she could stay longer.

I hug my dad and kiss him goodbye. "Thanks for dinner."

"Keep up the good work," he says to me.

"See you in a few weeks."

I hug Karen, knowing that next weekend she will pick me up Friday evening to go to her apartment for the weekend. We'll eat whatever we want whenever we want, watch movies, stay up late talking. We'll be free.

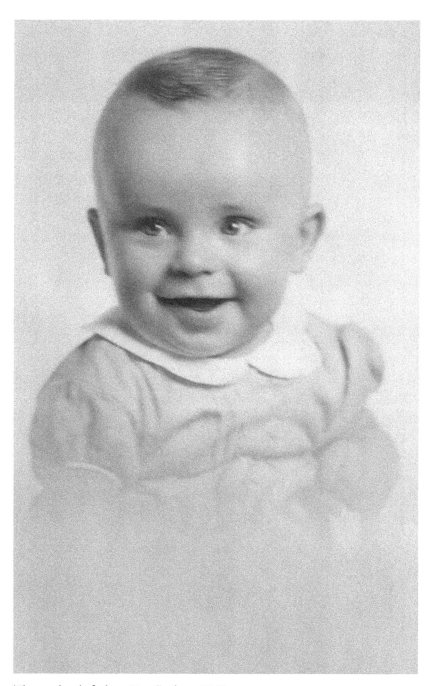

The author's father, Jim Stolpa, 1942

The author's mother, Marie Lebens, as a toddler in South St. Paul, Minnesota

Jim Stolpa at the organ, Church of the Incarnation in Minneapolis, Minnesota

Jennifer Stolpa Flatt (left) and Karen Stolpa Kruschke outside their home in Granite Falls, Minnesota

(*Left to right*): Karen Stolpa Kruschke, Jim Stolpa, Jennifer Stolpa Flatt, and Marie Lebens Stolpa at Jennifer's graduation from Winona Cotter High School in 1990

(Left to right): Jim Stolpa, Jason Flatt, Anton Flatt, and Marie Lebens Stolpa reuniting in St. Cloud, Minnesota

(*Left to right*): Edward Flatt, Marie Lebens Stolpa, Anton Flatt, and Jim Stolpa in St. Cloud, Minnesota

Edward Flatt and Grandpa Jim at Jim Stolpa's home in Waite Park, Minnesota

16

Seeing in the Dark

In my 19 years teaching at the University of Wisconsin-Marinette, I had more than just a few students in my office in tears, talking about their battles with depression or other mental illnesses. They seemed to see me as a safe person to whom they could turn when life had become too much. In most of those situations, and with colleagues and friends, I recommend a counselor and try to normalize their tears by sharing my own experiences. I try never to compare our journeys, just to share enough of my own to give them hope that someone can survive these feelings and even get rid of most of them.

I tell people that they deserve help, that they deserve to feel better because they are worthwhile and valuable. On his good days, my dad used to tell me that God doesn't make junk, that although we are all flawed, we are also amazing creatures. On his good days, he used to tell me he was proud of me, and I know he meant it.

I wish when people had told him he was amazing that he could have believed them. I wish he had been able to see his own value more clearly. It might have helped him work on seeing his way out of the darkness.

His journals teach me that his depression was often debilitating, preventing him from going to work on time, staying there all day, doing what he knew he needed to do at his job or at home. He asked himself, "Why do I continue to succumb to the darkness? What can I do to begin a real commitment to life?" His mind wandered to suicide more than once:

> The time goes so fast. I feel overwhelmed. I guess I'm in the blackness again because I'm bored and the future doesn't appeal to me. I hope I'm not in too deep trouble right now because although it repels me, the thought of ending it all occurs. Scary.

I was surprised when I first read those words in his journal about three years after he died. I stopped reading but kept rocking the porch chair. I looked up at the bright summer world around me and then reread his words, uncertain if I had interpreted them correctly. It was easy enough to transport myself and inhabit my dad's sense of failure, of aching loneliness, of despair. I just had to remember those moments in which I had questioned the very validity of my own existence.

When depression consumed me, I thought about suicide a lot, and it became a comforting thought. Now when I think about dying, I panic. I see that panic as a gift, a reminder that I no longer suffer from the perspective-altering mental illness I battled for so many years.

For a while, my dad's journals talk about going to see a spiritual advisor once a month. I'm sure Sister Myra was a wonderful person, and I'm sure my dad gained important perspectives from meeting with her, but I think it was not what my dad needed. When he writes in his journals about their conversations, they all come back to his relationship with God, as if having a deeper relationship with God will fix everything.

I believe he thought it would, but I'm not nearly as sure. In the journals he wrote, my dad spoke to God on a regular basis, so I can see how that relationship played out. There were beautiful parts to it; I admire the way he turns to God in a persistent, personal, and precious way, in almost every difficult or joyful moment.

Yet his turning to God and his self-loathing intertwine in a dance that never ended and wasn't always so beautiful:

Does it matter to you that I want to do this for you? Are you angry with me? Do you find my work wanting? Do you find me wanting? I thought you chose the weakest to be your instruments. How much worse can I get?

I hear the catch in my dad's voice that it sometimes had when he became angry, or deeply sad, or both. He is with me, reading these words aloud and pouring out his tortured soul, crying out for help.

I believe my dad's most important relationship in life was with God, which may sound wonderful and full of faith, but the inequality of that relationship haunted his every thought, action, and self-evaluation. Turning to God and God alone, focusing exclusively on that relationship in counseling and in his internal conversations, heightened his feelings of inadequacy: "I have let God down miserably with the poor use of the gifts he has given me." His journals show a willing servant of the Lord, a child of God, who knew from the start that he could never be adequate or sufficient: "You have never let me down even though I have let you down so many times"; "If you want something else, you must show me, but, please be gentle. I know I don't deserve that, but you know me."

I talked several times with my dad about poems by the nineteenth-century Jesuit priest Gerard Manley Hopkins. I came to love Hopkins's poetry about his own depression and doubts because of how perfectly I felt he articulated my own anguished moments. In one of my favorites, Hopkins's speaker questions God, something I now know my dad did regularly in his own journals. The poem is now titled "No Worst There is None" because of its first line, one that forecasts the total darkness that is to come. The speaker cries out, "Comforter, where, where is your comforting?" I know that like me, my dad could relate to that cry of desperation. In his journals, he often asked God, "Where are you now that I need you?" or "Have you abandoned me, God?" The poem by Hopkins has an ending where he describes "a comfort" that only those who have visited total darkness could define as happy: "all / Life death does end and each day dies with sleep." As

I casually paraphrased for my literature students, 'take comfort in knowing that while life sucks, at least you get to sleep each night, and eventually you get to die!' Happy endings are relative.

Like my dad and like me, Hopkins struggled with faith, with deep depression, and possibly other forms of mental illness. Like the speaker in Hopkins's poem "Carrion Comfort," my dad was still "wrestling with (my God!) my God." My dad would argue that "wrestling" with God and wrestling with doubt in God's existence was itself an affirmation of God's existence, which is true. You can't talk to someone or wrestle with someone you don't think exists. Perhaps then in those moments of utter despair, my dad and I were not completely without hope.

In my dad's book collection I found a slim volume of Hopkins's poetry that looked as if it had never been opened, evidence of interest if not engagement. Maybe Hopkins's words were too close to his own. Maybe he didn't need to read what he already felt deeply. Yet my dad struggled to define himself as someone who suffered from depression and never once articulated to me or in his journals any possibility that there was something else, something even deeper wrong. He wrote after a fight we had, apparently a particularly destructive one, "Even now as I write the word, depression, I feel so hurt and destroyed. For it's like they—K&J—think I am responsible for it. That I am in it. They really do not understand." In the same entry he said, "They have left me with the perception that I am an evil person in need of help, that I am not a person they want to be around and that I am not a person they feel they can get close to." Part of me nods and feels that we communicated clearly with him—not that he was evil, as that was his perspective and not our words—but that he needed help, that we couldn't get close to him, and that we didn't want to be around him. Part of me feels so sad for him because of his pain at our response and because he just didn't see his own illness.

He danced around the diagnosis of depression, tried to deny its existence inside of him, and avoided his role in fighting it. He met with a longtime family friend who was also a priest and the priest gave him homework, designed to help him feel better. He avoided it. He said it was too much work. Then, a few months after he mentioned starting to see Sister Myra regularly, he wrote that he ought to reach out to her again. I realize that he didn't stick with those sessions for very long. "Really, when a person is depressed they don't want to talk and almost cannot talk." Maybe she had asked him to talk about a level of darkness he wouldn't visit.

※

My dad clawed his way out of the pit once. There's an amazing two-year period (1997 and 1998) when his writings include the most lucid and direct explanations of his feelings I've ever read or heard from him. During those two years, he was a healthy person exploring his feelings, his experiences, and his thoughts in a coherent and productive manner. The cloak is torn away, and I can see the real person underneath.

He was on an antidepressant that entire time, he had started seeing Sister Myra again on a regular basis, and his parents were both deceased. I can't help but imagine the latter had a helpful effect. His toxic relationship with his dad and challenging one with his mom were at rest. Perhaps he finally felt unshackled by his dad's death, able to explore who he truly was without risk.

He still beat himself up for overeating and talked about his food addiction, but he treated it like a problem he needed to solve. He still had self-doubts and work conflicts and flare-ups of temper, but he wrote about how he later apologized to coworkers or compromised over conflicts, something simply not possible in other years. There are entries where he moved from a place of despair to a place of hope—*on his own*—just by talking himself through his feelings. Sometimes he wrote about spending too much money on computer programs, but then he pivoted and mentioned how he used them for so much good. He talked about a tiff with my mom, but only later, when he could also say how they worked it out together.

Eagerly, I reread these years. I encounter him in these pages not in the darkness which fills so much of the rest of what he wrote, but instead in a place of greater clarity. I find myself in conversation with him as a human being.

> I feel good about these accomplishments and tonight in a strange way I feel I am able to accept myself a tiny little better in that I recognize some of my own good work, some of my own accomplishments. Not that for a moment I can forget that all of this is the result of your gifts and the gift of the people around me. Still, I see myself as responding to your call at least a little bit.

Thanks be to God, antidepressants, and therapy, which together brought him to this moment of self-acceptance. And then this moment of grace recurs, wonder of wonders, weeks later, taking a different form, one of an intense self-awareness, a sense of his own personal growth:

> Another point that occurred to me tonight and it has occurred off and on of late, is that my need for approval seems to be growing less strong. I think that is good. Too much of my Dad is in me. At least I sense this as being him. I have to impress people—that is my need, that was his need. Then, it becomes old and I have nothing more to say. How sad. Perhaps I can still change myself in this respect. I think it is already happening, but ever so slowly.
>
> Nothing is going to be done of any consequence unless I do it when it comes to my life. No one can live our lives for us.

I think about my own journey out of the darkness around that same time. When I was working on my master's degree in Duluth, Minnesota, in the mid-1990s, I sat in a counselor's office talking about all the work I'd done to "get better," but how I still struggled with the same issues and feelings. She asked me a question that startled me: "Who is Jennifer if she is not 'someone who suffers from depression'?" I realized

I had no idea. I had identified myself by my depression for over a decade. She challenged me to think about creating a self that was a survivor of depression. The work to do so took me at least another decade, and in some ways it's still in process.

For my dad, a few routine journal entries after his brief moments of self-awareness and self-esteem, this awakened section of his journals ends. I've read the rest of the pages he wrote or typed, and they're not like these. I know the rest of the story. Had he turned a corner in his self-development? Perhaps. The path he took later—including returning to graduate school for a second master's degree—is probably evidence of his growth, of his ability to value himself more deeply, to face his demons.

But there were also the times when he took himself off antidepressants without his doctor's permission. Or the time a few years after these journals when he was first diagnosed with cancer, and they didn't give him his antidepressants in the hospital after surgery, and days later he was so unbearable to be around that I sat in the car with my mom and my sister sobbing, not wanting to go back in to see him and endure his viciousness. There were caustic emails, hurtful remarks, intense mood swings, belittling comments about my mom, and many ugly days. Unlike a happy movie where the rest of his life was lived out in deepening self-awareness and honest dialogue, the window closed most of the way.

I share the unusual entries with my sister, my mom, and Jason. Together we marvel that he was able to value himself at all. I think they are less in awe because they have not read the hundreds of other pages filled with ever-present self-deprecating comments. I find myself wondering if I could have done more to encourage him. What did he think of the Jennifer I created who was no longer suffering from depression but was instead a survivor of it? Was he envious or hopeful? If he could have stayed out of the darkness longer, how much better could our lives have been?

In our experiences of depression and suicidal thoughts, my dad and I share a deep connection. I go back to that dark place in my mind sometimes, briefly, like a tourist now, so that I can better understand him. I take him by the hand and wander around, but if I move back into the light, I can't see him anymore. I don't know who he could have been. He didn't either. I go back sometimes to the shared pain so that my empathy for him grows a tiny bit.

And then we part ways. The truth is that I chose to get help, to act, to fight and fight and fight, while he embraced inaction. He didn't end his life, but after he had colon cancer the first time, he didn't go back for the required checkups that might have caught its spread to his lungs a little sooner. He didn't stay on antidepressants. He didn't see a counselor on a regular basis. He wasn't doing everything he could.

I'm not so naïve as to believe that my dad chose to suffer. He didn't choose to grow up in a society that discourages men from expressing their feelings. And he also didn't completely ignore the possibility that he had treatable mental illnesses. He took antidepressants off and on, and I know he read about depression and treatment. Maybe he was so deeply mired in the darkness that he couldn't see the problem clearly or see a way out. Maybe he tried other counseling and it failed, and he didn't write about it. Maybe once some counselor or doctor suggested a diagnosis more specific than depression and it scared him. Maybe his insurance didn't cover it, at least not fully, and he didn't value himself enough to spend the money and go into debt to pay for it. Maybe he felt ashamed to admit his mental illness because it's just not something you talk about. Considering myriad maybes, I feel sorry for him that he suffered and sorry for us that we did too.

I wish people talked about depression in the open and supportive way that we talk about other illnesses, the way we talk about cancer, for instance: "Bob has depression. He deserves to feel better and be healthy. Let's get him the help he wants and deserves." I wish men bought and sent greeting cards to each other that normalized seeking counseling: "Good luck in counseling, dude! You are going to kick depression's ass!"—complete with a picture of a donkey on the inside and a cartoonish guy kicking its butt. What if the TV shows my dad watched had shown men going to counseling, and not as a joke to save their marriage from some trite miscommunication issue? What if the society that surrounded my dad had made it seem normal for him to discuss his feelings? What if his employers, including the Catholic priests for whom he worked, upon learning of his illness, had given him paid time off and paid for his counseling? What if we began to see the cancer of the soul that is depression? I wonder if he would have had the strength to walk the path to light that would have opened to him. I'd like to think he would have.

17

1994 (Age 21): Because I Wanted to Go to the Movies

"Daddy?" I stand in our living room during a commercial break, hoping to catch him at a good moment.

"What?" he snaps back.

Now is probably as good a moment as any. "I was wondering if I could borrow the car tonight."

His feet slam down the bottom of the recliner and he sits forward, muting the television. "Where are you going? Do you have your group tonight?" he asks, referencing the Emotions Anonymous group of mostly 40- and 50-somethings who meet once a week, the only group I've found to replace the counseling opportunities I lost after my graduation from college this past December.

"No, not tonight. I was thinking actually about maybe going to a movie."

"With whom?"

"By myself," I try to say with conviction.

"What?!" He sounds incredulous. "Why would you go to a movie alone?"

"Well, Amy's not here anymore, and I haven't made friends yet in my grad classes in town …" I think about my hopes to get into a graduate program somewhere else for fall. If I were living in a different city, I could go to a movie and he wouldn't know.

"No."

"Why not?"

"It's not appropriate."

"What? How so?"

He puts his feet back up in the recliner, effectively ending the conversation.

"Why is it inappropriate for me to go to a movie?" I repeat.

"Alone?! What would people think? What if you met up with someone? It's a dark theater. Anything could happen."

"People would think I was going to a movie I wanted to see. I'm 21 years old, Daddy. I can handle this."

"Absolutely not. And where would the money come from anyway? What job do you have that pays for this midweek movie fun?"

"My scholarship is still paying my full tuition this spring. I'll be working this summer. I'd work more if I had a car to get to a job …"

"And who would pay for the car, I wonder. Hmmm?"

I turn around and head back to my bedroom so he can't see the tears in my eyes. They're mostly from anger, but I don't want him to see them as a sign of weakness. I sit in my room with my headphones on and watch sitcom reruns, grateful that my mom and I won the battle to have a cable jack put in my bedroom when I had to move back home temporarily. I want to block out his viewing of the conservative Catholic TV station. Why he's watching it, I have no idea. After he does, he's always angry, saying that it doesn't represent what the true church should be about, saying its values don't fit with Jesus's social justice mission.

I struggle to be engaged by plots I already know or ones so simplistic I can guess the jokes and the outcomes before they happen. I sit on my twin bed, the TV on a cart crammed between its foot and the familiar brown closet doors in front of me that take up most of the short wall, along with the door to leave the room. The door is shut, and I can see on its back the posters of Corey Hart and Howard Jones, reminders of my teenage years at home and my fantasies of escape. I think back to college and its stress and hard work, the small dorm rooms with no character and little comfort. It hadn't felt much like an escape, but in hindsight, it had been. I close my eyes and enjoy the darkness welling up inside of me. I lean back into the comfort of sadness and isolation.

I surface from my room a couple hours later, walking quietly down the dark hallway and looking into the garage to see if my mom is home yet. She's not. It's not quite 8:45, when she usually gets home on Thursday nights. She'll be tired—not as tired now that she works at a public library as when she worked at the factory, but it's a long day, cleaning and laundry at our house in the morning, working 12–8, driving 45 minutes each way. I don't want to need her when she's so tired, but I do.

I venture back through the kitchen and out to the living room. My dad's watching a rerun of *All in the Family* now. I sit on the couch across from him. He looks up. "So, you still pouting?"

I slow blink and look up at him. "I wasn't pouting. I was upset."

"Oh, poor Jennifer," he mocks. "Can't go to the movies … has to sit and watch TV with her stupid dad. Can't go out to try to meet guys at the movie theater …"

"Daddy, that's not what it was about. I just wanted to get out tonight."

"You got out today for classes."

"It's not the same thing. Sometimes, I just want to go and be out of the house."

"Well, that must be nice to have this budding social life. I wouldn't know anything about that."

I sigh.

"What! What! I'm sorry. Am I keeping you from something? You're such a child."

I hear the garage door opening and my mom driving in. I look at the TV, willing him to get interested in the plot again. It'd be nice for my mom not to walk in on a fight.

"Are you done talking to me now? Is that it?" He waves his hand dismissively and imitates a spoiled teenager voice: "You can stop talking now, Daddy. I'm done with you."

"Daddy, that's not it. I just don't want to fight about this. I didn't go to the movie. You got what you wanted—"

"Trust me. I did *not* get what I wanted here."

I don't even understand that comment, so I don't respond. I hear the door from the garage into the kitchen open and close behind her. I want to get up to greet my mom, but I'm worried my dad will misread that move as defiant.

"Hi, Mom," I say to her when she comes to the doorway between the living room and kitchen.

"Hi dear, hi Jim." She looks at me, and I try to telegraph with my eyes that all is not well, but of course it doesn't work. She's tired, and I don't know how to send mind messages.

"Guess what our daughter wanted to do tonight, Marie?" He stands up and fills the space between his recliner and my spot on the couch.

"What?"

"She wanted to ditch me and go to the movies in my car because our house isn't good enough for her anymore and she needs to 'get out' and 'see people.'"

I want to be somewhere else. I don't want to play this game anymore.

My dad is standing in front of me now, his finger jabbing the air between us. I've stopped listening to his words. I peer down the tunnel, not seeing him or my mom or the room anymore, just a spot on the cream-colored wall across from me. I briefly tune back in to hear him scream, "I guess you're just always right and I'm just crap! Maybe I should leave. Maybe I should just go kill myself. Would you like that?"

Through the darkness that inhabits me I feel a rush of energy, a current. The current drives my hand to pick up a pair of sewing scissors nearby. I pull off the plastic safety cover and let it drop from my fingers to the couch behind me as I stand. I face him, but I'm still looking down to the end of the tunnel. I don't really see him. I see a way out, a way for this to end.

I take the scissors in my right hand and with a sharp movement point them at my chest. I hear my mom's agonized scream and terrified cry of "no!" I stop the scissors an inch from my chest. I don't know what to do now. Forward or back? Which is which?

Someone's hand takes the scissors from me. My mom is by me now, and we cry together. I am shaking, the energy drained from me, the moment of decisiveness gone. My mom's arm is across my back and her presence begins to pour light back. I begin to see around me again. I don't see my dad. He's probably in the basement. When her words have restored my sight, my mom reappears before me and I see fear in her eyes.

18

Reading His Words

My journals from as early as age nine or ten hint at intense dissatisfaction with myself and with my choices. I've pulled them out once or twice as an adult to reread them. The parts that don't hint at my early depression are typical, full of young crushes—oh, that boy on the bus—or ambitions and dreams about keeping my room clean or somehow getting along with my sister. Like my dad, part of me was afraid to write all the truth on the page, so I must read between the lines.

My mom says my dad told her to destroy all his journals when he died. I thought about respecting that wish, of turning the scissors on what was left of his identity on the page. When we first began uncovering his journals, hidden amidst so many pieces of paper he kept—directions on how to play Doom or Fairy Godmother, paid electricity bills from six years earlier, or a piece of junk mail or old catalog—I thought about not reading his words, about putting them in a box or shredding them. During those days of intense physical and emotional work, as we pulled ourselves away from his belongings, I spent hours shredding documents with private information. I hunched over stacks of papers trying to make sure there was nothing valuable or important among them.

Each night, lying on the couch in the quiet darkness, I cried silently. The living room was still full of his possessions, the walls were covered with his memories, and his presence permeated the house. Each time when the realization of his permanent absence hit me, usually harder at night when exhaustion weakened my rational capabilities, the ache in my soul came back to me. I forgot about my frustration and anger and just felt empty.

In the end, the temptation to read my dad's words was too strong. I turned off the shredder, put the scissors down, and with my mom's permission, I took everything he had written. I started from a self-centered goal: I wanted to find anything that explained how he felt about me. Back at my own home, I would squeeze in time to read through his journals. I read them in the kitchen at night after my kids went to bed, bright lights on, my husband in the next room on alert in case their overwhelming honesty brought me to tears.

There were no immediate revelations that helped me understand his complexity, but I read on and tried to understand who he was when I was too young to see him clearly. I read his thoughts on education written while I was still a child. I read about his dreams of a new house with a fireplace and a family room. He never got either.

I read his journals written when I was a teenager and he was unemployed, then before that, when he was considering leaving his job selling insurance. I sampled, moving back and forth in time. Always, after reading for thirty or forty minutes, I'd end up crying, exhausted by his view of his life, our lives, himself. I'd take a break, sometimes for weeks.

After months spent sampling sections at random, I decided I would reread his journals more carefully, find out what I could from reading his thoughts chronologically. On summer afternoons, I spent hours on our front porch in the white wooden rocker, looking up to see the beautiful Menominee River, green grass, people passing by in cars or on bikes. I read diligently, for longer periods of time, trying to get the flow of my dad's life. I began with the beautifully handwritten pages in a spiral notebook, moved on to the typewritten pages I could picture him working on in our basement, and finally arrived at the entries I had printed out from computer files, pieces of paper he'd never touched himself. As I read, my feet, tucked under me, fell asleep, and the rocker was hard on my back, but I ignored these physical discomforts. I pushed through his repetition, pushed through his dark times, willed myself not to get sucked into the vortex of his sadness.

I heard his voice in every passage. It was as if he were narrating his life to me. I couldn't ask him questions, which was just like when he was alive, but now at least I was getting to hear the internal monologue that had altered our lives so greatly. I put post-it notes on entries I wanted to return to later to consider more deeply. Soon the colored flags mounted and nearly every two pages contained one. And then I stopped after a few years' worth of later entries, frustrated with how I was choosing to spend my time. What was I looking for? The passage that explained everything about his and our suffering? The part where he said he was sorry? The entry that fixed it all and could heal me? There was no passage I could read aloud to my mom and my sister so we could exclaim, "Oh, *that* was it! What a relief to know." His journals offered no magic elixir to help me turn back the clock and relive my childhood differently.

Every time I read, I felt a complex mix of emotions that included a deeper appreciation for the depth of his self-doubt, how he saw his life full of unfinished projects and unachieved ambitions, and his connection to God. Despite the ways in which his relationship with God was sometimes not building him up, it was also one of deep intimacy. Despite its questions about a frustrated sense of purpose in his life, he ends a journal entry written just months after his second cancer diagnosis with an affirmation of faith: "God, I do love you. I feel your love for me. I am grateful. Thank you."

It is on entries like that which my mind lingers. I marvel at how my dad, like the biblical figure of Job, could maintain *any* sort of relationship with God despite his anger and sorrow at the way life had turned out for him. I consider the innumerable times his mind and pen turned to God as I would turn to my husband, sister, or any intimate friend to share the good, the bad, and the inconceivable parts of my life. Maybe I return in my mind to these journal entries because I want my dad to teach me how to have a closer relationship with God. Maybe he still can.

❧

One evening, I settled in to read back issues of a spiritual magazine my dad had collected and put in a paper grocery bag, magazines he'd told my mom he thought I might enjoy. Tucked inside one of the first volumes I picked up to read was a set of lined, lime-green post-it notes with my dad's handwriting on them. His shaky writing laid out a set of reflections, a semi-poem he'd written, either in response to some of the readings in that issue or in response to that moment in nature and his life:

> empty—
> trees that are sticks
> reaching to the heavens
> thick
> broken branches
> waiting
> wild & overgrown
> dry
> bent every which way
> waiting for life
> will it come?
> gnarled
> broken bark
> time—long yet short

I picture my dad looking out of his living room window, pausing from his reading to experience uncertainty, to feel winter in his soul. I imagine his sense of brokenness, how long he waited for spring rains to come into his life sometimes, how long he lived with only hope for better times. Sometimes I feel dry, broken, and gnarled. I know my dad was waiting for God, pleading with God to come and give him hope. Sometimes, I don't know what I'm waiting for.

In the same journal, on a separate Post-it and with the heading of "Thoughts—overlay with Jesus Prayer," I find this quasi-verse in conversation with God. The purple Post-it is a splash of color against the beige pages of the journal. The lines are broken, maybe by the paper's limits more than by his choice, but I like the pauses and the surprising breaks, and I pretend they were intentional:

> Sometimes we try too hard—
> God is always near—even in
> those moments when we feel so alone,
> even abandoned. A mysterious God
> indeed. I am just beginning to see
> ever so little through the clouds. It
> is different now than even a year ago.
> I'm not sure how it all happened,
> but I am different today. It's not
> what I've done, but what God has
> done for me. What delights God
> places on my path! A beautiful
> cardinal singing to me! What joy.
> What comes next my Lord?
> Will you be there waiting for me
> When the time comes?

One poem answers the plaintive cry of the other. "Will it come?" Yes! "What delights God places in my path!" For a moment, hope and faith are restored. Then follows another, deeper question: "What comes next my Lord?" And the ultimate question of faith: "Will you be there waiting for me / When the time comes?"

As much as I revel in his use of poetic devices, his choice to write in verse frustrates me because so much is left out. What is different from a year ago? How had God worked in his life? What took him from that place of despair to one of hope? I yell at the page, "I can't go with you, Daddy, if you don't tell me the way to go!" And I want to go there, to that place of faith. I envy his devotion to prayer, to thoughtful reflection. I sink into guilt over my own lack of attention to my faith life. When do I talk to God?

My questions are different. What comes next, Daddy? After all the struggle and the doubt and the anger—what comes next? After the frustrations with hierarchical churches and male images of God—what comes next? After earthbound battles over weight and time and priorities and money—what comes next? After all the pages and pages of pain poured out—what comes next? I inherited from him pages and pages of words, but he never wrote down the answer.

A few times while he was alive, my dad shared a piece of his creative writing with me, a poem or set of reflections. As I got older and began to study literature in graduate school, I wondered if he was hoping for encouragement from an "expert" in the field. I always told him that I liked the piece (and I did), and we'd talk about its meaning to us, but I didn't know how to help my dad be a better writer. At that point, I barely knew how to help my first-year composition students, and they had far more obvious issues in their writing to deal with than my dad did.

Sometimes I thought he shared his writing with me because then I would feel more comfortable sharing thoughts with him, his way of trying to level our relationship. He used to tell me that one of the most important things we can do in our lives with those we love is to make ourselves vulnerable to them. It is in doing so—in asking for help, in recognizing our own shortcomings—that we enter a deeper relationship with that other person. In my experience of my dad, he gave this advice much more freely than he was able to take it.

I had the chance to remind him of this lesson just days before he died, when he was struggling to get a soda straw to his lips. Whether it was medications, or the cancer, or physical weakness, he couldn't do it. I asked if I could help, and he shook his head with frustration a few times. Finally, I reminded him that it was time for him to show his vulnerability so that, as a wise man once told me, we could deepen our relationship. He let me help him. Then I left the room to cry.

Unlike the exchanges we had during his lifetime, his journals spread out before me so many of his vulnerabilities. Reading his words, I enter a strange conversation with him, perhaps the safest conversation ever. He can't argue with me or make cutting remarks. He can't be the aggressor. I can try to see through the negativity towards other facets of his identity.

Still, reading my dad's journals is awkward, like reading letters addressed to someone else. Reading his final journals is especially painful—I know the end is coming even when he doesn't. The entries I have meander, cycle back over the same problems and emotions, and keep drawing me back in to try to work with him to figure it all out. He used his journals mostly to sit in his thoughts, to delve deeper into the mysterious darkness. I'm not sure writing a path out of it was even possible for him.

My dad writes several times that he should probably reread his own writing. He says he knows that's a common practice for those who keep journals and that they often then gain insights about themselves and their lives. But he never mentions having done it. I wonder what would have happened if he had reread them? Would he have cried as I do? Would he have been able to see what I see and find a way to love himself more?

I don't reread my own journals, so I can't blame him. In our living room, a collection of ten or so reading journals from the past fifteen or more years chronicle my responses to everything I've read and the life I was leading as I read them. On another shelf are my journals about my boys, in which I write less and less frequently, to my own disappointment, where I try to track their development, their precious moments not to be forgotten. Upstairs, more journals are tucked away in a box in our overflowing guest bedroom closet.

Perhaps someday my children will read them, struggling, no doubt, to decipher my cramped and horrible scrawl—the one that leaves even me guessing sometimes as to what I meant. They'll find in my early journals much more darkness than in those I keep as an adult, at least for now. Like my dad, I don't know what is to come for me, how I will handle the challenges and heartaches ahead. What insights could my boys glean from the random captured experiences and ideas I recorded?

I consider again my dad's wish for my mom to destroy his journals after his death and his decision not to do so himself. I can't imagine wanting my own words to be destroyed. Why did he ask her to erase those remnants of his identity, of the workings of his mind? Why didn't he put them through the shredder himself before he died? Did he fear no one else would want to read them, that no one would understand—or care? Did he secretly hope that someone would? I have saved these flashes of his thinking from the scissors. I value the chance to enter his mind, to wander in the darkness with him, to leave again enlightened, understanding him just a bit more.

19

1995 (Age 23): Because He Had Conviction

"Let's go out to lunch," my dad says to me on a spring Friday morning. I'm at home for the weekend from graduate school, and he's got the day off.

I'm taken aback by the offer of lunch at a restaurant. I can't remember many times we went out to eat for lunch that wasn't a brunch after church on Mother's Day or a special birthday.

"Sure," I say, wondering if he means McDonald's or homemade sandwiches down by the river.

We end up at the Country Kitchen, a sit-down restaurant across the highway from where my parents live on the outskirts of Winona as it blends into the small town of Goodview in one direction and a commercial district in another. The waitress greets us as if she has a thousand other lunchtime customers, as if this is nothing special, but here my dad and I are on a Friday, eating lunch in a sit-down restaurant.

I can't help looking at the prices that I'm sure seem modest to the other customers and wondering if my parents' financial situation has improved. My dad's been employed now for almost nine years at the cathedral in Winona, Minnesota, and my mom has been the library director in Arcadia, Wisconsin, for about five. I can't imagine either job pays all that well, and I know there must be debt to repay from their time of unemployment in my teenage years, but I also know they send me a check every month for $100 to help me pay my rent. When we'd gone apartment hunting in Duluth, Minnesota, where I was getting my master's degree in English, the only places I could afford on my teaching stipend were a little rough. My dad had said, "You need a place to come home to at the end of the day where you feel comfortable and safe—comfortable taking your shoes off and walking around in your stockinged feet." We'd found that place, and they'd agreed to help me make ends meet.

At the table, my dad spreads his thick fingers out as he places his palms down in front of him. "Tell me everything about yourself and your life," he says. The waitress brings us glasses of water, and I take a sip. "And don't leave anything out," he ends. This is a stock phrase of his. I never know precisely what it means, so I laugh nervously.

"Classes are good," I say vaguely as I look through the menu. I settle quickly on a cheeseburger, something familiar to me, and close the menu. I look down at his unopened menu.

"I'll have the special," he says as an explanation. "It was on the board out front. What are you studying?"

I begin to tell him about my class in medieval literature, telling him about the challenging textbook we're using, one written by our professor.

He raises an eyebrow high enough that it arches above the thick frames and lenses of his glasses. "Sounds like a professor just wants to make money by selling his own books!"

"Well, sure, but it's also because he knows it well. He's an expert in this area." I rush to defend my professor and then I worry that I shouldn't defend him. I don't want to pick a fight. There are people at most of the tables around us, groups of elderly women out for lunch with friends, a young couple behind us, a businessman eating alone. I don't want them to witness my dad's anger.

But he doesn't get angry. He shrugs, so I continue talking. "We're reading this really interesting manuscript by a fourteenth century mystic named Julian of Norwich."

"I've heard of her," my dad says, looking up as if to call down information from the heavens.

"She had this series of visions, and then she wrote about them. She was very young. What's fascinating to me," I lean forward as I get into the topic, "is that she talks about Jesus as our mother sometimes. I've also noticed that she doesn't mention Eve at all, but she talks a lot about original sin and Adam. She doesn't blame Eve all the time like you hear at church, in the Bible, or in so many other manuscripts. I think that might be something special about her."

The waitress stops by and takes our order. After she leaves, my dad leans back and puts his right pointer finger across his lips, his elbow resting on his left arm. He purses his lips. This thinking pose is one I know well. He taps his finger against his lip. "St. Augustine and others certainly had a lot to say about Eve, and not good stuff. You might be onto something. What does your professor say?"

I'm a little surprised at how the conversation is moving in this productive, almost collaborative way. I blaze a trail of honesty: "I haven't talked with him yet. He's so intelligent, and he has this gruff voice. I don't want him to tell me my ideas are stupid."

"But how can he help you if you don't talk to him?"

"I know, I know." I look down, and my shoulders slump.

"What's the manuscript called?" my dad asks.

"*Revelations of Divine Love* in translation or *Shewings* in its original Middle English. We're reading it in Middle English—with lots of notes of course."

My dad's eyebrows both move up. "Impressive. Do you think I could handle it?"

I'm hesitant. I don't want to diminish my dad's intelligence. "It might not be worth the effort. The translation into modern English has the same content."

"I'm intrigued," he continues, "by this notion of God as mother. It aligns so wonderfully with Isaiah's reference to God as a mother comforting her child or when Jesus refers to himself as a mother hen gathering her brood. To think that this book is hundreds of years old and yet has been largely ignored by the Catholic Church."

"Well, Daddy, it *was* written by a woman. The Catholic Church isn't so big on listening to women's voices."

He nods first and then shakes his head, sharing in my frustration. "I read a book recently, *She Who Is*, by a feminist theologian named Elizabeth Johnson. One of her main points is that if we make God into a male, we risk creating a false idol out of the divine. Then we end up worshiping God the man rather than God the divine beyond all knowing. You might like it. It might even prove useful to you."

My dad's suggestion comes in a different tone than usual. Instead of telling me what to think, he seems to be inviting me into a discussion. "Huh." Watching him sip his coffee, my brain is mostly still stuck on how to write a paper about Julian of Norwich's exclusive focus on Adam and not on Eve, but I'm interested in my dad's point.

Our food arrives, and I casually eat some french fries, drawn more to our conversation than to the restaurant lunch I had recently found so novel. "So why doesn't the Catholic Church ever talk about this woman, this Julian of Norwich? Why did I have to go to a public university and take graduate classes in literature to learn about her?" My tone has become a little angry, but I'm not angry at my dad. I'm angry at the Church.

"That's a great question," my dad says as he scoops some of the pot roast special into his mouth. His lips twitch forward in between his chewing. He's a careful eater when we're around others, using his napkin to wipe his lips even when I don't see any food on them, making sure no one sees him with anything astray. He swallows and talks while his fork hovers over his plate. "I think the male hierarchy would like to keep their grip on knowledge, on power, on truth. They don't want you and me to think things through on our own. They don't necessarily want us to know about movements that have existed throughout Christianity and throughout Catholicism's history that explore other ways to view women or the priesthood." Somehow, unlike other times, this doesn't feel like a lecture. Then he mentions another book that sounds relevant to my project. I begin to imagine with enthusiasm going back to school with two or three sources I could use for my paper, a theoretical foundation I hadn't had before.

"Jesus was far more of a revolutionary than the modern church is," he continues. I think about this for a moment. Jesus as revolutionary. God as revolutionary. God always seems so stable, so secure, so traditional. I think of the rituals of the Catholic Church that are centuries old.

"What was so revolutionary about Jesus, really?"

My dad has finished his lunch and pushes his plate away from him. He leans back in the booth and adopts his thinking pose again. He crosses his ankles—I know because the tip of his heavy dress shoe taps against my shin.

"What *wasn't* revolutionary is the right question. Jesus sat down with women, with tax collectors, with sinners—all people his society rejected. He told the Pharisees that what mattered more than the letter of the law was the spirit of compassion and forgiveness. Jesus wasn't about hierarchy. He wasn't about pecking order. When the disciples wanted to know who was first or who would be honored in heaven, he kept reminding them the last will be first, that to be a servant to others was the best and highest calling one could take. If that's not revolutionary, I don't know what is. It's just that the Catholic Church doesn't always embody or embrace that revolution."

I sit there taking it all in. I can understand why my dad would follow Jesus, would believe in God's ability to transform the world. I can understand why my dad doesn't seek after riches but revels in being a minister. "But then why do you stay … in the Catholic Church that is?" I've asked this a few times before. It's been in these honest moments, these conversations where my dad and I are meeting as almost equals, as two people of faith searching for answers. I want to know his answer. I want to know why I should stay.

He pauses and sighs deeply. "You can't change something from outside of it. If you want an institution to change, you have to stay inside and fight for that change." I've heard this argument from him before. It makes sense, I guess. But I don't feel I'm winning any fights by staying and feeling disgruntled. I think about the priests at the churches where I play organ up in Duluth, how I help pay for graduate school. I think about their sermons about Mary as wonderful because she obeys, about the disciples as wonderful because they're leaders, and about how that means I should obey and men should lead. That's what God wants.

"I don't feel like it's possible to make any changes to such a huge institution."

"That's just it!" he exclaims and leans forward with energy. "They want you to think that. But you have to stay and continue the fight. Think about the reading and research you're doing. The thinking you're doing. If you write this up, everyone who reads it will be challenged to think of God as mother, to think of God as more than just male. Everyone who reads your work will be inspired to rethink Christianity and to see its roots in social justice! And there are so many people like you in the church, more than you know. It's why we must stay. We have to be among the voices challenging authority from within."

He pauses for a moment, looks up in the air and seems momentarily at a loss for words. Then his passion takes hold again: "You'll see as time goes by that there are so many voices out there doing that good work, and the number is growing. Eventually, we will be loud enough to be truly heard. Eventually, we will bring the change Jesus would want to see."

For a moment, I allow myself to imagine a Catholic Church transformed by voices slowly gaining traction and changing the way leadership thinks and feels. As we leave the restaurant, I feel uplifted, inspired, transported.

"Thanks for lunch, Daddy. And thanks for your help!" I marvel at the conversation we just shared, at the ways in which he had hope to spare—to give to me. I sense an energy in him as we walk to the car.

"Of course! Any time."

20

Reading the Silence

My dad's bookshelves told a careful observer a lot about the man. Biblical concordances sat next to theological treatises; books about the apostle Paul stood next to books about Judaism. It turns out he wasn't an eclectic reader. Sprinkled in among these volumes were contemporary self-help books (mostly Christian) about death, dying, and ministry. From that array, a stranger could safely bet that his career at some point was ministry. The books on music and music history tell the story of an earlier era.

I used to think a lot about my own bookshelves and wonder what they would say to a careful observer. I thought that, like me, most people go into someone else's home or apartment and almost instantly begin to analyze the books that are there in order to better understand the person who owns them. I've since realized that most people are not like me, in this and many other respects, and don't give more than a casual glance at someone else's books. But I have been engaged in an in-depth character analysis of my dad based on his books for some time now. There are certain books from his shelves whose spines are so familiar to me that they bring back specific memories even though I've never actually opened them. Sometimes all it takes is reading the titles for me to feel engaged in a conversation with him about his interests.

Like many readers, my dad had so many books and magazines that they spilled over the bookcases onto tables and stacks on the floor. In this way, I am my father's daughter. My husband says that for every book I bring into the house, I should pay a bookcase tax—a small fee that would accumulate to buy more bookcases. I disagree and just keep on buying books because he likes hunting for antique bookcases almost as much as I enjoy filling them. The moment a new bookcase enters our home, it is instantly full. Like my dad, I struggle to let go of my paper companions.

My dad borrowed books from libraries, but as his financial situation became more stable later in life (or as he tricked himself into thinking that it was, or as he just stopped caring that it wasn't more stable), he bought more and more. A trip to a bookstore was a fun afternoon as long as it ended with a stack of new possessions. Possession of the book, in his mind, was perhaps 90 percent of gaining its knowledge. I believe that for him, as for me, the anticipation of the conversation with a new author or a beloved favorite kept him from feeling lonely or without companions.

Some books he read cover to cover soon after their purchase. Many books he left on the bookshelf with post-it notes marking the place he had left off or the only chapter he'd read—the one he felt was most important to him. These half-finished or partially read books were a fixture in his life and in mine. At different points in my life, I viewed them differently: a testament to how he couldn't finish what he started; an inspiration to me to stop reading when something was no longer of interest or use; a sign of a restless but obsessive personality that couldn't find fulfillment. My responses over my lifetime perhaps say more about how I was feeling about the man than about the man himself.

For my dad, the words in these texts were potential conversations made real when he wrote in the margins or shared their ideas with someone in his family or a colleague or a person to whom he ministered. He saw himself in conversation with writers, sometimes copying quotations into his journals. He would underline a passage and write an exclamation point in the margin. I reread the passage and wonder why. The full conversation of that moment is lost.

My dad loved the idea of words, the potential they have to encode and transmit meaning. We talked a lot about words and their power. He taught me to recognize when people used words to limit me as a woman, and he taught me to fight those limitations. He talked with me about biblical words that had been poorly translated and taught me the importance of examining a seemingly straightforward word more carefully. He always wanted to learn a foreign language, or at least he often said he did. He studied several in his lifetime, but none ever seriously or for very long. He said many times that he was in awe of my ability to speak Spanish with as much fluidity as I do. He would trot out his fun phrase, "*El caballo está en la casa verde*," not when it was appropriate to talk about horses in green houses (is it ever?) but whenever he wanted to be silly about language.

On his bookshelves after he died I uncovered a nearly pristine Polish verbs book (a nod to his Polish ancestry), dusty old 1960s reprints of French novels he'd had to learn to read for his first master's degree decades earlier, and Spanish books of all types, mostly workbooks, most of them carefully completed—until about page five or six. I found untouched books on how to study biblical Greek and Hebrew. I found Greek and Hebrew flashcards still in the plastic, plans interrupted or never begun. He loved exploring words, but he ran out of time to learn them all, to see how they fit together.

༄

Part of me wonders if my dad thought about his bookshelves the way I did—as a sort of résumé to the world. Very few people ever came to our house, but I wonder if reading itself was an opportunity to impress others, to learn something he could use to validate himself to others. I worry that my own obsession over my bookshelves and how they might look to others indicates my own reading interests aren't dictated by pure curiosity or pleasure. I wonder whether the books on my shelves are my friends, as I call them, or my badge of honor, my external validation.

When I was a teenager, I picked up a brochure at the public library that listed the "classics"—great literature everyone should read. I began to read what was listed. I was drawn to the thickest and oldest volumes on the shelves. Long before I was old enough to understand what I was reading, I plowed through texts like *Les Misérables* and Gogol's *Dead Souls*. I used books at school to impress my teachers, picking the three-volume *Kristin Lavransdatter* by little-known Norwegian writer Sigrid Undset when I had to do a book report during my sophomore year of high school. My teacher kindly let me do the report on just the first volume when I ran out of time, but I made sure to finish the trilogy that summer. I enjoyed my time reading classic authors like Charles Dickens, but often felt an internal pressure to read faster, to get through books more quickly.

Despite my voracious reading habits, I never felt accomplished enough in college or graduate school. There were always authors I'd never heard of and books I'd never read. I felt downright ignorant taking the literature-specific GRE exam for graduate school, reading questions about movements like Theatre of the Absurd with no idea which author listed best represented it.

I worry that I've always seen books as a path towards legitimacy, towards self-worth. Did my dad similarly feel that books could solve his problems? One night, my dad lamented in his journal that two new books didn't arrive in the mail that day as he'd expected. He was frustrated, almost angry, as if somehow those two books were going to fix everything and now he had to wait for the cure. But no book was ever enough. Books made him think of reading other books or reminded him of books he'd tried and failed to understand or enjoy or finish. Books made him think about writing something worthy of publishing, a task he wanted to accomplish but didn't want to undertake.

Once I started teaching, everything I read served a potential purpose. I could use bits of this book in a composition class, reference these ideas in my first-year seminar, practice my Spanish, or design a new class around a genre. I grew to feel guilty when I read something just for fun and eventually labeled these works as "medicinal literature," giving myself an excuse to recharge.

I wonder if my dad's obsession with productivity is what drives my reading, and yet, like him, I sometimes worry that reading is the opposite of productive. How can one feel accomplished when shelves of books await and the value of what you've already read cannot be measured? What utility does it serve? My dad struggled at times to value the life of the mind, but he loved to read. Wandering through texts and searching for meaning, for answers, for knowledge he could use to impress others—to prove his own value—my dad may never have felt more at peace and more restless at the same time than when he was reading.

Certainly, as for me, words had the potential to inspire him or to crystallize his thinking, to articulate what he felt better than he was able to express. One of the reasons he said he loved reading the journals of Henri Nouwen, May Sarton, and others was that their insights gave voice to his ideas. They were able to articulate what he was thinking or feeling.

I believe my dad thought that books could help him treat his own depression, self-doubts, and mental illness. He thought pulling out a book could solve every problem, and I suppose I feel that way too. When life presents me with a problem, whether it's with parenting, health, or my house, I wonder if there's a book out there that could help me with it. But there are limits to the helpfulness of these one-sided conversations. After he died, I began to wonder if his mental health would have improved if he had read less and talked to healthcare professionals more. I found myself rereading the titles on his bookshelves and wondering what they said and didn't say to him.

※

After his death, disassembling my dad's significant collection of books was necessary. My mom needed space for her mysteries, and the books my dad owned deserved to be read by someone else. It fell largely to me to go through his collection. Since I share some of his interest in Christian feminism, theology, and writing, I took what I wanted first. I sat in the living room, their bedroom, or the office—all of which contained completely full bookcases—and tackled them one shelf at a time. I considered each cover, read the back, imagined myself reading it, opened each one to look for notes, scraps of paper with ideas on them, hints of his mindset as he read it. Then I decided: take it with me, suggest it to someone else in the family, or let it go where it might.

Each trip across two states to visit my mom, I worked through more bookcases, resigning myself to many of the books finding a new home with a stranger. I talked through my bookshelf explorations with Jason, struggling to express my feelings. "I feel like I'm interrupting some sort of conference by splitting up the collection. Now the books can't converse among each other on the shelves. Plus, people won't be able to figure out who my dad was by scanning the titles. I won't be able to. I feel like he's dying all over again every time I let a book go."

"So take more," Jason always said.

"What about the bookcase tax?" I jokingly asked, hoping to cheer myself up.

"We'll deal with that later. Take whatever you want. Take everything you think you might someday want. Don't let something go if you feel you'll regret it later."

"Sometimes I think I'll regret not taking everything, but I don't need everything. I don't want everything. I just keep worrying that what I'm giving away has the answers in it."

"To what questions?"

"I don't know yet. That's the problem."

I took books because they relate to my interests. I took books that someday I might want to read. I took some because I remembered their spines. They can sit unread on my shelves. They can wait for the day when perhaps they have meaning to me beyond the covers that remind me of him.

Yet I couldn't take them all. I had to say goodbye to the memories that were triggered when I looked at certain titles or dust jackets. Around this same time, I often read to Edward a book called *Time to Say Bye-Bye*, which was designed to help young children with transition times, the painful movement from one activity to another. As he sat on my lap at story time, confused by my tears, I thought about saying bye-bye to the personality and the person who still seemed physically present in the book collection I was tearing apart. I faced my dad's death with greater difficulty and a deeper reality taking apart that collection than perhaps in any other moment.

In his journal towards the end of his life, my dad wrote about how at one moment he was reading six books at once: "I find them all interesting in one way or another, but why do I have this need to read so much at one time? Maybe I'm afraid of running out of time." In August of the year before he died, my dad bought a book designed to help the reader work during one full year towards a lifestyle that included writing. I found the receipt tucked inside it. He died before the year was up, and honestly, I don't know that he ever opened the book. I can't yet imagine what it is to face both the certainty and uncertainty of death, and I wonder if, as I would be, my dad was saddened to think of an end to reading—an end to the amazing conversations he could have with authors. What is it like to have to say bye-bye books, bye-bye bookshelves, bye-bye ideas waiting to be processed, conversations not yet begun, and friendships with authors never to be started?

※

When I was back at home, his books sat in bags near my already overflowing bookshelves for months, even years. Eventually, as we acquired new bookcases, my dad's books began to be integrated into my own collection, but I remember which ones they were. Most of them I haven't touched again. A few I have let go since then, knowing I will never read them and wanting the space. Each time I do is a struggle.

One day after Jason found two antique bookcases at a decent price at auction, we reorganized our entire book collection. Finally, we had a plan that would allow him to keep his boat history, engineering books, and large Victorian architecture books separate from my how-to-teach better, Victorian fiction, mystery, history, theology, *Star Trek*, and other random books. Finally, I could group similar books together in a way that would make me feel more organized, that would help the books have a more coherent conversation among themselves on the shelves. My kids helped haul books from room to room. They weren't paying much attention to spines or covers or order. Instead, they commented on how heavy they were or how many there were.

"How many of these books have you read, Mom?"

"Most of them."

"What?! That's incredible."

Then we started a new game. As they brought me a pile of books from the other room, they asked, "Have you read this one? How about this fat one? Ugh—this one is so heavy. Have you read this one?"

"Yes." "Yes." "Most of it," I replied.

For a moment, I wondered what this new knowledge made them think of me, how it affected their definition of me. I wondered if my kids would ever stare at my books. I wondered if they would try to define me by what I have read. I wondered what they thought about all my books *before* this project. Did they think I was acquiring all these books to someday read them? I laughed aloud at the thought. If so, they must have thought I was overly optimistic about my reading time.

And maybe I am. I have lots of books that I haven't read yet, and yet that doesn't stop me from buying more. I am my father's daughter. I have books with bookmarks halfway through where I lost interest, got distracted, or felt I'd learned what I needed to learn. I have my Japanese Kanji cards that are in nearly pristine condition because my brief time studying the language was interrupted by graduate school. I have my shelf of German language books and German language cards—not in plastic but still in crisp condition—because my slightly longer study of that language went by the wayside when my life became full with my children. I keep all these possessions. They are memories of the past, integral parts of who I remain, and tantalizing hints of who I might still become.

At times, unfortunately, they become a way for me to criticize myself for not being more than I am. I wonder if my dad's books served as both inspiration and critique. I wonder if he felt the weight of unfulfilled expectations when he looked around at them. And sometimes I wish someone would come in, admire my bookshelves, and think me more worthy because of them. I acknowledge the troubled nature of that line of thinking. I think my dad felt the same way, and so, for another moment, I feel I understand him better—his insecurities, his passion for learning, his desire to know.

Scattered among my books are some of the words my dad valued, words he read in the silence of his mind. His books contain within them pieces of him, the sentences and ideas that made him up as much as any of his molecules or cells did. As my books commune with his, ideas seep from one to the other. Perhaps he is still present and available for a quick chat any time I want to pick up one of them. Perhaps I can still learn from them and from his example how to be a better book owner, how to be kinder to myself and true to myself as a reader.

My dad was a pretty firm believer that he was making a transition into a time when he would be at one with a God who would share ideas and knowledge with him. One of his favorite faith one-liners was, "If I don't have individual identity after death, I am going to be really mad at God!" It takes a second to process the joke.

I think he was 99 percent certain that an afterlife contained a plurality of ideas, books, knowledge, and wisdom. If we dream up our own heaven, I can't imagine he dreamt up anything other than a giant bookstore with unlimited time to browse and read, discuss with the authors, listen to some music to help process it all, and then chat with the divine one to help explain the difficult bits. Then again, maybe the heaven my dad dreamt up wasn't like that at all. He knew that words interfere with meaning. I wonder if in the silence after death he has found the meaning he sought. I wonder if in his silence I will find mine.

21

1997 (Age 25): Because We Walked Together

My dad's putting on his perfectly clean tennis shoes. He's had them for several years now, but he rarely wears them, so they look almost like they're fresh out of the box. As he ties them, leaning down to do so and breathing heavily because of the exertion, I ask if he wants company on his walk.

"Sure, but only if you can keep up. I walk fast."

I shove my feet into my own beat-up tennis shoes and say I'll try. We head out the door in the kitchen, through the garage, and then outside. The sun is brighter than it has been for months, at least since the January days when it beams off the snow and blinds you. Now it's a March sun, the kind that melts anything that's left frozen but doesn't warm you enough that you sweat as you walk. It's not warm enough for shorts either, not that my dad ever wears them much. For him, it's polyester trousers every day, the kind that he's worn almost my entire life, the kind we've bought him for Christmases and birthdays. Now they make his tennis shoes seem even more out of character for him.

"Keep up!" he says firmly as we start at a quick pace down the sidewalk in front of our house, past the bushes that will soon be overgrown and need trimming again. He hates weeding and trimming but loves having a beautiful yard.

As we cross the street to the next block, I ask about his plans for the garden this year.

"I think we're going to keep it simple."

"Good idea," I say, beginning to pant as I almost run to keep up with his longer stride.

"I'd like to plant some new rose bushes on the side of the house if I have time and energy." I know he loves looking through the rose catalog. "And I'd like to get the planters that my dad built and put some new flowers in pots there—some coleus maybe." I picture coming back in June to celebrate my mom's birthday and Father's Day and seeing the colors of the planters.

I didn't realize how fast my dad meant he would walk until I skip a step or two to catch up with him. I glance at his face, and there's an intention there that goes beyond exercising off some calories. He's also exorcising some demons, perhaps of lethargy and dis-ease with life. Perhaps apathy or laziness.

"Look at the water," he says to me with a bit more cheer in his voice as we turn onto a side street where there is no sidewalk. I look down and see the steady stream of water rushing towards the storm drain, a subtle sign of the changing season.

"That wind is still brisk though," I reply as I feel the remnant of winter's bite.

"Not for long now."

I barely recognize the houses around us as we've walked in a direction we don't normally need to drive. I notice the trees have tiny buds and little leaves sprouting.

"How's your medication treating you?" my dad asks in a sudden change of subject.

I think about how every morning I take my antidepressant and then start chugging caffeinated soda to stay awake as I drive to Loyola in Chicago to teach and take my doctoral classes. The medicine makes me sleepy if I take it in the morning, but when I took it at night, it interrupted my sleep. I woke up with a racing heart, unsure where I was or when it was. I prefer to take it in the morning and fight off sleepiness with caffeine. But I don't mention any of this to my dad. There's no need to worry him about it.

"Fine," I reply. "It seems to be helping me stay on an even keel."

"Are you still in counseling?"

"I haven't found anything in Chicago, and I haven't figured out what my student health insurance would pay for. I think the tune-up I had in Duluth was enough for now."

"I haven't done much with counseling, but I find that my own experience of the antidepressant medication is a mixed bag," he replies. I'm a little surprised to hear him speak so openly. I knew he had started to take something a little while back, but nothing else. "I find I don't feel music the way I once did."

"Huh." I kind of know what he means, but I'm hoping he'll say more.

"The extremes aren't there anymore."

"Right."

"The highs aren't as high, and the lows aren't as low."

"I know what you mean. I sort of miss being able to feel the depths of despair in a piece of music. But it was hard to climb out of there after the music stopped. Nearly impossible. I don't miss that part."

My dad doesn't say anything. Maybe he misses the depths. There's definitely an appeal to them. After enough years dwelling there, it becomes a well-decorated home. I've felt that tug enough times to know it. I remember sitting in my apartment in Duluth, listening to a Beethoven symphony, the tempest matching my turbulent mood. Sitting there on my floor, staring out at a cloudy winter sky, tears streaming down my face, I would gently pound the floor with my fists and lament all that I hated about myself and my life. I wonder if my dad ever does that in the basement. I wonder how he experiences the deepest depths now that Karen and I aren't around to fight with, aren't around to see.

We round the corner to head back home. "I should really go to work this afternoon and practice. I'm not ready for Easter at all."

"Sure. I know there's a lot of music. I have reading to do for a paper that's due next week anyway. I can do that until Mom and you get home. Are we waiting to have dinner until Karen arrives?"

"Yes. I think we'll go out for fish tonight." It's not my favorite, but if my dad is going to remain relatively upbeat like this, I want to go. Maybe the walk has done his endorphins some good.

I picture us later at the restaurant, laughing and talking, seated around a table overlooking the river, other people wondering if that family always has such fun together. It won't happen that way, I know, but the dream seems closer than before.

22

Self

By the time I was a teenager, my dad drove me to school every morning and I didn't have to take the bus any longer. Normally our trips to school in the morning were quiet, both of us in our own stressed-out cocoons. Sometimes he would ask me about my upcoming day. A few times, he would ask me what I was thinking. The ensuing conversation felt awkward, probably because I was a teenager and I was thinking about Duran Duran or Corey Hart or some other rock star, wishing I could escape my reality and go on tour with them. I would never have to worry about money again, I'd get to hear music I loved all the time, and I'd have some incredibly hot guy tell me he loved me all the time—typical teenage stuff. That's not something you tell your dad. It's highly unlikely he would have understood the seriousness with which I dreamed. If he was trying to see the real me, I kept that hidden, protecting it from any derision it might have faced from him.

At different stages and with different levels of confidence, my boys have told me their dreams. My older son talked about his dreams of playing professional sports and my younger son spent a summer telling us about how he was going to be a billionaire. As their dreams evolve, I try to see both the dream and behind the dream to something I can nurture in them. I'm grateful for their honesty and openness with me. I want it to continue.

I look at my children sometimes and try to see them as people, not as my children. I think it's possible, but only for brief moments, for glimpses. Sometimes when they're talking, I watch them intently. Sometimes I even stop listening to what they're saying. When they were little, I would stop trying to follow the rules to a game they made up that seemed to change even as they told me about it. Instead, in those moments, I noticed the animation in their faces, the way they moved their hands, the way they couldn't sit still. Even now, I try to hear past the words of the moment. I try to see my kids as individuals developing their own interests, passions, dislikes, dreams, and identities separate from my own.

When Anton was a baby, I sat on the edge of the daybed in his room and held him one night as he tried to fall asleep. I looked into his face and pictured the teenage Anton. I watch him now and try to see him as an adult, coming home for a visit, telling me about life's problems and joys. I catch glimpses of their potential future selves as well as their current selves. Or at least I think I do. As hard as I look and as much as I try to set aside my own preconceptions about them, I still see parts of me. "Oh no," I think, "Anton has my perfectionism," or "Edward has my driven nature." I struggle to see *them* and not to see them as my children, my "creations" or "productions." How can I truly support my children in their dreams as individuals if I can't stop seeing them as my children?

I feel I have more success when I try to look at my husband as a person and not as my husband, not as my children's father. He's been an adult the entire time I've known him, and although he's changed, he was a more fully developed person I could get to know from scratch when we first met. I sit in church sometimes and practice this way of seeing him. On Sundays when I play organ, I'm off to the side of the pews facing the front. My angle allows me to observe him as much as the pastor. I think about Jason's pains, concerns, joys, and dreams. I try to see the world he sees and consider what thoughts he may be having. I look at the progress of his white hair overtaking the black. I think about his perspective on church itself. He wasn't raised in any religion, so he's attended more services with me than he ever imagined he would in a lifetime. I consider why he comes. I wonder why he's participating in this moment but not in the next. If I remember to ask him after church what he was thinking about, I'm never even close in my guesses.

I think about my dad asking me how my day was or what was on my mind. I think about how many of my dreams I kept hidden from him—even the more prosaic ones like earning a PhD in English or traveling to foreign countries. I know I was developing an identity, a self that transcends nameable characteristics, but that self was a mystery to my dad.

I suspect the reverse is true as well. All along, living side by side, my dad and I were two separate individuals, interacting as parent-child, unable to see the other clearly even if we had tried. I ask myself why I'm still trying now, given how much harder it is to see him clearly now that he is gone. Yet his voice walks with me still. His perspective on my choices is still there, and I want to find a way for it to be present without it controlling me. I want to establish who I am, who he was, and where the line is between our two selves.

❧

Somewhere between ages four and six, a child becomes intellectually capable of imagining life from someone else's perspective. A great example of life with small children before this developmental milestone is when a child stands in front of a television blocking your view. Sometimes that's just carelessness, but for a very young child, it's different. *They* can see the TV, so they assume anyone seated behind them can also. They can't imagine that the person behind them could have a different perspective.

As I grew older, as it does for so many, reading became a way for me to practice imagining others' thoughts and feeling empathy for their situations. I took my interest in narrative and made it into a game for dull moments. When I was very young and we lived in southwestern Minnesota, we'd take the long drive across the state to visit my dad's parents in southeastern Minnesota. I began to play a game: "What would it be like if I switched places *right now* with the person living there or driving in that other car?" Part of the fun was imagining escaping the tension of the car (my dad was not generally pleasant on long car rides—something I can appreciate a little more now that I too have made long car trips with two children). Part of the fun was imagining the shock of the transfer of consciousness from one set of surroundings to another. It appealed to the budding science fiction fan inside me. Total chaos ensues inside the minds of the two who have just swapped bodies, while they decide whether to tell anyone. Who would believe them?

I remember frequently ending the game with the realization that challenges existed in that alternative world just as in mine. Farm life could be isolating, big-city life complicated, and other cars too might have dads who yelled for no reason.

I realize now that I never imagined switching places with my dad. I vaguely recall imagining being my sister, but that wasn't all that different, or so I thought. I imagined being my mom suddenly, offering us more hard candies to pass the time, asking to turn off the radio, or finally understanding why she didn't. Maybe if I had played the game and imagined being my dad, I might have begun to understand him earlier in life. Maybe my imagination, robust as it was, couldn't manage to invent the thinking behind his actions and choices. Perhaps I already knew there was a darkness there I didn't want to inhabit.

Several times before he died, my dad said that he wished he could live long enough to see my boys grow up, to see what sort of people they were going to become. At the heart of his wish was, of course, a desire to live longer, but there was also a deep desire for connection: to be remembered and to *know* another. At the heart of his wishes was also the belief that he *could* know them, could see them truly.

Despite the impossibility of the task, I find value in seeking to know those closest to me. I sit in wonder staring at my children and trying to see what is unseen, what is perhaps unseeable. I want to know my children. I enjoy watching them grow into the world and into themselves. I love the moments when they say what they're thinking with honesty and directness. Perhaps because my dad and I didn't succeed at doing so, I will practice truly seeing my children. I will listen to their conversations for what is said, what is unsaid, and who is saying it. I will hear in their voices echoes of who they were and who they will become.

23

1999 (Age 26): Because He Didn't Get Help

"What's that on your chin?" my dad asks me as we sit in the living room after church, after brunch, and after his nap. Karen and I went for a walk to give him time; playing organ in the morning for two services always makes him tired. Then we sat in the living room with my mom for the better part of two hours, having a half-whispered conversation so we wouldn't wake him. At one point my mom dozed off, but when she woke up again with a start, she rejoined our conversation about the weather, people in our lives, stresses we face. My dad had reclined in his chair, snoring in interesting ways for the better part of three hours.

"It's a zit," I reply with a sigh.

"You still get those?"

"Yeah."

"Do you have one on your nose too?"

"Yes. Thanks for noticing."

"Well, it's pretty big and the one on your chin is big too, so it's hard to miss them."

It's amazing how quickly I can feel awful about myself. I shift uncomfortably on the sofa that faces his chair.

"You know, Daddy," Karen says, "it may be hard to miss them, but you don't have to point them out."

"Was I talking to you?" he asks Karen.

"No, but I just wanted to point out that it's not always nice to tell someone about the thing that makes them feel self-conscious."

"Thank you so much," he says sarcastically, "for teaching me how to be a good person. I'm so glad my daughter is here to help me learn how to behave."

"I have to go to the bathroom." I get up to leave. I don't have to go to the bathroom, but in my parents' house, it's a place to which I can retreat, sometimes with my book, when I need a break. The noisy fan blocks out so much. When I was younger, I could hide in my room all afternoon and read or listen to music. Now when I come home from graduate school for a visit, I am expected to spend time with the family.

"Want to watch TV?" I hear my mom ask as I walk out of the room.

"Marie, I don't want to watch TV," my dad snaps. "The girls are home. We shouldn't watch TV but spend time talking to them. They leave tomorrow morning."

I think back to the night before, when I was trying to fall asleep at 11:00. The TV had been on since 9:00, blaring. And it didn't go off until midnight. The thin wall between my bedroom and the living room didn't deaden the sound at all, and my dad's slight hearing loss meant it had to be at a high volume. I hope that no one mentions the hypocrisy of my dad's statements. But if they do, the resulting explosion will be their problem because I'm headed to the bathroom.

When I come out ten minutes later, nothing has improved. In fact, conditions have deteriorated. My dad and sister are fighting about teaching. I'm not sure how they got on the topic, but here we are. I suspect that Karen didn't want to talk about it. It's the weekend, and she has a rare Monday off the next day. Bringing up work on a mini-vacation like that is something my dad would do, either unaware of or unconcerned about the other person's feelings.

My sister is talking about the challenge of making parents realize that math has value for their kids. "Bo-ring," my dad says. "I'm bored."

"Wow, that's rude," my sister replies, her earlier choice to be honest with him continuing. Normally we just ignore such comments. I walk to the kitchen to get a drink of water. How much longer can I delay going out there? What hope is there that by the time I do things will be resolved?

"I'll never understand how you can like math anyway."

"You sound just like the kids' parents."

"Well, how do you respond to them? Let's practice."

"I don't need practice. I deal with the real thing every day from the kids and their families and even the other teachers and administrators."

"Fine. Obviously, you think I have nothing to offer you. You don't value my teaching experience or expertise at all." My dad walks into the kitchen and I am caught pretending to look for a snack. He's sighing heavily with irritation and mounting anger. He pushes past me to reach into the refrigerator for a can of Pepsi, which he pours into a glass over ice. When he's angry, he stomps, like a little child. I walk back to the living room after he does, and I sit on the sofa. Karen's at the other end. My mom's in her chair at the head of the room. Karen and I glance at each other.

"So," my dad says to me, "your sister doesn't like it when her students complain about math. Do your students complain about having to work too?"

I think about the college composition students I've had over the years of graduate school. They're 18-year-old students being forced to write papers for a purpose they don't understand. Of course they complain about it.

"Sure. Sometimes."

"Your sister says that her students complain a lot about having to learn. How do you handle it?" His tone is not conversational, and I know this topic is a minefield. I don't want to tell Karen how to teach, and I see where this is headed—he's trying to pit us against each other so we fight. But if I don't answer a direct question from my dad, then *we'll* have a fight. For some reason, he wants someone to fight.

So we do. We argue about teaching as my dad preaches: "You have to stand up to your principal more, Karen!"

"It's not that easy, Daddy, and I do, when it's appropriate."

He makes more snarky comments about math: "You know, maybe the kids and parents are right. Maybe most of what you're teaching them won't be useful in the future. I can tell you, I didn't get much usefulness out of what I learned."

Karen replies in anger and pain, "So there's no math in music or in finances or in mortgages or anything like that?"

"There's so much math all around us," he says in an exaggerated and mocking tone. "Yeah, right," he responds to himself. "You have to do better than that if you're going to win an argument against parents."

I try hard to stay out of it, but he pulls me in from time to time. Sometimes I say things I don't mean that I know will hurt Karen's feelings because I've now got anger built up inside of me and she's a safe target.

After a while, Karen decides to take a different approach: "You know, Daddy," she says with forced calmness in her voice, "we were having a nice conversation until you woke up. It's like you wanted to start a fight. Do you recognize that? Do you realize that maybe there's something 'off'—that maybe your depression is affecting all of us? Are you still on your antidepressant medication?"

I did *not* see that coming. Karen and I have talked about it a thousand times, and of course I've fantasized about saying such things to my dad, but I haven't ever had the courage to do so to his face. It goes over about as well as I'd expected it would.

"Who the hell do you think you are?" He jumps up from his chair. "What right do you have to talk to me about my behavior?" His face contorted with anger, his eyes narrow and his mouth opens wider as he spits words at her. "Maybe you should remember to honor your father. Or doesn't what God has to say to you matter anymore? Maybe we should just throw all those commandments out the window. They're just shit." He waves his arms around as he yells. "I'm just shit," he says slowly and his finger jabs at the air between them, as if he almost wishes she were right in front of him and he could poke her in the chest to emphasize each word.

"Jim," my mother begins, but he glares at her. She holds back what she was about to say.

"Sometimes I think you'd prefer it if I just got on a bus and left and never came back. Maybe I should do that. I'd like that. Would you, Marie? Would you?"

At some point, I dive in. I can't let Karen and my mom swim in this river alone. I stand and move closer to him where he is hovering over Karen on the couch. Like Karen, I try to keep my voice level and somewhat calm. "Daddy, maybe we can all calm down a bit and talk about this. No one's saying you're shit or that we don't respect you. This just feels like a lot and all of a sudden."

But it's impossible. "I'm going downstairs. I don't have to take any more of this abuse!" he shouts. "How dare you come here to my house and tell me that I have a problem." He takes a step towards me and points at me, as if accusing me. "*You* have the problem! You're the one who had to go to counseling!" He says the last word as if going was a reason to be embarrassed.

For a moment, I am shaken. Am I in the wrong here? Have I disrespected my father? Should I apologize? I think back to conversations I've had with my counselors over the past several years and I try to remember that I'm not a bad person. I'm not a bad daughter. I look at my dad and say with sadness, "Maybe if you got some help, you would be nicer to be around. I've been in counseling off and on for years now. Why is it good enough for me but not for you?"

Daddy takes two steps towards me, reaches out, and slaps my left cheek with his right hand.

It is the third time in my life I remember my dad striking out at me physically. My mind rushes to the two other times—when as a small child I refused to eat what I was given and he slapped my bottom, and later when as a teenager I challenged him while we were talking in the basement and he kicked my shin with the tip of his hard dress shoe.

"We're leaving, Jennifer." The firmness and depth in my sister's voice surprise me. She's not crying anymore.

My mom is crying louder. My dad stares at me for another ten seconds. We lock eyes as if to see more clearly in each other what has happened. I search his eyes to see if I can see behind the anger and the depression. I can't. He looks at me for something and, not finding it, turns on his heel and marches downstairs.

I look to Karen. I feel the sting of the slap on my face and inside I feel empty. Karen looks me in the eye and says again, "We're leaving, Jennifer." I see the resolve in her eyes. I feel the possibility of escape—the thrill of freedom—and I walk down the hall to my bedroom.

As I pack in my room, I hear my mom sob from time to time and I know her shoulders have heaved. I've seen it so many times before. I want to run to her and tell her to pack and come with us, but I know she won't, and her tears will weaken my resolve to follow Karen's lead. I picture her leaning over in her chair, making herself smaller, curling up inside and out.

I meet Karen in the hallway between our two bedrooms with our suitcases packed. I look at her again. Are we really going to do this? What will this mean? "What's going to happen?" I whisper to her.

"I don't know," she says. "But we can't stay here after that. We'll drive back to my house or to a hotel here in town."

Somehow my heart is both leaping for joy and drowning in sadness at the same time. We pause by the living room to look in at my mom. Karen's voice falters as she says through quick-sprouting tears, "I'm sorry, Mom. We can't stay after that. You see that, right?"

My mom's sobs renew. We pause a moment longer and then Karen turns to walk through the small kitchen and out the door to the garage. I follow.

We get out to the driveway by our cars and I notice it's gotten dark outside. The fight lasted long enough to erase the rest of the day's light. We walk first towards the trunk of her car and I can hear Karen crying. I don't know what to do. Should I be encouraging her or resisting her? How did she decide to do this so quickly and with such conviction?

I start to put my suitcase in the trunk and pause. "I just can't believe this, Jen," Karen says. "I can't believe he did that to you." Her sadness turns to anger again. "I don't understand how he can't see that he has a problem! He couldn't have his own way so he hit you?! He doesn't want to admit he has depression and that he needs medication and counseling. I don't want to deal with this anymore. His mental illness isn't my problem."

I wonder, how will I feel if I leave? Which side of my emotional struggle will win out in the end? Will I feel relieved, or will I be haunted? What will he do and say to my mom when we're not there? What if I never get to see her again? What if they're so angry with us that they cut off all contact? How will Karen cope with that? How will I?

My suitcase at my feet, I put my hands to my mouth and close my eyes. For some reason, I am not crying. I open my eyes and look at Karen. She is looking to the sky and then to me, searching for an answer.

"Karen, I don't think we should leave. Not right now. Not like this." I pause and let her think for a moment. "I know this was awful and he was wrong. I don't want to be here either. But if we do this … We haven't thought this through fully. I don't know if we're ready for what comes next."

"Jen," Karen says through tears that distort her voice a little. "I'm 30 years old and I feel like he rules my life. You're 26. Aren't you ready to make decisions on your own and not worry about him? Aren't you ready to be treated with respect?"

I look up and see the brightest stars and planets have appeared above us. I sigh with exhaustion. "I think I just want to figure this out with you some other way, some way where we can make sure Mom stays in our lives too."

At my mention of our mom, I can tell the last of Karen's conviction melts away.

The sting of the slap on my face is gone, but I feel wounded. Still, after a few more minutes, we go back inside. We meet my mom coming up from the basement. She has been downstairs, perhaps trying to calm him down, perhaps trying to convince him to come back. Without words, we hug my mom. "I'm sorry," Karen and I say to her. "I'm sorry," she replies through tears. I think I am apologizing for the trauma caused by walking out, but I'm not sure.

I freeze in the kitchen when I hear my dad trudging up the stairs. Like a character in a play who can't escape my prescribed role, I say "I'm sorry, Daddy." Karen apologizes. My mom apologizes. We hug together.

Instead of an apology, my dad says in a shaky voice, "God blesses us with each other. We must always remember that. We have to keep our fights together in this circle so that we can resolve them together and stay united." Through tears, Karen and I agree.

The next day, before we drive away, we both kiss my dad on his lips, the way he still requires of us even as adults. I feel no affection as I kiss him. I tell him "I love you, Daddy." At that moment, it's not true.

24

And Then I Remember

In the first year after my dad died, I talked through memories with my sister, revisiting what we'd experienced growing up with him. Sometimes I'd get stuck in a positive childhood moment. "I miss the fact that I'll never get to hear him play the piano again," I would say.

"I don't miss getting the silent treatment if we said something that pissed him off," Karen would reply.

"I sometimes wish I could have just one more day to go back and say, 'I love you' one more time," I'd say to her.

"And what do you think he'd say back? It might be 'I love you too,' but it might also be something cutting like, 'You have a funny way of showing it,'" she would reply.

I knew Karen was right, that I was idealizing the past, letting one positive memory wash over hundreds of negatives. Forgetting the dark matter surrounding these pinpoints of light felt easier than moving through it, than trying to understand it. But the effects of the dark matter lingered all around me, calling to me to consider how both the good and the bad helped shape me.

Having kids myself made me realize that I never once asked my dad to do something with me, to play a board game, to play hide and seek, or to go outside to toss a ball around. I was too afraid that his "no" would be shouted rather than spoken. My boys regularly ask me if I can hang out with them, and I ask them too. Our answers aren't always "yes," but it's not like what I experienced as a child. I went downstairs to my dad's office with trepidation when I wanted to ask him if I could go to my friend Amy's house next door to play. Her home became a safe place for me, her basement a space for stupid soap operas, MTV, and teenage conversations. Many days, to get to this haven, I had to go through my dad, but I never knew how to ask. If I asked too quietly, he might yell, "I can't hear you—speak up!" If I came in and said nothing at first to let him finish whatever he was working on, he might yell, "What do you want?" If I boldly stated my request, "Can I go to Amy's to play?" he might yell, "Why did you have to interrupt me?" The threat of the violent outburst was so constant that I'd often wait until my mom was available to ask or just stay in my room.

I wonder now if I could classify my fear of my dad's outbursts as phobic. The only other thing I've ever feared in the same way is bats. I'm scared of many things—spiders, snakes, heights, horror movies—but I have just one real phobia, one truly irrational and crippling fear: bats. Over the years, I've tried learning about them, combating my irrational fears with knowledge. I've tried watching bats through a window, seeing their arcing flights in the backyard, noting how beautifully they swoop, knowing precisely where they're headed and how to get there. I've tried thinking about how they eat mosquitos and other pesky things. But for the first eight years of my married life, there were enough gaps in the boards of our Victorian-era home that my husband and I were visited by bats. After bats invaded my safe space, I began to wonder where the next one would be. I would walk into a room where I had seen a bat in the past and check for it. And then one night there was a bat in our bedroom. I didn't feel safe. I was on edge.

There was no safe space in my house growing up either, no space my dad didn't have the right to enter. Like the bats who seemingly pop up out of nowhere, my dad's mood could shift from neutral to furious in seconds. He also understood the power of silence, of withdrawing from the family completely and giving us the silent treatment. When I was as young as five or six, my dad would not speak to me for hours over something I had done. Sometimes I never knew what had happened. Other times I had been cranky or disrespectful. In my room alone, I fretted, trying to distract myself, hoping that it would blow over. Then I would tentatively step out of my room and back into the rest of the house to see if he would interact with me. "Daddy, can I practice piano?" I might ask. Or "Daddy, can I watch TV?"

Most times, whatever had angered him hadn't blown over, and my tentative question would be met with icy silence, a turned back, or a huffy reply: "I don't really care what you do, and you obviously don't care at all about my feelings or opinions, so I don't know why you asked."

Sometimes I would cry alone in my room, tracing a spot on my bedspread over and over as I replayed an earlier conversation looking for my fault. Sometimes I would pick at a spot on the carpet or on a stuffed animal, toying with the textures as my mind roamed back to earlier fights. Sometimes I'd find my mom or Karen and I would cry with them. Whatever option I chose, hours later I would come forward and apologize to my dad, almost always unsure what I had done to give offense. He'd lecture for a little bit, and then we'd return to "normal." My dad knew how powerful his silence was, how I couldn't go back to enjoying life or focusing on anything else until I had stepped forward to resolve the problem.

Sometimes now I find myself briefly giving my kids the silent treatment; usually for me it's because I don't want to yell at them. Maybe that's why my dad was silent. I don't know. Usually now after I've yelled at Anton or Edward or walked away from them, I go after them and try to talk more. My dad's hours-long silences manipulated me into apologizing profusely for minor transgressions. I don't want to subject my children to that.

❧

After I moved out of my parents' home, I started to feel less of an irrational fear of my dad. Instead, I started to feel anger. Sometimes even now, long after he's dead, I get angry when I think about him. I'm confident some people would tell me that feeling anger at a dead person isn't a productive emotion. I wonder though. I read online that the word "anger" comes from the Old Norse word "to grieve, vex." Other origin words mean "distress, grief, affliction." To grieve has two meanings: to feel a loss and, the lesser-known definition now, to afflict. I know that even the dead can vex us, can distress me. My dad's presence after his death lingers in many ways. Maybe anger at a dead person isn't so strange after all. Maybe it's a way of considering the lasting afflictions that even those who are dead can cause us.

Part of me knows that my dad's controlling behaviors were a form of emotional abuse. In our twenties, before his death, my sister and I would spend hours processing events of our childhood and our ongoing relationship with our dad, trying to make sense of it. We would sometimes venture the claim to each other that his behavior was abusive. We would stay in that moment for a while, considering the possibility. Then we would back off from the gravity of that claim, afraid that we were being too hard on him. Part of me can see how that too is a symptom of his controlling nature. Part of me knows that victims of emotional abuse are reluctant to call it abuse because there are no bruises. I know the research, the theories, but sitting with the claim is much harder than it sounds.

All the tiny hurts don't seem like much as I list them. I wonder how others would perceive them and worry that outsiders would say I am making too much of disciplinary choices my dad made. I wonder, how could all these tiny instances cause me to feel so damaged? So angry? The logical part of me suggests that the cumulative effect of so many tiny, controlling, manipulative statements can be so much stronger than the sum of its parts, but still I hesitate.

And then I remember that there were also deeper betrayals—betrayals of values. This man who taught me about a loving and all-forgiving God after whom we were to model ourselves would withhold forgiveness in petty ways and use God as a weapon to justify his treatment of us: "You don't respect my opinion enough to just sit, listen, and then follow my advice. God tells you to honor your parents, but you treat me like shit. How do you think God looks upon that behavior?"

My dad, who taught me to be a feminist in many ways, would, when the mood suited him, throw up my biological sex as evidence of my inferiority: "You're so cranky right now. It must be your period. See, that's why women can't be president because you can't be trusted near the button to send off nuclear weapons." This same man who told me I could be anything I wanted to be when he was in his right mind would deny my full humanity when he was in a dark place and needed to lash out at someone. I'm sure he thought it would help him feel better. I'm confident it never worked.

So many memories overtake me at times. They overwhelm the understanding of his pain and suffering that time, distance, and hard work have helped me gain. They overwhelm my compassion for his untreated depression, his worries over money, his love for us, and his desire to give us (and himself) a good life. In those moments, I just feel angry.

Over the years, people have told me that I shouldn't hold on to anger. It only hurts me. People have told me I need to forgive my dad for all he did, that he did his best and that it's time to move on and not blame him for what he did to me, my sister, and my mom. Yet I know that sometimes any reaction other than anger is wrong. Sometimes anger is justified. Sometimes to reflect on a situation and not become angry is unhealthy.

Like my dad did for years, some people bring in God to tell me why I should "forgive and forget," "bury the hatchet," "let it all go," "be the bigger person," or whatever cliché they want to share that would smooth away all obstacles between me and my dad, leading to a perfectly happy father-daughter relationship. One woman at work, when I explained why I wasn't going home for the holidays, trying to put into words my pain, reminded me that Jesus wants us to forgive seventy times seven times: "Remember that God asks us to forgive and forgive and forgive over and over," she said. The message to me was: "This is your father. Suck it up. Accept whatever he's given you and continues to give you. Forgive no matter what. That's what God would want."

I think it's much more complicated than that, even within that seemingly straightforward biblical text. I think it's important to note that what Jesus said about forgiving someone up to seventy times seven times doesn't mention anger. The text proves that the practice of forgiving is important, but that doesn't mean anger doesn't come back again. Maybe we need to forgive that many times because we get angry that many times. And maybe that's OK.

This interpretation fits better with my understanding of a God that recognizes that people do harm to each other and says that while vengeance isn't our go-to strategy, neither is the right path forward being oblivious to the wounds caused by others. Jesus as the suffering servant, an image my dad taught me to value and believe in, isn't an image of a God who says to the victim of emotional abuse, "Suck it up. Forgive and forget. Your anger is only hurting you." Instead, I think the suffering servant sits next to the victim of emotional abuse and feels angry too. I think Jesus, in that moment, would say, "I'm angry. That was wrong. Let's forgive one more time for now until the anger returns. Then we'll do it again."

I think what happens too often when people try to informally counsel victims of emotional abuse or when we as the afflicted try to counsel ourselves is that we rationally think there should be and will be an end to the anger. We think forgiveness will free us from that anger. I don't think that's the case. Instead, I've come to believe it's OK for me to feel angry from time to time. It's natural and even rational. Trapped in his darkness, my dad spewed poison from time to time as a release valve. My sister, my mom, and I suffered collateral damage from his survival attempts. I shouldn't have had to be afraid of his reactions, of him. What he did—how he acted—was unjust and hurtful. I can be angry about that whenever I want, and to suggest otherwise is in a small way to endorse the abuse.

Perhaps the more important battle is what I am to do with my anger. A friend once said to me that responding to an unjust situation by saying, "That's sad," is empathy, and of course that response has a place. But responding to an unjust situation by saying, "That makes me angry," is much more powerful. She said that feeling anger suggests impetus to act, to change, to move in a new direction.

My anger at my dad does act as an impetus for change. When I get angry about his lack of treatment for depression, I am more likely to make an extra effort to reach out to someone who might need a referral for mental health counseling. And when I get angry over memories of him, I try, ever so briefly, to be a better person, a better mom. I try to be more aware of how my destructive emotions are forging memories in my kids.

The day my younger son said to me through tears, "You never say, 'I forgive you,'" I listened.

"I always forgive you, Edward," I replied. "I've told you before, there's nothing you could do that I wouldn't forgive. That doesn't mean I won't get angry or you won't get a time-out or get yelled at."

"But you never say, 'I forgive you,'" he said.

So I did. And I try to remember to say it again.

I forgive my children as they learn how to navigate relationships. I forgive them for saying, "I hate you, Mom," because I know they don't. I still feel hurt, but I forgive—I accept the limitations of being a child, of being a human who is wounded or tired or has lost all perspective on what matters in life. My dad was once a child too, of course. I wonder why no one ever helped him learn what I hope my sons learn, to share their feelings, to use words to help tame and navigate emotional storms. I wonder why no one ever helped my dad see the power of saying "I'm sorry" and "I forgive you." I wonder why he seems to have seen both phrases as weak, only for others.

I don't know that I forgive my dad every time my anger resurfaces. If I did, I'd probably be approaching seven hundred times seven by now. I also know that I won't "cure" myself of the anger I have felt by forgiving him completely and letting go. Instead, I have worked harder towards forgiving myself for not being able to fix our family, forgiving myself for never finding the right way to help my dad.

I think about how my dad's moods ruled the day, how his darkness and despair and depression on certain days—manifesting themselves in angry outbursts—were like a black hole to which the rest of the family was inexorably drawn. Like a black hole, he had too much mass, too much power in the family structure for us to escape. Luckily, unlike a black hole, sometimes he was able to escape the event horizon, taking all of us with him to a happier place and moment. But still, I need to remind myself that it wasn't possible for me to "choose" to be happy when my dad was in his darkest places. I couldn't pick myself up, so I can't blame myself for that. And since that situation was unjust, I am allowed to be angry at him and at every person and every system that didn't help us.

To be true to myself, I can't respond to my memories of hurt by saying, "I forgive you, Daddy, so I won't be angry with you anymore." Maybe the best I can do and maybe all I *need* to do is respond to my memories with "I forgive you again, and I am still angry sometimes."

25

2004 (Age 32): Because I Don't Believe in Angels

My dad is talking about angels as he and I sit together on the couch in my sister's house in northern Wisconsin. I look out her front window and see the expanse of grass and the tiny flower gardens she and her three neighbors have planted to make these homes in the country, a few miles south of Rice Lake, seem like they are a part of a settled neighborhood.

I'm only half listening to my dad. I just drove four hours to get there in time for a birthday weekend celebration—my thirty-second birthday on Sunday and my mom's to follow on Tuesday. We'll celebrate Father's Day as well, even though it'll be the following Sunday. My sister and I have gifts all ready for my dad and my mom. The semester has ended and I'm off contract. I should be writing, working on projects to earn tenure, but I've taken a couple of weeks off to read for fun on my balcony, taking walks to feel reinvigorated and take a break from my academic preoccupations.

I tune in when I hear my dad talk about angels as if they are physically present with us. "Well, sure," I say, "I believe in the way that we act as angels to each other. The way we reach out to help each other in hours of need. But obviously not in angels with wings, right?"

My dad, who is sitting close by me on the couch, shifts forward, his size 13 feet in their solid brown dress shoes pressing up against the side of my stockinged feet. I am sitting on the end of the sofa. I begin to feel cornered as he shifts his body to half face me.

"No, I do mean angels with wings," he says. I'm taken aback by this. I've always felt that my dad didn't believe in that kind of angel. I thought it was one of the many points of agreement we had about our faith and religion.

"What are you saying?" I ask.

"The Bible is very clear about the existence of angels as semi-divine beings," he begins in a kindly but condescending lecture style. He begins to name names and quote passages. I listen for a bit and then interrupt at one point.

"But isn't it possible that we need to interpret those passages not in a literal sense but in a figurative way? Like other parts of the Bible?"

My dad raises his right arm, the one closest to me, and brings it down quickly to his knee, like a director using a clapboard to call for quiet on the set of a film. I shrink back further into the couch. "I can't believe you're saying you don't believe in angels," he barks. "It's an essential tenet of Catholicism. Are you rejecting the teachings of the Church?"

I'm not sure where this is going. There are lots of essential tenets of Catholicism that I don't believe, that my dad doesn't believe either. I let him talk a while longer, thinking about my recent attendance at a Lutheran church in my community. I am hoping to tell my dad the truth about my exploration of Lutheranism this weekend. I am hoping to tell him about my meetings with a local Lutheran minister, himself a convert from Catholicism. I met him because his background in theater led him to an interim job directing a play on our campus.

I want to tell him about the watershed moment when this pastor told me that I don't have to stop being Catholic in order to begin practicing my Christianity in a Lutheran church. I want to tell him about how the ELCA allows for ordained women and bishops and views women differently than the Catholic Church does. I want to tell him about how they have communion every week and that so many of the prayers are the same that I feel like it's almost the same service, but in an institution that values me more. I want to share my growing enthusiasm for this new faith community, one that also needs an organist.

I decide to dive in and say what I'm thinking: "But there are lots of Catholic teachings we don't agree with."

"Such as?"

"Papal infallibility, women priests, married priests, annulment, birth control …"

"And what do you think about birth control? I'm not sure that's something we agree on. Do you have anything you want to tell me about?" His voice is condemnatory and not an open door to conversation.

I think about the other secret I have to tell them, that my attempts to meet someone through online dating sites have resulted in meeting a guy I really like, a divorced man who was raised outside of any organized religion. I wish I hadn't said that last one on the list. I avoid the topic of birth control for now. "I just don't understand why you're saying I have to agree with everything the Church teaches."

"I'm not saying you do, but I don't understand why you're rejecting my belief in angels. Why you're saying that's stupid."

"I never said that!"

"Yes, you did! You said you don't believe in angels with wings and all that stupid nonsense."

"Daddy, I never said that. Listen, I just drove four hours, and I've only been here thirty minutes. Can we wait and talk about all this later?"

"What's 'all this'? Do you have something else to say?"

I sigh. I want to get up from the couch. I want Karen and my mom to come out from the spare bedroom where they've gone to admire Karen's new comforter and pillows. I start to suspect they've heard our raised voices and they're hiding. I don't blame them, really, but I could use a diversion or some backup.

"Well," I say with trepidation. "I wanted to bring this up in a different way and at a different time, but I do want to talk to you about the fact that I've been meeting with a Lutheran pastor and attending an ELCA church the past few weekends."

I don't get to say anything else. My dad's face shifts through disbelief into anger. "Marie!" he shouts. I start to stand, and he stands too, turning quickly on the carpet because of the smoothness of the underside of his shoes and stomping loudly down the hall. "Marie!"

I hear voices down the hall, but I can't concentrate on the words. All I can think is, *Shit*.

※

We're sitting around my sister's kitchen table, dinner plans put on hold while my dad seethes. I wonder if Karen is peeved at me for ruining night one of our visit, wishing I had found a way to avoid the outburst. But the only direction in which her annoyed glances move is towards my dad.

We're seated just steps away from the couch where the fighting started this time, the open concept living room and dining room allowing me a complete view of that space that I'll always associate now with that conversation about angels.

"I blame you, Karen," he is saying now. "How have you let Jennifer get so out of control? You've always had a tremendous influence on her, and I always thought you would use that for good."

"Daddy!" I yell out. "That's not fair. I'm almost 32 years old! I get to make my own decisions about life. And this isn't the first time I've mentioned leaving the Catholic Church."

"It is to me."

"That's not true." He turns his glare from Karen to me as I continue. "I mentioned it at Christmas and after Easter."

"I'm sorry. I wasn't a part of those conversations. And if I was, I had no idea you were actually serious about contemplating such a move. My suspicion is that Karen *was*."

I try to keep my tone even, to avoid the pleading child tone that I know will annoy him and ought not to be there anyway. "I guess I'm just surprised you're so shocked, Daddy. I mean, after all these years of feeling spiritually unfulfilled, of being angry after every Mass, of coming home and being angry about the sermons and the way women are talked about …"

"How dare you make this final decision without even talking to me? Why did you hide this from us? Why didn't you tell us you had stopped going to church and started to become a Lutheran?"

Because I thought you might try to stop me, I think.

Aloud I say, "I don't know."

"Daddy," Karen begins, but his glare cuts her off.

"You don't get to act all high and mighty, Miss Karen. You turned down a perfectly good teaching job an hour away from us so you could move all the way across the state in two months to be closer to your sister. You didn't consult me about that, either. What else are you doing that you're not telling us about? What else are you hiding from your parents?"

I'm taken aback by the directness of this question. I look at Karen, thinking about the time we've been spending on dating websites, the online conversations and dates we've had. My hesitation tells my dad all he needs to know.

"So there's more! What do you two have cooking that you're keeping from us?!"

I look at my mom, who has remained silent this entire time. Karen speaks about her experiences with online dating sites, while I look at the wooden tabletop in front of me. When I speak, I look at Karen for support. I glance at my mom occasionally. She's crying quietly now. I don't know if it's because of what I'm saying, what Karen's saying, how my dad is acting, or a mixture of all three.

"Just what type of men do you think you'll meet online? What are you hoping to get out of these hookups?" My dad's words slap me.

"It's not like that. Jason's not like that."

"So we get to know his name. How generous of you. This 'Jason,' this man you're dating, is someone we know nothing about."

"I'll tell you all about him! He's an engineer, a naval architect. He's kind and generous. He owns his own home."

"How old is he? What's his past? What religion is he? Do you even know?"

"Yes, he's been very honest. He was raised outside of religion, but he's a very spiritual person. He's divorced, but she was a terrible person to him—cheated on him, did drugs, stole money from him …"

"This is the kind of man you choose! How does that honor your father and mother? It would have been easier for me to deal with it if you had brought home a Jewish man."

"What does that even mean, Daddy?" Karen begins. "You need to meet him. He's great."

He shifts his entire body to face her. "Oh, so *you've* met him! How nice for *you*! When were we going to be let in on these little secrets?"

"Daddy, I just wanted to wait until I knew if it was something serious or not," I insist. "There wasn't much point in getting you upset if it was nothing."

"Thank you so much for protecting me," my dad says in a patronizing tone. "I really need my little girl's protection. So, I was just going to find out about your online hookup with a divorced man when you wound up dead in his house?"

"Daddy!" Karen says in exasperation. "Calm down and be reasonable."

"Don't tell me what to do! You're hardly honoring your father and mother by moving so far away from us. Who will take care of us when we get older?"

"What?!" Karen says in shock. "You've always made such a big deal out of saying you wouldn't expect us to take care of you as you aged because you didn't want to be the burden your own parents were to you."

"How dare you!" My father's finger wags at my sister. "Who the hell do you think you are? My parents were never a burden, and I never said any such thing. Oh, it's all clear to me now. I can see it all. You two hate us. You want to be as far away from us as possible. And you want to reject everything we ever taught you, every value we ever tried to give you. I'm going to bed. I couldn't possibly eat dinner in this situation with these ungrateful children."

He leaves the table and my mom looks at us helplessly. "Why didn't you just say something earlier?"

"You really think this would have gone any differently over the phone two months ago?" Karen asks.

"No," my mom admits. "Jennifer, I do worry about you. What do you know about this man you met online?"

"Mom, I'm not stupid. Give me some credit. We met first in public places. I asked around and found out that he knows one of my colleagues, and she and her husband say he's a wonderful guy and worth trusting. I've been careful."

"Well, you have to understand that your dad's anger comes in part from a desire to protect you—that he loves you."

"Mom, come on," Karen says. "What part of that is love?"

"Why can't you just talk with him before you make decisions?"

"Maybe because we want to make our own decisions," Karen replies. "I'm 35 years old. I get to decide where I live, where I work, who I date. And Jennifer gets to decide where she goes to church. These aren't his decisions to make. Don't play the peacemaker here, Mom. He doesn't deserve your efforts."

"I know, I know." My mom sighs deeply. "I don't know what he wants sometimes."

"I do," Karen says. "Control."

❧

That night as I lie on the air mattress in my sister's office, I cry instead of sleep. I lie on my back and cry about religion. I turn on my side and cry about all the fights we've had as a family. I roll to my other side and cry because I know if I want this to be resolved I will have to say I'm sorry the next day, but life with my dad has emptied me of insincere apologies.

At some point, Karen sneaks into the office. "Are you awake?" she asks.

"Yes," I sniff.

"I figured. I can't sleep either."

"I don't want to apologize ..." I say with tears streaming down my face. "I don't believe in angels with wings coming to earth ... I want to keep going to Bethel Lutheran Church ... Jason is a good man ... You're moving to the right place for your life ... We're not wrong. We're not bad children."

"Then let's not apologize tomorrow."

I stop crying. By the lights of the power strip and the electronic devices it powers I see her face. Her eyes aren't red or puffy. Her nose isn't red either. I look her in the eye and see her strength.

"Daddy's out in the living room right now," she whispers. "I just went out there to check on him. I asked if he was OK, and he was just so rude back to me. He only wants to fight. He wants to have a big blowup to get his venom out, but I don't want to be the collateral damage to his untreated depression anymore." I'm surprised by Karen's clarity and conviction. I want it for myself.

※

We don't apologize, so my dad doesn't speak to us. All morning, all through lunch at a nice café in town, into the afternoon at her house. My mom speaks to us, and we speak to her and each other. It's beyond awkward. We've entered unfamiliar territory.

And then he goes to lie down in the guest bedroom. And then he talks with my mom for a while in hushed tones.

"We're going for a ride," he says as he stalks past the couch where Karen and I are sitting. My mom silently follows him out to their car.

For almost an hour Karen and I talk. "He's giving us an opportunity to play the game again," she says. "I just can't anymore."

I don't feel her strength, but I know in this moment of decision, I choose Karen, so when they come back and he demands, "What do you two have to say for yourselves?" instead of apologizing, we say calmly that we need to make our own life choices. My parents go to the guest bedroom and come back down the hallway with their suitcases packed.

"You don't want us in your lives anymore. You've made that abundantly clear." His lips twitch in anger in between each sentence. Part of me realizes he's right. I don't. Not like this. Not anymore. His words snap as they exit his mouth, whipping the air between us. "You don't value my wisdom, my life experience, or my opinion. You'd rather I were dead or just gone. That's clear."

While that's not fair, I can't engage, or he will stay. If I say a word, he'll know he's won, and we'll fight until we apologize. And will that mean I have to go back to Catholicism? Will that mean I'll have to give up Jason? I'm not willing to do that, so I stay with Karen, motionless on the couch.

My mom looks at us questioningly. She is crying quietly. I want to reach out to her, to ask her to stay. But I know she won't. She can't. I look again at Karen. Her lips are set firmly, and she blinks slowly a few times. I hear the opening and closing of a car trunk and two car doors. I hear the engine start, the tires on the gravel after the car leaves the concrete apron in front of Karen's garage. Through the front window facing the couch, I see their car back up, its wheels spin, and my parents drive away.

26

Searching

A couple of years after my dad died, I realized he probably enjoyed the conversations we had about religion. I'd never even considered that before. I listened to what he had to say, took him seriously, and sometimes said something that made him think in new directions. In some ways we were friends discussing a common interest. Sure, it was a troubled relationship, but it was an intellectual collegiality I don't know that he had with lots of other people.

So when I left the Catholic Church—his church—*our* church, he hurt. It turns out I don't need to find pages in his journals to know that to be true. Maybe I broke my father's heart when I left the religion of my upbringing and the religion of his entire life. Or maybe I made him angry. Perhaps it would be most accurate to say that my father lost control of my life when I left the Catholic Church, of defining who I was, and that bothered him.

Perhaps it's unfair to give just one explanation for his complex response. Maybe in all those conversations we'd had about his disenchantment with the church's hierarchy he felt he had an ally. And when I left, he felt alone. Maybe he was surprised I had the courage to leave. Maybe he was envious. Maybe he wished he could leave too.

I didn't feel I had deserted him, but maybe he felt that way. Bill Shepard, the ELCA pastor I met with, reminded me that I would always be Catholic: "When we change and grow, we don't lose our past identities—we add to them. You are choosing to practice Lutheranism right now and to grow in your faith and spirituality in this church community."

I wish my dad had been able to see that, to accept my decision, but I don't think he could ever fully understand just how rejected I felt by my own religion. As much as he had read and thought and discussed, he didn't know what it felt like for me as a woman in the Catholic Church.

I'd love to say that ever since I started attending a Lutheran church, all has been well. Certainly, my worship in an ELCA church has contained moments where I felt more accepted as a woman: visiting women pastors celebrating the Eucharist, discussions of gender from the pulpit that weren't about separate and definitely not equal. Yet some Sundays I still feel trapped in an earthly religion that hasn't embraced the social justice message I think the divine wants us to see, particularly surrounding gender equality.

I know preachers are fond of reminding congregations that the Holy Spirit transcends gendered pronouns. But each week, the amount of time we spend talking about Jesus and about a masculine "Father" so far outweighs the amount of time we talk about a non-gendered spirit, it's hard to keep it in mind. Yes, there are prayers that talk about how "like a child in its mother's arms, so we rest in God," but these prayers are comparatives, not direct statements about God as mother. God is like a mother. God isn't depicted *as* a mother. To add to it, mothers—and by extension, women—are figured as caring, loving, supportive. Why not strong, decisive leaders?

Each week everyone says, "Our Father" and my own troubled relationship with my father is not a model I want to apply to my relationship with God. And no matter how hard I have tried to think about something else, no matter how often I say, "Our Creator," instead or omit male pronouns in prayers that allow it, I still think of God as male. And that creates distance. When I picture God as male, I picture myself as an incomplete copy of a part of God. I feel unlike God.

Still, I fight within myself. Largely because of my dad, there are *never* times when I pause to consider, "Maybe I am, because of my womanhood, just lesser, made to serve and not to lead." Of course, it's also because of the evidence I have from existing in my own skin for a lifetime. I know what I was made to do. I know who I am. I am not lesser. I am equal. I was made to serve *and* to lead.

※

With my two sons, I tried from an early age to refer to God with either no pronoun or switching between "he" and "she," mother and father images. I read books to them over and over that compared God to all sorts of creatures and that talked about how trying to name God is futile because God transcends all labels we want to use. We read books about Native American traditions that often show women in powerful divine roles and show the presence of the divine throughout all nature. I hoped to make some progress by helping my boys to grow up picturing all sorts of things when they imagined their creator, not just the guy in the white beard with the flowing white robes. I wanted more for them than that cliché. It's so unhelpful.

And then when my older son was around six or seven, I said something to them about God and used a female pronoun, and Anton "corrected" me: "You mean 'he,' Mom. God's a man." When my younger son was about seven, he too described God as a man with a beard (and with hairy toes for some odd reason).

I felt like a failure.

And I don't think my dad could have understood how awful it felt and how awful it still feels to know that is what my children believe, to know that it will forever alter the way they look at everything—every woman, every man, every part of our culture.

I worry that I am repeating my father's choices, repeating what I sometimes see as a mistake. He stayed in a religion with which he had problems, one of which was its treatment of women and the non-ordained men like himself who serve in ministry. I stay in a religion that teaches gendered ideas of the divine that I do not believe, that I believe warp us and our understanding of humanity. And I am raising my children, as I was raised, in a faith that is flawed in ways I can clearly see and articulate but seem to accept by staying.

Ultimately, I know I wasn't a failure as a parent because I didn't refer to God enough with something other than male pronouns. I was fighting a losing battle from the start because believing in God's masculinity is pervasive. No matter what we taught at home, once I chose to take my kids to church—almost any church—I lost the ability to help them perceive God as anything other than male.

I think about the stereotypical, damaging images of women that my children and I hear read from the Bible at church. I think about how confusing it must be for my kids to hear our pastor talk about equality, and then hear lines from the "most important book" that say something else. I think about all the parishioners around me who unthinkingly say "he" and never once imagine that God could perhaps not be a man. There's no revolution afoot in the Lutheran church either. Some weeks I know my dad was right—nothing's different even if you change churches.

I left and lost, but what have I gained? I often wondered, do I pull myself and my family away from church or from any organized religion? I find tremendous value in the community, in the ritual, in the coming together to learn more, to pause to reflect. I leave the sermons I hear inspired to try to be a better person. I enjoy seeing people I know, having a church family who knows me and understands parts of me at least, if not this important part. To leave again may take more faith than I have. I begin to doubt I could find some church tradition that expresses more accurately the full social justice message I believe exists in the Gospels if you read beyond the bias of the men who wrote the stories down.

Maybe this next phase won't be an active leaving but a passive and slow removal. My busy life means I can no longer accompany the choir. Our weekends away for work or family lead me to attend only the every-other Sundays when I play organ for the service. I stopped pushing my kids to attend.

I asked my sister if I am a bad person.

"Your boys are good people with a strong conscience and social justice convictions," she reminded me.

"But what if they don't believe in God?" I paused and looked at her. "What if I don't? What if within two generations I've taken our family from a strong faith in organized religion to nothing?"

Karen had no easy answers for me. She has her own struggles. I want to believe that my dad, on his good days, would have entertained my questions and assured me that God believes in me even if I don't believe in God. I want to believe, too, that a strong faith in organized religion isn't the same as a deep faith in the divine.

Sometimes I tell my boys that the divine is reflected in all things and all people, and we should strive to see it and sense its presence everywhere. On a beautiful spring day, I pause and tell them to soak in the divine presence in the gentle breezes. In the cold of winter, I remind them that God is present in the warmth of a fire or a hug or a cuddle under a warm blanket. I tell them the divine spark is in them too.

I remind myself the divine is in me too. And then I see myself, my fully female self, and I remember all the messages I've heard over a lifetime from organized religion of "he" and "his" and "father-God," and "Jesus-man." It's harder for me to believe what I want to believe. It shouldn't be so difficult.

27

2005 (Age 33): Because I Never Really Moved Out

One Thursday afternoon, two months after my wedding, the phone rings. I see my dad's name on the caller ID. It rings a second time, and I consider not answering it. What could he be willing to say? What will I say? After the third ring, I pick it up.

"Jennifer," my dad's voice is instantly familiar, as is his dismissive tone.

"Hi, Daddy."

"Hi, Jennifer." My mom's voice on the other handset is even and controlled.

"Hi, Mom. How are you?" A stupid question, but I don't know what to say. I sit on a kitchen chair and look down at my work shorts splattered with paint from outdoor projects on our Victorian home in Marinette. The two shades of purple and dazzling pink overlap each other, while streaks of white and yellow complete the abstract painting on the black canvas of my shorts.

"How do you think she is?" my dad responds. I realize this is not a call to reconcile our relationship. "What are you doing?" he asks.

"I just came in to take a break. I was outside working on a project for our house." Perhaps this can be an opportunity for me to talk about normal things, to draw them into my daily existence again. "It's a Queen Anne built in 1881 and needs some restoration work. I've been learning about priming and painting, and I'm redoing our front doors."

"We're moving," my dad says abruptly.

"What?" I stand up from the kitchen chair and walk over to the blue countertop across from me.

"I've left my job at Cathedral. Your mom retired from the library. I'm going to St. John's to get a Master of Divinity in Theology, and we're moving to St. Cloud."

"Wow." I turn and lean my back against the countertop. "Congratulations, I guess. That's awesome that you got into the program and you're doing this … I know you've wanted to do this for a long time."

"I got a scholarship too," my dad says.

"That's wonderful."

"We leave in a couple of weeks. We're calling to tell you that we're having a garage sale this Saturday. We're getting rid of things that you left behind. We just wanted you to know."

My mind reels. Moving in two weeks. Garage sale this Saturday. My childhood possessions. What was left? I think back to the room in the back of the basement with shelves lining the far wall. What had my mom and I put there? A box with play items from my grocery store. A wooden gas station we played with as kids. My dad's old fire truck toy. Pull toys. I see the old yellow drop leaf kitchen table in the basement that would fit so well with my older home, the dress-up clothes in the old dresser in the basement—clothes and hats from my grandmother, mother, and aunt. I think of my train set, my closet upstairs with boxes of children's books, my beginner trumpet, the framed cross stitches I completed after spending hundreds of hours on each one. What will be sold? What will be kept?

I picture the house in Winona and my childhood bedroom with the wacky carpet and the leaky window. I think of the kitchen, redone years after I left, with its glass doors to display dishes and glasses. I think of the bathroom, also redone after I left, the old yellow tiles that had been falling out, covered with a black plastic garbage bag at one time to protect the inner drywall, replaced later by gleaming new fixtures and tile.

"I … I … What are you selling? What are you keeping?"

"If you left it here, you obviously didn't want it."

"I don't know if that's true," I say. "I didn't have a chance to come back and see things and to decide what would forever go away and what I would keep."

"Well, if you want anything, you'll have to come get it."

"Jennifer, you don't want any of this old stuff," my mom says. "The toys and games that are left are so old …"

"What if Jason and I have kids?" I ask. "What if I wanted to pass some of those along to them?"

"You'll want to buy them new things, not all this old stuff," she replies.

I think about the antiques throughout the home I now share with Jason, the love of all things old that imbues our relationship. I want to ask more questions, but this conversation is ending and my dad is saying, "Well, we just wanted to let you know." We say goodbye.

I sink to the smooth coolness of the vinyl floor in the kitchen. My eyes fix on a blue diamond shape in its pattern which quickly becomes obscured by tears. My mind can't center on any one object or image from my childhood home but continues to repeat the mental list I've already created. I dial my husband's work number, hands shaking, and punch in the extension, getting it wrong the first time. He answers at last, "Hello, this is Jason," with a smile in his voice, and I hear one of his coworkers laughing in the background.

The sound of his voice unhinges me. "They called me!" I blurt out through sobs. "My parents. Come home now please. I need you!"

"I'm on my way." His tone is serious. In just minutes he is in the kitchen, on the floor next to me. As he holds me, I tell him everything between sobs.

"We'll go then. We'll get in the car tomorrow and go down there and get what you want."

"The sale is Saturday. We wouldn't get there beforehand."

"Then we'll go to the sale and buy what you want."

I briefly fantasize about getting there before the sale, telling everyone outside to please let me have the first chance at purchasing the memories I want to keep, begging my dad to let me walk through the house one more time, renting a trailer and taking all the things my dad doesn't value.

I tell Jason about an earlier garage sale, the one when we moved across southern Minnesota, from Granite Falls to Winona. I said I wanted to keep my beloved desk lamp, a rose-and-white swirled ceramic base with a painted picture of a Georgian lady and gentleman. "Keep it. It wouldn't be worth more than a quarter to anyone else," my dad said to me. "What?! It's beautiful!" I replied. "It's a piece of junk," he said.

"He doesn't understand what I value …" I say to Jason now. "We have always seen things differently. I just don't know what to do. It hurts."

Jason lets the silence of the kitchen and the safe space he has created for me give us time to think. Then he takes a deep breath and says, "It may feel like your parents are eager to invite strangers to walk through a lifetime collection of objects that mattered to you, but they are less interested in ensuring you have one last look."

I look at the bushes outside the kitchen window. "I think that's it. It just feels so … weird and unnatural. I just wonder sometimes why I didn't take all my things years ago, back before we stopped talking."

"Well, you were in an apartment and maybe were waiting for a house. And you were going home so often. I'm sure you just always imagined you'd see it all again someday."

But now I won't.

I know Jason means it when he says he will drop everything and take me to the sale. As my crying diminishes, I picture it more, playing with the idea of running there. This time, as I imagine showing up before the sale starts, I add in dialogue after the garage door opens. I see my mom, her startled expression at my presence. I see her start to cry, while others look at her strangely. My dad fumes and asks me who I think I am. My mom disappears inside as confused garage-sale buyers drift around me. There is no reunion hug, no "I'm sorry" from my dad.

I can't go. I can't walk into their garage and beg for or pay for or take from them for nothing things they hope to get a few dollars for to finance this move. I can't have that be our next meeting, maybe our new last meeting.

"I don't want to go," I say to Jason with more certainty than I feel. "I don't know that I can be that close to the house with them still in it, that close to all the memories. I'm not sure it's worth it for the chance to get … I don't know what. I don't know that I want to risk going back there and having some new ugly encounter or sliding back into the old relationship."

Jason stands up and reaches down with a hand to pull me up. "I think you don't want to risk your future happiness for a relic from your childhood, and I get it, but that doesn't make it easy to let go."

I feel numb. I let Jason hold me up, supporting me in his arms as I am unsteady on my feet. The shock and emotions of the past half hour have drained me. "Do you need to go back to work?"

Jason turns to look at the clock behind him. "No, it's close enough. I can go in early tomorrow. What do you want to do? What will help?" I step away and try to imagine what will restore some peace to my afternoon, what will stop me from thinking and rethinking this conversation all evening.

"I don't know. I didn't see this coming … and I don't know where we go from here."

28

Estrangement and Normalcy

Those closest to me knew within a week about the initial break from my parents. Others found out in subsequent months, usually around a holiday. Acquaintances knew that holidays, major and minor, were important to my family, so they would ask if I was headed home. I would stumble over what to call what we were going through: A break? A pause? A breakup?

I didn't use the word "estrangement," not until long after it ended. I suppose like any historical, musical, or literary era, it didn't feel like it needed to be named or could be named until after it ended.

And I didn't know how long it would last. The first Christmas, Karen and I resolved to enjoy our lives even though every moment was steeped in memories both bitter and beautiful. We celebrated that we could spend holiday times alternately at our own homes and then reminisced about holiday traditions at the homes of our grandparents and parents.

The first birthday I ever celebrated without my parents was the day after they walked out of my sister's house. I don't remember much except sitting in a restaurant across from Karen, asking each other, "What just happened?" I am confident Karen tried to make it as celebratory as possible, but I have no obligatory picture of myself by a cake like I do for every other year of my life.

For Karen's birthday in January, the first after the break, I made her a cake like my mom used to when we were kids, complete with seven-minute frosting and the store-bought pink and white candy decorations for the top. I drove the two hours to her house to deliver it, not thinking through how the temperature changes of the freezing cold outside and the heater on high in the car might impact the cake in the back seat. By the time I arrived, the top said something like "app rthd re" and the rest of the sentiment had slid down the sides of the cake. We agreed it tasted fabulous even as we laughed and cried.

Easter one year we tried not to see each other. Life was full and neither of us got time off for the holiday, so our new tradition, we decided, would be to talk on the phone for a good long while that weekend.

That tradition lasted one year because we decided it was awful. We missed each other too much. Slowly, we adapted and developed new calendars and new approaches to celebrations. Through it all, I was grateful for Karen. She was my family. She was my connection to my past.

※

A few months after the break, we wrote a letter to my dad's doctor. I don't remember what we said, but our hope was to tell his doctor what we wanted to say in person—that my dad's depression was worse than he was letting on, that his angry outbursts were more severe than he would ever admit to anyone outside our family. I don't know what we hoped, except maybe that his doctor would ask him better questions the next time my dad came in for a checkup. I don't know if we should have written the letter, but we did.

My dad wrote a letter telling us his doctor had given him the letter. He said never to interfere in his life again. He told us that our mom was crying every day and every night. He told us that we were the most ungrateful children he had ever heard of.

We wrote my mom a letter and sent it to the library where she worked. We wanted to tell her how much we loved her and how much we missed her. We told her that this break wasn't about her, that we just were not willing to tolerate his behavior any longer. We told her that if she wanted to get out of the relationship with him, we would help her. I don't know that we believed she would reach out to us and say, "I'm coming!" I don't know if we wrote it to help her or to excuse ourselves.

In response, my dad sent me an email saying my mom had brought home the letter to share with him. He said it had upset her a great deal to receive such a letter at all, but certainly at a place where she couldn't read it in private. He told me never again to try to divide them. He said he didn't know where he went wrong to raise such hateful children.

A few months after that, I sent my dad an email to tell them I was engaged. My dad emailed back to ask how I could possibly think it was appropriate to send such news. He asked how I could possibly think this would bring them joy since they would never know my husband. He used a phrase I remember him using many times during our break: "I do not know who you are."

I sent an invitation to my wedding in the mail, months before the date. I couldn't decide whether to do so or not, but part of me hoped it would trigger a reconciliation. I wanted my mom at my wedding. I was excited to have my dad hear the great music we had planned. Mostly, I decided I would be able to look myself in the mirror if I knew I had tried.

I was in the kitchen a few days before the wedding, taking a break from the preparations since the reception would be at our home. The mail came and there was a card from my parents: "We couldn't possibly attend," my dad had written. "We think you know why. We wish you congratulations but cannot be a part of your lives." I fell into Jason's arms, crying.

Three years into the break, my mom was turning 70. Karen and I talked about how hard it was to be away from her for every birthday, for every holiday, for every celebration. Her birthday had become almost a day of mourning for us. We opted not to send a card because we didn't want to get the nasty message back from my dad. Shortly thereafter, we got a note from my dad saying we were horrible people for not even acknowledging her 70th with a card or a call.

At least that's what I remember him saying. I printed out every email he sent me during the break and, for a long time, kept every card and note he sent as well. When I would wonder if I had made a mistake cutting off contact with him, made a bigger deal out of his behaviors than I should have, I would look at the growing pile of reminders that I hadn't.

Years later, I got rid of them all. I felt like it was the right thing to do. I remember agonizing over the decision. Now, as time passes and I can't remember precisely what he said or wrote, I worry that I have become the unreliable narrator of my own story. I know deep inside I am not, that when I say "it wasn't that bad" or "he wasn't that mean" I am gaslighting myself, perhaps as my dad's proxy in this case.

The truth is that I do not remember every note he sent. I do remember that in all the communications, my dad never reached out to say, "Let's find a way to talk constructively," or "Let's find a way to be peacefully and harmoniously in each other's lives." He never wrote, "I'm sorry if I hurt you." To be fair, unlike the rest of my life, I didn't write "I'm sorry" to him either. But I did repeatedly write to him, suggesting that we could move forward, not revisit the past, not rehash the argument of that final day together at Karen's house. For a long time, he just wasn't interested.

❧

Over a decade after I reunited with my parents, about seven years after my dad died, I asked my mom to tell me more about those years we were separated—what life was like for *her*. I asked her if she hoped for a reconciliation.

"I didn't expect to ever see you again," she told me. "I couldn't see a way forward. He wasn't changing, and I couldn't see it happening with him the way he was."

Karen and I eventually found out after my dad died that my mom never knew how much we had communicated with my dad during those years. She never knew he called and left a message for Karen demanding back the $10,000 gift they'd given her as a down payment on her house. He said that since he didn't get to have any say in where she lived and what house she owned, he wanted the money back. Karen ignored the message but didn't forget it. My mom never knew that he would periodically send a note, a card, or an email with a mean-spirited or sarcastic reminder of how awful he thought we were.

My mom said she thought of us often, but she knew that Karen and I were together and always would be. "That gave me peace." Somehow she knew we were happy, so she went about her life, enjoying her work and reading books. Sometimes, something would set my dad off, and he would launch into an extended rant against us. "I was never the one to bring you up," she explained. "I didn't want him to spew out evil about you. It was like he hated you in those moments." No wonder then that she didn't hold out hope for a reconciliation.

"You know he wanted to come to your wedding," she said to me one day.

"No, I didn't know that … I mean, I had invited you after all."

"But not in that way. He wanted to come and sit in the back. He wasn't going to go so he could get together with you again. He wanted to punish you. He wanted to embarrass you. I kept thinking, there we'll be in that itty bitty church and we will ruin Jennifer's wedding day. I couldn't let that happen."

"Was he going to come talk to me? Come to the reception? What was the plan?"

"I don't know. I don't think he had one. He was just angry at you. Maybe he envisioned you seeing him, feeling guilty, rushing to say you were sorry. Or maybe in that moment he just wanted to see pain on your face because he was in so much pain himself." She paused for a moment. "I never stood up to your dad. He said I did all the time, but I really didn't. I did that time. I told him no. We were not going."

I think for a moment about how awful it would have been had she not stood up to him. I picture the joy on my face in my wedding photos replaced with pain and tears. I am so grateful to her.

"He wanted to go to Karen's wedding too. She didn't send us an invitation but somehow he thought we could figure it out and go anyway. He gave up on that one more quickly. I just can't imagine what he was thinking …"

※

During the years of separation from my parents, every day as I drove to work at UW-Marinette, I rounded a corner and spent a few blocks driving right alongside Green Bay, part of Lake Michigan. Regardless of the season, the view is stunning. It is nature at its most glorious: sunrises, clouds, waves, ice, birds rising and falling, an empty boat waiting for adventures. The immensity of the view is overwhelming. Almost without fail, I thought of my dad and I would feel a tightness in my chest. He loved looking at nature, big and small, and enjoyed taking pictures of roses and waterfalls and sunsets. I would sit on the front porch of our home looking at the Menominee River, trees, and a walking bridge. I would think of sitting with him on that porch, talking about life, religion, mortality, birds, and flowers.

I missed him, or at least I missed the good days with him.

Listening to a Tchaikovsky symphony or a George Winston piano solo, I would know that he had felt it deep within his soul as I do. He surrounded me with wonderful music from birth, and as a result the soundtrack of my life has been diverse, rich, and powerful. I thought of never hearing him play the organ again and I felt deep sadness.

Even as we settled into what was to become our estrangement, even as it became normal for us to be apart, I felt unsettled and uneasy. I felt a sense of loss.

At the time, I thought how much easier it would be to deal with my grief and loss if he had died. Now I know that his actual death presented challenges I could not rehearse for, a grieving process unlike any I could imagine. But during our separation, I would imagine what I would do if he were dead. It felt predictable and known. I would deal with the funeral home, arrange a Mass, select the music, and perform the rituals.

In reality, I struggled to know what to do, say, or feel knowing he was alive but gone from my life. There is not a socially accepted process for grieving the loss of parents or loved ones during a period of estrangement. Instead, we often feel a sense of guilt or shame and hide the reality when possible. Still, I have come to know that it is far more common and normal to experience this type of grieving than many of us want to admit.

For my mom, my dad, my sister, and for me—like for all in these situations—our lives went forward, every day both normal and strange. Although life sometimes felt disjointed, everyday events reminded me time was moving forward as usual. New holiday traditions, new friends, vacation trips, new opportunities at work all served as reminders that despite the surreal backdrop I felt my life now had, my life was straightforward.

Even as I held onto hope for reconciliation and building something better, I enjoyed the pause from the drama and pain. I came to understand that life with my dad in it was exhausting. Even when he was doing better, I lived on the edge, wondering if it would last. I needed time away from the uncertainty and the arguments. I needed time to begin to forgive *myself*, not him, for something I couldn't even define. I needed to be OK that I couldn't fix things. I needed to forgive myself for not missing him more, for letting life be normal, for being OK with the separation. In the end, I needed to forgive myself for finding happiness without him in my world.

29

2006 (Age 34): Because I Worry He's Right

"Nothing fits," I say to Jason for what must feel like the tenth time in two weeks. I turn away from our bed covered in clothes towards a closet with little left inside it.

"We need to go find you the next set of maternity clothes," he replies, and before I can raise the objections he knows are coming, continues: "I know we couldn't find anything in town here, so let's go somewhere else. You deserve to feel good about yourself every step of the way."

"Maybe this weekend?" For now, I pull the same pair of stretchy black pants I'd worn today out of the dirty clothes basket and put them neatly to the side, grabbing a shirt from the bed that I don't love but that will work for tomorrow.

"Sounds good."

And suddenly I am crying. Almost immediately, Jason is at my side and pulls me in for a hug.

"We'll get you new clothes …"

"Actually, it's not even that right now … It's …"

I can't continue at first, so I just drench his shirt in tears and stand there for a moment.

"I keep thinking about my mom and dad, at least once a day. I just … I never knew for sure I'd have kids, but if I did, I never imagined my parents not knowing their own grandchild."

I pull gently away from Jason's hug, walking over to my side of the bed and sitting down, pushing the clothes into the center and out of my way.

I take a deep breath, grab a tissue from my bedside table, and blow my nose.

"Today at work, someone said to me, 'Oh, your parents must be so excited. Is this their first grandchild?' It's one of the new part-time instructors so they don't know that my parents aren't in my life. So I had to say, 'yes, it's their first, but we aren't in communication much these days, so I don't really know.' They just looked at me funny and said something like 'sorry to hear that' and then walked away."

"Well, that person isn't an integral part of your life, so their opinion isn't truly important."

"I know. It's not that—well, it is that because it's embarrassing on some level, but I also just feel like, do people think this is easy? Do they think I don't think about my parents every day?"

"Do you?"

"Yeah. I mean, almost every day. At least my mom. I worry about her. And then I get angry because she's choosing his side and sticking with him. I have no idea how my mom even feels."

Jason shifts more clothes to the middle and sits down on his side of the bed.

"It's hard for me to explain it all," I continue, after wiping my face again. "It's like, every day, I go about my day and I'm happy most of the time, don't get me wrong, and then something will make me think of my mom or my dad and sometimes there's an ache and sometimes there's anger and sometimes there's worry."

"What do you worry about?"

"That I am the bad daughter he says I am. That I messed up. That it really is my fault and has always been my fault and every time I said 'I'm sorry' I should have and then some."

I let the silence be for a moment, giving Jason time to think and respond. I know I need his perspective.

"If you had them in your life right now, would you be better or would you be worse? What energy are they going to bring into your life?"

I look down at the new tissue I've been playing with in my lap, folding it and unfolding it. "I don't know …"

"Really?" His voice stays calm and even. "Listen, Jennifer, he's looking for you to grovel. The only way to satisfy him truly is to go back in time and redo it. That's impossible. It's not logical."

"Don't you ever wonder if I've made the right choices along the way to this moment?"

"I don't ever question the choices you've made. Sure, there's a part of me that wishes they were in our lives. I feel guilty sometimes that I'm the reason they aren't, that because you chose me, a divorced man, they won't let you back in."

"That's not it," I rush to reassure him. "I guarantee it. This is about me standing up to him and wanting to make my own decisions. It's about me leaving the Catholic Church. It's about … well … I don't know. I don't know sometimes what it's about. That's part of the problem. And that's when the doubt comes in …"

I start to cry quietly again.

"All right. Time to call for reinforcements." Jason reaches across me for the phone and dials.

"Hey, Karen," he says in the almost goofy voice he uses to break tension. He pauses. "I'm mostly good, but Jennifer is broken again." He smiles at me. "Karen, you have the memories and the right approach always. Fix please!" As he hands me the phone, he lies down on the bed. I turn and lean against the headboard. As Karen starts to talk, Jason rubs my right arm soothingly.

"Hey, what's up?" Karen says.

I try to communicate but hearing her voice has made me feel safe and made me cry again. Jason reaches for the phone. "She is feeling guilty and worried that she hasn't done enough to reconcile with your parents. She worries she's the bad daughter your dad says she is." Then he hands the phone back to me.

I hear Karen sigh deeply. "Jen, you have done so much more than he deserves. He's the one who went nuclear, left, and cut us out completely. You need to stop hearing his voice in your head. You need to stop victimizing yourself."

She pauses, but I'm not ready yet to speak. I need her to keep going, to somehow pull me up out of the spiral.

"Do you remember when Daddy sent me the snippets from his journal? Do you remember how hurtful that was? He sent me like three or four pages of typed thoughts. It was full of how we were both just terrible and then it was all about how I was terrible, how he didn't understand where he'd gone so wrong in raising me, how it was up to me to help keep you on the right path and I had failed. I remember just sitting on the floor in the bathroom sobbing. And do you remember what my counselor said to me? She said 'you need to move on. He's not going to change.' My counselor told me I need to treat it as if they have died. You need to let them go. There is no way he is going to change. Honestly, Jen, I don't know why you're still trying. I don't know why you're expecting it to be different when you reach out to them."

Karen pauses and I take a deep breath. "I do remember that."

"What did your counselor say to you, when you were getting married without them there?"

"Well, just that it's normal to feel sad that I'm experiencing milestones that I can't share with my mom. That it's normal to feel sad that I can't celebrate events with my parents."

"Sure. That's true. But if they were in our lives right now, how would Daddy react? It wouldn't be in the fabulous way you wish he would. Who knows what he would say? I mean, we never knew how he'd react to anything, so why would this be any different? I've told you before, I think you're a little crazy to reach out to them."

"I know. I just …" I sigh. "I don't know, Karen. I just wish …"

"Just be prepared. I don't think it's going to be successful. I don't want to see you get hurt any more than you already are."

"So you don't have any doubts about the path?"

Karen is quiet for a moment. "No, I don't anymore. Do I wish he were different? Sure. Do I have hope that he will be different? No. I've grieved losing Mom from my life and when I think of her, I hope she's doing OK. And with him? I've just moved on. I don't want him to control any more of my emotions than he already has."

"I wish I were where you are."

"Well, I know I sound like I have it all figured out and everything's just fine, but I suppose the truth is that I can be a mess sometimes too."

"I know. You always have been a bit of a mess sometimes," I say with a lighter note to my voice.

Jason squeezes my arm, gets up from the bed, and walks out of the room.

"Jennifer, you know I love you. You're awesome. You are going to be a great mom and Jason will be a great dad. You have his parents in your life. You have me and Mike in your life. You have so many good friends who will want to know your child too. Your kid's life is going to be full and rich, even without Mom and Daddy. You will make sure they have enough."

"Thanks." I wipe away a few stray tears. "It's hard, but you're right. I have to think about the pain he might cause my child too, through me, through Jason, and directly. For now, this is just what has to be. And I love you too."

"So promise me, you will keep trying not to let him hurt you?"

"I'll try." I take another deep breath and let it out slowly. "Oh, and Jason says he wants to go maternity clothes shopping this weekend. Any chance you and Mike are free to join us?"

30

Not about Him

My view of my mom is a textbook case of how easy it is to see a survivor of intimate partner abuse as a victim and nothing more. After my dad's death, Karen and I pushed her to see a counselor, to talk openly about what her marriage was like, but when she went, she tended to sugarcoat her experiences. We saw her as vulnerable, unwilling to leave her house on a regular basis because she was afraid. We cried over her loveless marriage, her painful life, her dreams unfulfilled.

A conversation with my pastor a couple of years after my dad died started me down a different path. "How does she talk about your dad?" he asked me when I was sharing my view of her.

"I asked her one day at a restaurant if she misses him, and she said she doesn't. I think she felt guilty, but I told her not to. I told her I understood."

Pastor Scott seemed impressed by her answer, and I felt confused.

"So she's able to talk about him in a realistic way?" he asked. "She doesn't idealize him?"

"Not at all."

"What about all of his possessions?"

"Gone. We got rid of his books and papers. I took his journals. She's turned his office into a guest bedroom and puzzle room …"

I could tell by my pastor's expressions that I was supposed to get some insight now. I was a little slow in seeing it, so he pointed it out to me: "Do you know how many people after the death of a spouse, even one who was challenging in the ways your dad was challenging for your mom, can't see reality? It sounds to me like your mom has been extremely brave and has changed a lot in her life. She's been willing to change her entire living situation."

"Good point." I thought about how she went out to buy a new couch and new chairs a few months after my dad died. Their sagging furniture was replaced by beautiful new tan and brown pieces with red accent pillows. My mom did it all by herself.

Years later, she moved across two states to be closer to us. She was excited about everything new to her—a new home in Menominee, Michigan, a new identity as a Yooper in the Upper Peninsula, a new car, a new church (mine), new friends, new restaurants. As my sister and I packed and later unpacked boxes, we marveled at her willingness to part with pieces of her past.

One day she told me that at Bible study at her new church, she described her marriage with honesty for the first time to someone other than me, Karen, or her counselor: "I just said in the context of our conversation, that my husband was verbally and emotionally abusive."

"How did it feel?" I asked.

"Good!" She seemed to surprise herself with her response.

"How did people react?"

"They listened to the rest of what I had to say and then mentioned a couple they knew that was similar."

"I'm glad you said it. I hope you say it again sometime."

She looked out the window behind me and smiled faintly. I could tell she was proud of herself. She should be. I'm proud of her, and I tell her that.

I remain protective of my mother. I don't want my dad or memories of him to hurt her anymore. But I must be careful not to infantilize my mom. She is not a small child. She is not just a victim. She is also a survivor. I recognize those times she propped us all up despite her own inner pain. I see the strength it took to hide so much from her children. I see now that she is, without a doubt, one of the strongest people I will ever know.

Even after all these years, part of me still feels guilty. I stayed in my family to fight for change from within for as long as I could. Ultimately, I didn't see change as possible, so I left. Sometimes I feel as if I deserted my mom. How might her life have been different if I had stayed? Should I have apologized my way back in sooner so I could help her? Should I have gone back to get her out? Would she have left with me?

I believe that if I had stayed, if I had apologized to my dad and allowed him to control my choices, I wouldn't be married to Jason, and my two beautiful boys wouldn't be in this world. I hope she knows that I had to escape, to forge a new path, while she retreated.

She brushes aside my concerns and worries. "You had to stay away. Things happened as they needed to happen. And I have you and Jason and Anton and Edward … It's all wonderful."

※

My mom now speaks of my childhood with honesty, showing me what I could not see then, especially her sense that she was not in control of her life. "I was too weak to stand up to your dad. I learned to keep my mouth shut because otherwise I'd just get yelled at. Other times it came back on you kids, and I didn't want that."

One afternoon, I asked her again if she ever thought about leaving. On that afternoon, the memories tumbled out one after another with more anger than usual after so much time. "I remember in Winona, some days it felt so unsurvivable that I would go in the bedroom and check the newspapers for classified ads, looking at apartments for rent. Then I would realize that I didn't have a job with enough money, and I would worry, what would it do to Jim if I left?"

"Did you care?"

"Of course I did. I loved him, and I always hoped that the next thing would make him happier. When we left Dubuque and he stopped teaching at the college there, I thought he would be happy teaching choral music at the high school in Granite Falls. But there were always battles with administrators there, so when he started to sell insurance for the Knights of Columbus, I thought he would be happy—connecting with his Catholicism more. Well, that was such a bad fit for him. He couldn't get himself to call people he didn't know and try to get them to buy something, even something he believed in. When we moved to Winona, I thought he'd be happier being closer to his parents, but that was both good and bad for him … And then ultimately he was asked to stop working. Well, he was fired, but we didn't want to call it that."

She paused and looked over at me. She had been staring at the wall across from her recliner, lost in so many places and times, lost in so many hopes that amounted to nothing.

"Even when he was working, I always felt bad about money. I was afraid to call my mother because it cost money. I remember I didn't take pictures of you kids … Didn't want to waste the film. Then one day you were out in the backyard with Karen, both so little and adorable. I ran inside and got the camera to take a picture of you both. I felt so guilty afterwards, it's all I could think of when I saw the picture printed out months later."

"Did he say anything?"

"I just waited anxiously to see what would happen when the film got developed. Thankfully, he never said anything. Maybe he thought he'd taken the picture! I don't know."

I thought about all the old photos we had been going through lately. I had asked her to put names on the backs of them if she remembered any, or any other details like locations or dates. I wondered which picture it was—wondered if she remembers or if we could find it. Suddenly it seemed so precious to me, wherever it was, this stolen moment captured at some risk. She was still remembering, however, and still angry.

"When you were so little, we were at his parents' house. We hadn't talked about having another baby, so I didn't know. I put you down for a nap in the basement and came up the stairs. I overheard his mom say to him that we shouldn't have any more children. 'Marie can't keep the two you have under control, so she can't handle a third.' I remember thinking to myself, well, that's that decided then."

I had heard her tell me this story a few times before, but its cruelty and pain was still hard to hear. "Did you say something to him later?"

"No."

"Why not?"

"I was scared of him," she said and looked me in the eye. "I knew he'd yell or put me down or something."

I tried to imagine what that would have felt like, how hard it was to hear those words and not have anyone to talk to about them.

"I'm so grateful that we reunited so you can be in my life," I said, trying to shift the subject.

"Even when it came to reuniting with you, I don't remember him asking me. He wasn't talking through his feelings with me. I was happy that maybe we were going to see you again, but honestly, until you were there, and even after you left and it was still OK for us to talk about you and to see you again, I wasn't sure what would happen. I didn't let myself hope too much."

In every story she told me that day, there is a constant theme of control. My mom always felt like my dad was in control, like she didn't get to make decisions, small or large. In a similar way, long after Karen and I became adults and moved away, she and I worried and wondered and put my dad at the center of our decision making. I wish I could say that after our time apart and then our eventual reconciliation that I felt differently, but I didn't entirely. I remained on high alert. Ultimately, his endorsement of any decision or plan, big or small, mattered, sometimes even more than my own. My need for his approval put him at the center.

I think to survive her marriage and living with my dad, my mom often did put his daily wishes at the center. I assumed for decades that that meant she was miserable. I connected the dots from lack of control to frustration to sadness to depression.

I didn't have it all right. In some significant ways, I've come to realize my mom figured out some things a lot sooner than I did. In fact, I think she's been ahead of me for decades. I had a vision of her life and her marriage as a miserable experience from start to finish, but that's not accurate. As I listened more and more to her honest feelings about her marriage and her life, I learned that I wasn't hearing regrets. I wasn't witnessing her descend into a pit of despair over a wasted life. She was reflecting honestly on what had happened and the anger she felt. At the same time, she was also able to tell good stories about her life, her work, and us, her daughters.

I have learned that my mom realized she could be happy whether he wanted her to be or not. She could be happy whether he was or not. Her happiness wasn't about him. She could read a book or enjoy a day at work or savor food at a meal whether he was doing so or not. Yes, he may have controlled decisions. Yes, he may have made her feel inadequate. But time and again she was able to remind herself that her life itself was not about him.

I can't go back and learn from that perspective in time to deal with it in my living relationship with him, but since I still hear his voice in my head quite regularly, since I still hear his advice and comments, wisdom and criticism, I can try to take my mom's approach. I can choose to listen to the parts of him that were valuable. I can retell his good advice and give him credit for those bits of wisdom without being untrue to myself. My life and the wisdom I have chosen to take from him are in fact now about me, not about him. I can say "I learned from my dad" rather than "My dad said," not to take agency from him but to recognize my own.

With great clarity I now see that my mom is not a victim. She doesn't look back at her married life and see it as a tragic waste. If I do so, I am the one who is wrong. I do her a disservice. She deserves my compassion for her sufferings but not my pity. I picture her going to work and coming home during our separation, able to live with my dad but not be subsumed by him. I have much to learn from her about putting myself at the center of my life, of creating my own happiness, of balancing my relationships with others with my sense of self.

I can even apply my mom's lesson to my relationship with my own children. When I worry about my role in their lives, the way that I may be trying to control who they are or how they spend their time, I can try to take a step back and remember that the goal is not to be the center of their lives but the foundation for their character. I can separate my dad's definition of a "good family," one that fights together, has forced time together, and keeps secrets together, from my definition of a good family. I can remember that my kids wanting to spend time following their own passions and friendships is an indication that I have created a secure foundation for them which is allowing them to explore and develop who they are as individuals. I can remember that when they come to ask me to play a game, it's a sincere wish to spend time together, and I can know how precious that is—how affirming of our good relationship.

But it is so hard not to want to be at the center. I feel sad when they declare they hate doing the very things I love. I cry because we don't read together like we used to when they were younger. It is so incredibly difficult not to try to manage our family, to try to script or craft experiences together. It is hard not to force conversations or prescribe the path we walk together.

These difficulties remind me to have some sympathy for my dad. More importantly, they remind me I have more to learn from my mom's life lesson. Just as I can learn from her that my life is not about my dad—he's just *one* presence in my life and not *the* presence—my children need and deserve to say to me, "Our lives are not about you." Perhaps these lessons could free me up to live in greater contentment.

Perhaps I have even more to learn from my mom if I am willing to listen and stop assuming. Recently, I was sitting on my mom's couch, enjoying a cup of coffee and a chat. I was thinking again of what I could do to help her enjoy this time that remains. I asked, "If you got a diagnosis and you knew you had six months left to live, how would you want to spend your time?" She looked around at scattered mysteries, at her house, and at me. She swept her arm in the air and said, "This!" Then she smiled.

31

2008 (Age 36): Because of My Son

I'm holding my sixteen-month-old son in my arms, his warm skin cooling in the air-conditioned lobby of the grocery store in my parents' neighborhood. As the doors to the outside open and close for shoppers departing the store, the hot July air drifts in. Anton is in just his diaper for now. I'll find clean clothes for him in a minute, after he's calmed down and after Jason's done in the men's bathroom trying to rinse out Anton's car seat cushion and cover. He washed it out last night in the hotel tub down the street and yesterday in a store bathroom as we drove across Wisconsin and Minnesota to visit my parents.

"I'm so sorry you keep getting sick, Anton," I say to him softly in his ear as he nestles his head on my shoulder and begins to breathe more slowly, his crying subsiding. "Dad's going to be out soon, and then we'll get you dressed again and you can sleep a little. Maybe that will make you feel better." I rock back and forth, side to side, hoping he will relax even further.

I glance at my watch and realize we're now 20 minutes beyond when I told my parents we'd likely arrive. My stomach squeezes again as it has for the past two days every time I think about seeing my parents. Actually, it's been almost three months of worry, three months since my dad miraculously agreed via email to a summertime meeting in their home near St. Cloud. Three months of wondering why now, of long conversations with Karen about lowering my expectations, of brief email exchanges with my dad to clarify where they live and when we'll arrive and what hotel we'll stay at during our weekend visit.

There's so much I don't understand or know, but I do know he graduated with his Master of Divinity last December. I know he's looking for work. I know just a few weeks ago he emailed me news that the doctors have found some abnormalities on his chest x-ray. I know he went in because of a persistent cough. He asked me to forward the email to Karen since they still haven't spoken. I know in my heart it's probably the colon cancer back and now metastasized, and while it seems irrational to think this way, I wonder if somehow he intuitively knew months earlier that something serious was wrong and that's what softened his heart enough to allow us to meet. But that storyline is like a movie that will end with a family that is fully healed, that decorates for Christmas together while happy music plays, that supports and accepts each other unconditionally. That's too much to expect. I need to see another path forward and to imagine a different narrative.

For the past three months, I've imagined narratives based on past experiences and that's been the cause of my anxiety. Now, standing here dealing with Anton's persistent upset tummy, probably not a manifestation of his own anxiety since at his age he has no idea what's going on, I decide to call my parents, to tell them why we're late.

"Hello?" My dad's voice on the other end sounds upbeat.

"Hi, Daddy. It's Jennifer. I wanted to let you know we're going to be a little bit longer. Anton was sick in the car yesterday a couple of times, but we thought he was better this morning so we let him eat whatever he wanted this morning at the hotel. Apparently, that was a mistake. Peach yogurt did not sit well with him, so we're cleaning him up right now."

"Where are you?"

"I think we're not far from your house. If I understand the directions you sent, we're near the corner where we turn left. We're at the grocery store on highway 15 … that's close, yes?"

"Oh, you're just a few blocks away. You can clean him up here, you know," my dad offers.

"Oh, OK. I just didn't want to show up and say, 'Hello, where's the bathroom and the washing machine?' right as I introduce you to your grandson."

"Oh," his low and slow chuckle surprises me. "Don't worry about it. Just come. We'll get him cleaned up. Poor little guy …"

"Yeah, I don't know what's wrong, but hopefully it'll pass soon. And I hope it's not contagious."

"Don't worry about it." I'm surprised at his casual acceptance. "We'll be here and we can get him all cleaned up."

"That was your grandpa," I say to Anton after I hang up the phone, tears springing to my eyes. "I think they must be excited to meet you because they don't even mind the thought of a stinky mess," I say in a silly voice. "You're worth it!" I nuzzle Anton's head as it lies on my shoulder, and I move in a small circle in the lobby, staying close to the diaper bag and my purse on the floor. Confused shoppers look me up and down. I feel a bit like a failure as a parent, unable even to dress my child for this public place. I focus on Anton instead. "And you know, you're the one who got your grandparents to open their doors again, right? I knew if I sent enough pictures of how cute you are that they'd say, 'Come on over!' I knew you'd melt their hearts!"

The noise of pouring rain draws my attention back to the exterior doors. "Oh great … Just what we needed."

"It's not great, but it's better," Jason says as he walks out of the men's room holding the car seat cushion. "It really needs to be washed in a machine."

"Well, good news," I respond.

Jason raises an eyebrow in suspicion of any good news at this point. "What? The rain will wash it off?" he says, gesturing to the doors.

"No, genuinely good news. I called my parents, and they said to come over, mess or not. My dad sounds upbeat. He even chuckled. I think they're just so excited to meet Anton that they don't care."

"That's something in our favor," Jason says.

"So let's wait to get him dressed when we get there. Anything we put on him will get soaked now anyway."

I watch as Jason runs to the car ahead of us, gets in the back seat to reassemble the now damp car seat, trying to avoid the mess in the rest of the back seat as he does so. When I see he's finished, I grab the diaper bag and my purse on one shoulder, balance Anton gently against my left shoulder, and half-sprint to the car. By the time Jason and I are in the front seat, we're soaked. I turn to look at him.

"If this isn't evidence that this is a terrible idea, I don't know what is," I say.

"No, it just makes it more of an adventure. And just think, if this hadn't all happened as a distraction, you'd have been even more sick with worry over seeing your parents for the first time in four years. And I would have been able to spend the past 24 hours thinking exclusively about meeting my in-laws for the first time and how much they hate me."

"They don't hate you. They don't even know you."

"Yes, but I'm the divorced man who defiled their daughter and took her away from them."

"Hardly. But I guess I didn't realize I wasn't the only one sick with worry. I'm sorry."

"I don't think Anton's sick with worry …"

We turn to look at him in his car seat. He's not crying anymore, so his belly must not hurt. That's a good sign. His skin isn't as white as it was before either.

"I just hope he doesn't have some virus that will get us all sick."

"That would be quite the reunion gift," Jason says.

The blocks to my parents' house fly by, and the tension in my stomach spreads to every part of my body. I'm trembling on the inside. I want to scream, "Turn around!" but I also want to deal with Anton's car seat somewhere other than a hotel bathroom or a grocery store lobby. I want to clean up the car. I want to give him some time to rest and not be in the car. And I realize that part of me wants to have this meeting over with, to know that I have met with my parents again, that all the cards and letters and emails and photos I sent over the past four years have resulted in a face-to-face meeting. I want to know that we can move forward without having to rehash everything.

And then we're there. The sudden summer downpour has ended, and my dad has the front door open in greeting. He looks a few years older, with a bit less hair, a bit more silver in what's left. My mom is behind him in the doorway. I want to push past him to her. I want to say hello to him and then hug her, but I can't do it that way. He's the entrance fee I have to pay to gain access to my mom.

I lift Anton's damp body from the back seat and walk with him towards the front door. "There he is!" I hear my dad say. "Ohhhh …" my mom says from behind him. I see her hand go up to her mouth. I hear Jason behind me. As I approach the door, I realize that Anton in my arms prevents me from a full-on hug from my dad and means I can only half-way hug my mom. That will wait until later. For now, it is enough to hear them welcome my son and offer him comfort, to feel Anton's warmth in my arms, and to hear my parents finally say, "It's nice to meet you, Jason," as they shake my husband's hand.

32

What Grade Do I Get

Perhaps it's because of all the years I spent teaching, but sometimes I think I'm trying to grade my dad's parenting. Teachers create rubrics that have categories to help students understand and learn from the grades they earn. With my dad, it's as if I've been creating a rubric for good parenting, determining the categories as I reflect on our relationship. Ideally, a rubric is created in advance of a graded assignment so that it can serve as a goal and a guide for those completing the work, but I wasn't capable as a child of telling my dad what I needed from him as a parent, and I'm certain he would not have enjoyed listening.

If I'm going to grade my dad as a parent, I feel comfortable excusing some of his failures because of his untreated mental illness. I also feel comfortable giving him credit for some great successes. Still, even after all this time reflecting, I have no idea what overall grade I would give him. There doesn't seem to be a rubric diverse and complex enough to cover all the facets. It also doesn't feel fair to grade someone who's dead. Grades are meant to assess performance, yes, and are best delivered when the learner has an opportunity to take feedback and use it to improve. My dad's done being a dad, so feedback won't help. And the older my own children get, the more terrified I am by the idea that someday my kids might give me a letter grade, especially if one day they realize I've done the same to my father.

My dad said several times he tried to be a better parent than his parents. I believe he succeeded. For all his flaws, he was far more affectionate, more communicative, and more open than I know his parents were with him. I try to be a better parent than my dad was. I try to learn from the mistakes I believe he made. Then there's the half-serious joke I sometimes make when talking to my husband about a parenting decision: "Do you think *this* will be the issue the kids go to therapy about?"

During one chat alone with my mom some years after my dad's death, I was telling her about how sometimes Edward, who was maybe five at the time, yelled for no reason and then said afterwards that he didn't even know why. I believed him. I had been reading books about how to help him deal with his emotions and learning a lot about what might be causing him to act out as he was. With my mom that morning, lingering over cups of coffee and uncleared breakfast dishes, I said what I was really afraid was true.

"I see Daddy in me. I think Edward yells sometimes and Anton feels like a failure sometimes because I'm like Daddy too much." I choked on the emotions welling up inside me, and I forced the truth out. "Sometimes after I yell at them, I can't remember why. Sometimes while I'm yelling at them, I think how minor it is what they've done. Sometimes I hear myself saying things he said."

"Oh, but it's so difficult to be a parent, Jennifer," my mom said. "And all parents yell from time to time."

"I worry that I'm repeating all his behaviors, that I *am* him. That I do what he did even though I know it's wrong."

"You're going to make mistakes. Your dad's problem wasn't that he made mistakes. It was that he never admitted it. You do. And he never got help for his depression. He never dealt with his own issues with his parents. And," she sighs, "oh, so many things were wrong, Jennifer. Not just yelling once in a while."

I want to believe her.

My husband and I took a local version of a nationally acclaimed parenting class. In eight hours spread over four weeks, we learned nine strategies for dealing with various parenting issues. I'll admit a small part of the draw was the free childcare each week. Jason and I got to sit together with other adults, no immediate parenting responsibilities. At the end of the four weeks, we got a certificate. As we walked out of the building for the last time, my kids asked what I was holding, and I said it was proof that we would never make a mistake as parents again. Then I laughed and said, "Oops! It says right here on the certificate that the road to good parenting is always under construction. I guess that means I'm going to make lots more mistakes." I'm pretty sure my kids already knew that.

What the certificate represented, according to the presenters, is that we're working hard. The class facilitators were great at boosting our self-esteem, saying from the very beginning of the first class that "the best parents take parenting classes because they know there's more to learn." There were moments during the class when I felt awesome about myself as a parent because a technique they mentioned trying was something I already do. As new strategies were explained to us, I had moments of clarity when parenting seemed so easy—a series of dialogues that I would more carefully and calmly have with my children.

And then I'd spend the week with my children. I'd yell. They'd react. I'd be distant. I'd make so many mistakes.

On the first night of the class, one of the teachers said, "Wouldn't you like to start enjoying more of the time you spend with your kids?" I thought about it, and my answer was a resounding, "Yes!" My kids are awesome people. Everyone tells me that—teachers, friends, people at church. My kids are funny, smart, kind, and interesting. I want to enjoy time with them. What a cool concept, I thought. If I stopped yelling, policing, nagging, and a host of other activities, maybe I could start enjoying. Maybe I could sit back more often and just be there with them.

I wonder if my dad truly enjoyed spending time with me, especially when I was younger. I remember family meals growing up, how sometimes the food was long gone and we remained at the table. Sometimes it was an uncomfortable, forced decision to stay. My sister or I would have challenged something my dad said or brought up some idea he disagreed with, and until he was done preaching, we weren't allowed to leave. There were other instances, however, when the family would stay at the table long after the food was gone and no one felt forced. We were engaged in genuine disagreement or dialogue. We talked about faith, politics, life, school, the future. I learned from these conversations a lot about being a teacher, about debating, about defending my position.

On good days, my dad was fully present for us, and it was fabulous. And on bad days, my dad was there in some pretty negative ways. On those bad days, the really bad days when the depression was sucking him into a black hole of negativity, I wish he hadn't been there for me.

And so I walk away sometimes from my kids. I go somewhere else to fume for ten minutes. I try to remember that sometimes being there is the worst thing I can do for them because I can't be there in a positive way. I see this as progress, as proof that I have learned from my father's mistakes.

※

My dad told me on more than one occasion that he was proud of me. I'm pretty sure my dad admired the person I was becoming and became—most of the time. Sure, it was confusing to be told those messages by someone who also flew into a rage for no reason sometimes, someone who would also find ways to put me down or put me in my place. But I recognize that it would have been much worse if he had never said, "I'm proud of you."

I tell my kids I'm proud of them for all sorts of things: being generous, smiling at someone in need, making friends, getting a walk in a baseball game, cheering on their teammates, expressing emotions, learning something new, trying something new. I know that there are things I have said to Anton and Edward that will stay with them in positive ways for years and years.

When I set aside my fears about parenting, when I put down the rubric where I've circled "needs improvement" in too many categories for myself, I can be genuinely proud of the parent I am. I know I have handled some situations with Anton and Edward worlds better than my dad would have or did. But it is difficult to maintain that positivity. Every time I start to feel proud of myself as a parent, I worry that I am just deluding myself.

Maybe I should try to turn my skill for post-conversational paranoia into an aptitude for post-conversational celebration. Maybe I need to spend more time thinking about how a positive thing I said to my children (or a student or a colleague or a friend) may be carried along and have an impact on them, on their children, and on their children's children.

My sister does not have kids and knows me so well that she has been a tremendous sounding board to me as a parent, letting me vent and helping me see my children's perspectives. She has reminded me that I've spent a lifetime battling my own perfectionism, and it haunts me still as a parent. If I'm grading myself as a parent, I probably need to accept that "effective" doesn't have to mean "A plus." And sometimes I have to be willing to give myself a good grade. Sometimes I need to celebrate my parenting wins.

I wonder about the effects of perfectionism on my dad. Would he have been a better parent if after he made mistakes, he had been able to see that failure for what it was—temporary? Perhaps an important lesson awaits me there.

My relationship with my kids is fraught with challenges, just as my dad's relationship with me was. I will try to live the moments. I will be present in a game of cards with Edward or as I listen to Anton talk about his friends. I will try to enjoy spending time with them every chance I get. Maybe it is by being there in the moment with them, holding both the wisdom and the mistakes of previous generations, that I can best honor my father's desire to be a better parent than his parents. Maybe I will make the most progress when I let go of trying and worrying. Maybe it's just like what I told students for years: when we forget about the grades, we learn and achieve more.

While I'm not willing to grade my dad's performance as a parent, a lot of what I've written about my dad was also written partially *to* him. I think of my writings as a chance to have a conversation with him, to try to explain my side of things, and, yes, to give him feedback on his parenting choices. I picture my dad as I write and revise. And then I hear my children's future adult voices say to me, "Want to read the essays I wrote about your parenting choices, Mom?" In my imagination, I reply, "Hmmm … Maybe wait until I'm dead and come read them to my grave."

Perhaps this is the pinnacle of post-conversational paranoia—imagining the memoir your children write that evaluates you as a parent. Perhaps it's different after death. Perhaps my dad, his spirit freed from the body he rejected, at peace with life's unfairness, is now free of the paranoia of being judged. Most days that sounds like heaven to me.

33

2011 (Age 39): Because Change Is Complex

"What was that all about?" I ask Karen as we finish getting Anton into his booster seat and Edward's car seat settled in. We are standing outside of my car, under a streetlight, my parents' church a block away. Our visit alone, without Mike and Jason, has had some interesting twists and turns, but before we go to the restaurant for dinner, I need to understand better what I missed during the end of Saturday evening Mass.

"I mean, I know Edward was fussy, but I took care of it by taking him to the back of church. Then Mass ends 15 minutes later and Anton comes running back to me crying and Daddy comes to tell me I need to work on my parenting skills. What happened?"

Karen is clearly angry and trying to hold it in. We know we have a limited window here before our delayed arrival at the restaurant will be noticed, causing more trouble.

"He hasn't changed at all, Jennifer. Sometimes I wish we'd never reconciled with them." Tears start to come to her eyes and she fights to hold them back so there will be no breakdown, no sign for them later that anything is wrong.

I want to know what happened—I feel like I need to know to help Anton—but I don't want her to get even more upset. I decide to talk a bit to give her time to gather herself. "Listen, don't get me wrong. I know this is hard. I just keep focused on Mom and on knowing that

Anton and Edward will be able to say they knew their grandparents. Now that Daddy's stopped treatments, we have no idea how long it'll be, but at least I can tell the kids later that they met him and he knew them."

"But will they want to have met him? I mean earlier today with Anton's blanket … that was just so typically Daddy and just cruel."

"I know." I think back to watching my Dad torment Anton by pulling his beloved yellow blanket away from him and hiding it behind his back, putting it above his head, not stopping even as Anton cried and appeared visibly upset.

"Stop, please, Daddy," I had said, trying not to use the voice I'd had as a child.

"*Stop, please, Daddy*," he had mocked me.

"He's tired and he can't handle being teased right now."

"Oh, thank you so much for telling me how to be a good parent. Otherwise, I would never know."

"I'm just saying please let him have the blanket so he will calm down and I can get him to take a nap."

"*Fine*," he had said, throwing the blanket at me. "You are no fun at all and your son needs to learn to take a little light-hearted teasing."

Bringing myself back to this moment with Karen, I say, "So, deep breath, can you tell me what happened in there quickly, before we go to the restaurant and before we freeze to death out here?" I try to make a little joke to keep her from crying.

Something works because anger replaces tears. "So we're sitting there and after you took Edward to the back, Anton clearly wanted to follow you. He was sitting next to me and turning around to look to the back of church. He didn't stand at the right times and was fidgeting. Daddy just reached out and grabbed his arm, I think pretty tightly because he managed to pull Anton to his feet. Then Daddy leaned down and hissed in his ear, 'turn around, stand up, and pay attention.' Anton just freaked out, I could tell. I'll admit I sort of froze because it just took me back to so many times when we got yelled at like that for not being perfect. Anton leaned over towards me and started to cry. I felt awful, so I reached out and put my arm around him."

I look into the back seat of the car at Anton. He is rubbing his fingers along the edge of his blanket and looking sleepy. Edward has actually fallen asleep, tired out from crying in the back of church and from a long two days of travel and schedule interruptions. My stomach turns because I think of how I didn't protect Anton from that moment.

"Then Mass ended and Anton ran to the back, as you know, and was still crying. He just wanted you to comfort him and tell him it was OK. And you were back there with Edward, calming him down. So I tried to hurry back there to be with you …"

"And that's why Daddy came back and told me that I need to teach my kids to behave in church and that apparently he didn't raise us right either since you couldn't manage Anton and couldn't even get him to stay to listen to the postlude music."

"Yup."

I sigh and feel so tired. "We have to get to the restaurant. We can do this. We can do this for Mom, and for whatever other reasons I once thought were important. We can survive this. And we can even have some good moments, like we did earlier at lunch."

She nods and we hug briefly. I get in the driver's seat and in just a few minutes we are outside the buffet restaurant, Edward waking up as I carry him in. I snuggle my face against his neck, give him a few soft kisses there, giggle at him. I hold Anton's hand and squeeze it, asking him if he's going to have ice cream after dinner, getting him excited about dinner out. I am trying to be in this moment and love my children.

There's a part of me that really doesn't want to be at this restaurant, the same chain where I can remember so many ugly dinners with my dad. They are waiting when we arrive. "Want to sit over there?" I ask as we move into the restaurant.

"Sure," my dad says, and I think *we can do this.*

Anton runs to the end of the table. "Aunt Kaykay, you sit here, and Mama, you sit here," he gestures to his left and right.

"I want to sit there," my dad says, pointing to the same end of the table.

Karen sighs and says, "Can't you just let him sit there? He's four."

I don't know if it's the sigh or the question or the words or the day or the fact that he's struggling with my kids not growing up Catholic or this moment in his life or nothing at all or everything, but my dad is done.

"You always do this," he says. "You always put me last. You always have. What I want doesn't matter. You don't respect me and you don't respect my authority within this family." His voice is rising in pitch and in volume.

Karen stands next to the chair Anton had selected for her and looks directly at my dad. "I am not doing this tonight," she says quietly but firmly.

"*I am not doing this tonight,*" he repeats in a mocking tone. People at surrounding tables are watching, unable to avoid hearing him as he is almost yelling. The staff person bringing the highchair for Edward is looking to me for guidance on where to put it. My dad continues, "What is it that you *will* do tonight? Will you respect your parents? Will you help your sister's children learn to behave and respect their grandparents?"

I gesture to a spot, the highchair is placed there, and the staff person disappears. I want to follow.

"I am going to the salad bar," Karen says firmly, "and when I come back, I will eat dinner with the family. But we are not doing this. Whatever it is that you need out of this fight, I'm not giving it to you." I can see, despite her outward calm, that Karen is shaking. I take Anton's hand again, still holding Edward, and head towards the drinks.

Anton and Edward are quiet, which is not normal. Do I say something to them? Do I pretend this isn't happening? I'm not sure what the right thing is to do. "Anton, don't worry about any of that," I decide to say. "Grandpa is not feeling well right now and we are going to hope that he feels better soon. Let's just try to behave super well during dinner, OK guys?" I help Anton get a glass of lemonade and we walk back to the table.

Karen is back, seated with a salad plate. She and I exchange a glance. "Can I leave Edward here while I go get some food for the three of us with Anton?"

"Of course!" She looks across at Edward in the highchair and starts to talk to him about how much food there is and what he hopes to eat. I smile at her, so grateful she is here, so grateful she is helping me navigate this situation.

Anton and I bring plates back for me, him, and Edward. Everyone is eating, but no one is really talking. Like usual, I try to engage my mom. She is, after all, a large part of the reason I fought to have them back in our lives.

"Have you heard from Aunt Oney lately?" I use the pet name she had for her favorite sister. She tells me a bit about a conversation she had with her and her husband recently, mostly her husband due to some health issues Oney had experienced. Too late, I remember that my aunt and uncle aren't a popular topic with my dad, but he doesn't appear to be listening, eating his food and staring off into the distance.

Karen, Anton, and I end up talking a little bit about one of his favorite shows. He starts to relax and talk more about a game he's been making up, how he wants to play restaurant when we get home, how he wants to call his dad later. "I've never eaten in a rest-er-not like this before," he says, using his word for restaurant and gesturing to the buffets. "Has Dad ever eaten in this kind of rest-er-not before?"

"Oh yes, many times," I tell him. "I think you have too, but maybe not … I can't remember. Let's ask him when we call him tonight to say goodnight."

"That's nice," my mom says, "that this is a new experience for you, Anton."

I smile at her. My dad still isn't talking, but I'm hoping he's thawing and not escalating inside.

"Ice cream?" Anton says to me, remembering what I'd said outside. "Yes!" I say and lead him to the soft serve. He takes far more than he will eat, but I don't even care. I just want him to be as happy as possible in this moment.

Dinner ends and we drift out to the cars. "Thanks for dinner, Daddy, Mom," Karen and I say a couple of times. "We'll see you tomorrow morning around nine then," indicating we're headed to the hotel for the night. I can feel myself almost free. We are tucking Anton and Edward into the back seat when I see my dad's window roll down. He waves me over.

I don't want to go, but I do. What choice do I have? These times, they are the price I pay for knowing that I will not feel as much regret later. I take a deep breath, prepared for anything.

I stand a few feet away from his car and see my mom staring straight ahead out the windshield.

"Jennifer, you are an amazing parent," my dad says. "I'm sorry about all that."

I freeze. I look into his eyes and see sincerity there. I think I might also see a little bit of fear. Fear that I won't come back tomorrow after all, or later? Fear that I will keep him from his grandchildren? Fear that when he dies, which he knows is coming sooner now that the cancer will grow unabated, he will be alone—or that my mom will be alone? Fear that he will have regrets?

I don't ask. I simply smile and say, "It's OK. Thank you. See you tomorrow morning." He half smiles and rolls up his window. I turn and walk back to Karen and my boys.

"So?" Karen says to me as I get in and buckle my seatbelt. I sit for a moment, my hand resting on the buckle, unable to find the words.

"He apologized," I whisper. "He said I'm an amazing parent." I look up at Karen and see my surprise mirrored in her eyes.

"Well, huh." She looks out the front windshield. "I did not see that coming. What did you say?"

"Nothing much, I don't think. It felt so strange. I think he really meant it. Like, I don't think it was just an 'I'm going to die and what if it's tonight and this is the last interaction with her that I have' sort of thing."

"And if it was? Do you care?"

"Not really!" I chuckle. "I'll take an apology from him any way I can get it. Sorry you didn't get to hear it."

"Whatever," Karen waves her hand. "It wasn't really about me. Something bugged him about church and the kids' behavior or ... I don't know. I have never understood him and I probably never will. I don't know what set him off tonight any more than all the other times. Honestly, like all the other times, it was probably something else entirely, not even about Anton or Edward in church."

"True. Was it ever really about them—or us?" I start the car to turn on the much-needed heat. My hands rest on the wheel as I look up in the rearview mirror and see Anton watching me, looking maybe scared, certainly unsure. "What's up, Anton? You doing OK?" He nods. "Ready to go back to the hotel and go to bed?" He nods again.

"And tomorrow we go home," Karen says.

"And see Dad!" I say to Anton with a smile into the mirror. He is looking out the window now as the view changes, watching buildings, seeing the lights, looking into other cars, dreaming and thinking and growing in beautiful ways I cannot even imagine.

34

Not about Me

One woman who attended my dad's funeral was a fellow student of his at St. John's University when he returned there in his sixties to earn his Master of Divinity in Theology. She was probably in her twenties or thirties, and I met her briefly in the back of the church as she expressed her condolences.

"I was your dad's classmate," she said to me. "I'm so sorry for your loss."

"Thank you."

"It was so wonderful having your dad in class," she said. "He added so much to our discussions. He had insights into life experience that the rest of us didn't have. And he was so kind and generous. It was great to have someone from his generation in our classroom, but especially great to have him."

I smiled and nodded. I thought about my dad as a returning adult student for the first time. I always loved having these students in my classes. They come from wide-ranging backgrounds, always have loads of real-life experience, and almost always are highly motivated to work hard and learn a lot. They recognize references to cultural moments that many of the traditional-aged students don't, and, more importantly, they can act as a reality check on the other students. They reinforce messages I give and challenge my thinking more readily than younger students do.

I can see my dad thriving in that situation. If I put myself in the role of teacher, surrounded by twenty-somethings who want to be prison chaplains or ministers of care, guiding people through some of the most difficult of life circumstances but having little to no life experience of their own to help guide them, I can see how valuable my dad would be as a student.

Still, because of my life experiences with him, I was surprised at this woman's completely positive comments, even a little angry at the way she was going to remember my dad. I suspect she never imagined that beneath the soft, helpful, life-enriching exterior lurked a man who was haunted by demons of negativity, anger, and depression. Or if she did suspect it, she didn't know what an absolute pain it had been at times to be his daughter. She saw only one side of him, as most people did.

I remembered as a teenager imagining his funeral and how I would tell the truth about him, shocking many and validating some. I never gave the revenge eulogy I imagined and I don't believe it would have helped me feel better if I had.

I realize that some people beyond my sister and my mom share my experience of my dad. Others in his life dealt with his prickliness and his mood swings. I read about it in his journals and witnessed the awkward tensions with some coworkers. But I suspect a lot of other people didn't know that side. From their perspective, he was "a great guy," "a wonderful support," "a fabulous musician."

For a long time I resented that. How dare the world label my dad in these positive ways? How dare they proclaim his goodness? They needed to know the truth. They needed to stop saying that he was wonderful. They needed to stop measuring him based on only their experiences of him.

Then I had an important thought one morning: maybe it's not about me.

To be fair, I've known for a long time that I'm not the center of the universe, not even of my own little universe. I don't consider myself an exceptionally narcissistic person, no more self-absorbed than the next person. But still, this realization—this sudden awareness that maybe my dad's life wasn't about me—came to me as a shock. And then I burst out laughing.

Why would I ever have imagined that my dad's life *was* about me? Why would I ever have tried to define or validate or understand my dad's existence solely from the perspective of his relationship to me? My dad was a person and should be seen as a person, not just as my dad.

As a parent, I try to show my kids that I'm a human being first and foremost, not just their mother. When I'm exhausted and stressed and frustrated and I yell at them, I remind them in my apology later that I'm a human being who makes mistakes. I try to share with them bits about my work life, my thoughts on politics, my day, my likes and dislikes, all to help them see me as a human being distinct from themselves. Sometimes it seems to be working.

"How was your day, Mom?" Anton asked me at dinner one night when he was just nine or ten.

I looked up with surprise and saw genuine curiosity on his face.

"It was OK," I said, struggling to remember what happened. It's a tough question, and for a moment I felt sympathy for my children, faced with that question from me every day. "I had good classes. I met with some students. I think I helped."

"Good!" he said and continued scooping up mashed potatoes and corn.

I have reminded them often enough that I am more than just their mom, but I realized I need to remember that too. I take being their mom very seriously, but I have to be careful not to take it too seriously. I can't be Supermom because I'm also busy being Jennifer. And I think that's as it should be. Mom is one of the roles I play, albeit perhaps one of the most important, but it's not the only role, and it shouldn't be. As they grow older and I am less a part of their daily lives, it is essential that I stay their mom and also give myself permission to be all that I am: a vice president at a technical college, a writer, an organist, a reader, a daughter, a friend, a baseball fan.

While I was busy explaining to my kids (and myself) over and over that a parent is much more than a parent, I forgot to apply it to my dad. I forgot that when I contemplate my dad's life and whether it had value or whether my dad was a "good person," I have to take in lots more data than just what he was like as a dad. I have to consider him as Jim.

I have to remember all the elderly people to whom he ministered when he was in charge of the Apostolate for Older Adults and later the Ministry of Care at the Cathedral in Winona, Minnesota. I remember reading notes and cards from these people and from these people's children after their deaths, cards which sang his praises as a caring, loving, and faith-filled guide through their difficulties.

In his good moments, he knew they valued him. He wrote about how they enjoyed his coming to see them. "From their comments I can tell that at least for some of them, my visit is important." He talked about visiting a parishioner to give communion, to pray together, to talk, or just to be with them in their suffering. He wrote initials or only first names most of the time, and I find myself thinking about how Leola or KL or Bertha viewed my dad. They probably saw him as his classmate did, as a generous, warm-hearted person. Perhaps they saw within him a spark of the divine coming to care for them. I know he learned a lot from them as well:

> So many of them allow me into their lives, some more intimately than others, but nevertheless they allow me to walk along with them, so to speak, for a while, sharing with me their life stories. In this encounter I am convinced I am also encountering the Divine.
>
> Some of the stories people share about their lives are profoundly moving, some are tragic, some are of joy-filled times. All of these stories are better than anything I could read in a book because they are stories of real people living real lives. And when I try to reflect back to them something of what I hear, they so often welcome the opportunity to be heard and come to see things in

a different light in their life because they have had a chance to be heard, to be listened to.

And what a blessing this is for me. I have learned so much.

I can imagine how he listened to these people, validating their experiences. I can see how they would have loved him for it.

I have to remember the countless people over the years who came up to me and said how lucky I was to have my dad in my life because he was such an exceptional musician. Someone would stop me after Mass and tell me how his music was so helpful in their prayer life or that they "just loved that piece at the end—what a joyous celebration of the Lord!" His performances gave thousands of people great joy and moments of deep contemplation. I was one of them.

I think of the applause I heard and added to after a particularly amazing postlude. I think of all the people whose spiritual lives were uplifted because of his divine music. That's not about me. If I measure Jim in these moments, my assessment of him shifts considerably.

Of course, these people didn't know him very well. And some of them did know him and never let on to me that they saw his problems.

I met up to have breakfast with one of his former coworkers several years after my dad's death. Because of the abrupt nature of my break from my parents and the fact that they moved before we reconciled, there were a number of people who were a part of my adolescence from whom I was abruptly cut off. I wanted to reconnect with one man who had meant a lot to me and, I believe, to my dad as well. After we discussed our kids' lives and what we were doing now, almost as we were about to say goodbye, the conversation shifted to my dad. I took a deep breath and told him the truth—that life is easier without him.

No shocked expression crossed his face. Instead, he gave me an understanding smile, took a deep breath, and told me the truth: "I'm sorry I wasn't able to be for your dad who he needed me to be." We let a moment of silence pass before he continued. "I knew he was hurting sometimes, but I wasn't trained to help with that. I know at times he wanted me to help him with some deep issues, but …" He lifted his hands and let them fall on the table between us. "I couldn't help him."

"No one could," I said. "He wasn't ready for what help would have meant, I think." My dad's former coworker looked a bit relieved, and I realized that other people too had dealt with, in some small measure, the frustration of knowing my dad needed help. Months after I absolved this man of not fixing my dad's problems, I came to absolve myself more too. I didn't ruin my dad's life. I wasn't responsible for getting him the help he needed. Just as I can step back and judge my father's accomplishments without factoring myself into the equation, so too must I remember his mental illnesses were not about me.

※

A few months after my dad died, my mom showed me a letter she had received. "It's from the man your dad visited in prison the last couple of years." I asked my mom for more details. "He was convicted of murder but claims he didn't do it. Your dad believed him, and apparently so did a lot of other people who worked hard for his release. It hasn't worked yet."

"What's the letter like?" I asked my mom.

"Read it yourself if you like. It's long."

I told Jason about its contents when I returned home. "It's full of these incredible statements, all high praise for my dad. It's like this man knew a completely different person than I did."

"Maybe he did."

Later, I asked my mom if I could have the letter. For a moment, she didn't remember where it was, and I started to panic. The letter had come to represent something important—a view of my dad from the outside. I wanted to understand better who the man was that interacted with this prisoner. I wanted to gain that perspective more clearly. My mom found the letter in a manila folder with the others the man had written to my dad over the years. "Can I take the whole file?" I asked.

"Sure, I don't want it."

The letters helped me bring closer the idea that was then hovering on the horizon, that my dad's life was not about me. This prisoner wrote that "Jim was an amazing man, and I want as many people to know this as possible." Perhaps this truth deserves to be read as much as any other truth I experienced.

The man enclosed an essay he wrote, "The Difference a Person Makes," that he was sharing with others to honor my dad's memory. I see in what he describes what I'd heard others say throughout the years. He said my dad encouraged him and guided him. He wrote that my dad was "a very close and dear friend—who impacted my life in a major way." I wonder if this man realizes how few true friends my dad ever had in life.

He called my dad's heart "more precious than gold" and marveled that he came out weekly to visit him. I didn't realize the visits were every week. He called my dad an angel of compassion who accepted him for who he was. My dad helped him learn to process life events and helped him be open-minded. This man wrote paragraph after paragraph about lessons learned, in poignant and authentic ways. He used my dad's initials in the same way that my dad used initials throughout his journals to refer to others whose paths crossed his:

> By opening my heart to J.S., I found what it is like to experience life's greatest gift—unconditional love. Even though my philosophy for avoiding emotional pangs was to keep people at a distance, J.S. had an effortless way of turning cement to putty. Immediately, we had an immense connection and a close-knit bond soon followed. I discovered in order to freely love anyone—especially 'self'—I must allow myself to be vulnerable, which I am now OK with doing.

My dad helped him to value himself. "In spite of being incarcerated for 4+ years, I have more liberty now than I have had in my entire life." I marvel at lines like "what many of us dream of accomplishing, but so few of us ever ascertain, in my opinion, J.S. gracefully achieved."

My dad—Jim—changed this man's life. His willingness to visit this man in prison opened doors for him that had been closed before.

Thinking of the impact my dad had on this man, on all the people to whom he ministered over the years, makes me consider again that while my dad helped give me life and a few good lessons along the way, maybe, just maybe, he didn't live his life for me. Maybe his life had value not because of me but because of something else he did. Maybe in the end he was able to set aside or understand all his darkness and anger and depression and negativity long enough to do some greater good.

This man's essay included a belief that he helped my dad. My dad willingly shared information and stories with him. He wrote, "A part of me believes we gave each other a sense of peace and tranquility, so to speak, which enabled each of us to take the next step towards reaching our destination."

I wonder what my dad said to him. I wonder if maybe finally my dad found a confidante. Maybe my dad was able to talk freely to this man, a total stranger with whom he found an intense bond. Did they see in each other's brokenness an invitation to be fully themselves? Did he talk about his own troubled relationships, about his flaws, his realities? Maybe my dad was able to unburden himself at last, to share the things he alluded to but never wrote down even in his journals.

Part of me feels instantly resentful if that is the case. What right does this total stranger have to know my dad more closely than I did? But I push down those feelings of resentment and replace them with my new insight. This relationship wasn't about me. And I don't need to know what they talked about. I just need to remember this man's words when I take the measure of my father. When I measure the value of his life, I put myself in the correct proportion.

My dad's mind is gone, his accumulated wisdom with it. His book collection is dispersed, his papers all filed or recycled. His work is done. His pain and suffering are at an end. But his influence lives on.

I'll tell my children about their grandfather—the truth about him. I'll tell them about his depression and his anger. I'll tell them about his musical ability and the plague of self-doubt. I'll show them the essay from the prisoner. I'll tell them how others saw him. In telling these stories, I'll remind myself that my father's life cannot be defined solely in relation to me. And even as I remember the pain, I will celebrate that our lives have meaning if we look at the ways in which our small actions diffuse throughout the world and work for good.

Postscript

Permission

Since I brought them over from my mom's place, my dad's journals sat in stacks in various locations throughout the house often in precariously balanced piles on chairs and countertops. I've communed with them from time to time over the past twelve years. In the in-between times, they were a physical reminder of this project, of my attempt to make sense of my relationship with my dad.

I used them, perhaps against his wishes, to try to gain some measure of peace. Whenever I felt guilt over reading his words, words he perhaps didn't want me to read, I reminded myself how much he valued reading others' journals, how from time to time his own journals beg for an interested audience—asking, "Do I have anything to say to others?" I heard his sadness when he thought of how "in the end it can all be chucked anyway," all his papers and files. I remember the poem he wrote in one journal on his forty-fifth birthday that contained the lines "When we are gone, what is left behind? / Will anyone notice where we once were?" I tell myself that by reading his words I can bring meaning to his suffering—to our suffering.

Some days, I'm convinced that my attempts have failed because I feel I don't know him any better than I did the day he died. Other days, I see how communing with his spirit has helped me grow in ways I never anticipated. I can read his words with compassion now. I can open his journals to any page and readily identify the themes that run throughout them. I understand better how he viewed the world, himself, his work, and his family. I know somewhat better the role I played in his life. And I know he found joy in the love of his wife, the accomplishments of his daughters, the beauty of nature, and the marvel of music.

When I see a beautiful natural setting and I think of how much he would have liked it, I pause and treasure it, aware of my own mortality in ways I wasn't before reflecting on his. From time to time, I stop and look at my children, really seeing them in a way I didn't before thinking about identity so deeply. And when people give me sympathy about my dad's death, I can accept it a little more easily. I can say to myself, yes, there was a loss there, of what was, what could have been, and what never would have been.

It's easier now to say, "I don't miss my dad," than when I first realized it was true. It's easier for me to take a deep breath and know that's OK. Part of me thinks that if he were here right now, he'd say he understands that. He might even say that's natural and normal. He could surprise me sometimes with the profound ways he understood the mysteries of life. I think he'd tell me to hug those beautiful grandchildren of his, treasure every moment, admire the bird soaring through the blue sky, give to the poor, and live my life.

I think he'd tell me it's time to put away his journals too. I think he's right, and yet I cry at the thought of it. I continue to worry that there are some lessons in there that I need to learn better. I wonder if I need to dig deeper into my past in order to avoid going along the same path with my kids that he went on with me. I know that's just part of the legacy of an emotionally abusive parent—the constant self-doubt that I am good enough. I need to tell myself that even if I stop reading his journals and stop having conversations with him on the page, if I stop writing and revising about *his* parenthood, I will continue to grow into the best parent I can.

As a parent, my children are in my thoughts every day and they will be forever. It turns out being a child is also forever. Regardless of whether your parent is a hero or a villain in your story, or something in between like mine, it's not possible to write them out of the script.

From the moment I had consciousness and far past the moment of his death, my dad has been on my mind. But he doesn't need to be at the center. I need to claim the lead role in my own life.

So I grant myself permission to walk on with memories of him that I accept more fully as reality. I grant myself permission to think of him sometimes and not miss him, knowing that the absence of grief is still painful. I grant myself permission to feel sad for him and for myself—even to miss him for a brief moment—and to know that my ungrieving is a lifelong journey. And I grant myself permission to continue to ask myself the question my dad once posed in his journals: What is it that life is calling me to at this moment?

Acknowledgments

A couple of weeks after my dad died, I couldn't sleep. The events of the previous weeks were on constant repeat in my mind and when I tried to shut them down, I worried I would forget important details.

One night around midnight, I went downstairs to the computer in our study. For a couple of hours, tears streaming, I typed up memories of the last moments with my dad, of the trips we'd taken to visit him in his last few months, of his funeral and how I had felt.

In the days and weeks that followed, I returned to write more. I first shared the essay I wrote about my dad's books with two close friends—Amy Reddinger and Crystal Hendrick. Their early encouragement helped me continue to use writing to explore my feelings and document my journey through a strange sort of grieving.

Amy later read a long series of essays and then connected me with a friend of hers, writing coach Elizabeth Jarrett Andrew. I am grateful to Elizabeth for showing me how important it is to put myself and my reader into key moments. With her guidance, I wrote the alternating narratives and learned to map and remap my way through the insights of the essays I had written. Elizabeth also connected me with Beth Wright, who challenged me to revise deeply. From her, I learned more about how to let go of what I thought I wanted to say so that readers could see better what they needed to hear. A friend, former colleague, and amazing poet—Carrie Shipers—provided a fresh set of eyes and line edits at a time when I really needed both. Thanks to the collective wisdom of many, I have eliminated at least as many words as remain. I alone am responsible for the ultimate decision of which words I kept.

When I felt ready for my manuscript to become a book, I was fortunate to read the amazing memoir by Shenandoah Chefalo, *Garbage Bag Suitcase*, and see inside it the name of Mission Point Press. From my first interactions with Doug Weaver and Tanya Muzumdar at MPP, I felt I had found the right company—in both meanings of the word—to move to publication. Tanya helped me see the overarching structure anew, inspiring me to write new pieces to fill in gaps, and Tanya, Doug, and Chris Johns all helped me begin to see potential audiences and how to reach them. Every interaction I had with MPP staff made me feel valued and heard.

I learned more about writing and revising from this memoir project than anything that came before it, including teaching writing for 19 years. Over the years I learned a lot from colleagues, students, and teachers who influenced me, and I am grateful to them all.

Working full time while writing and revising this memoir has been a challenge at times. My husband, Jason, always told me to prioritize it. He and I had hundreds of conversations about content, sequencing, doubts, fears, and moments of triumph. Jason always tells me to go for it, almost always has the perspective I need, and never fails to make me laugh at a time when I am taking myself too seriously. Jason, all those years ago you wooed me through your beautifully written emails. I am so fortunate to have a talented thinker and writer like you as my forever partner.

My mom, Marie, was a tremendous support to me through the long journey of writing and revising my memoir. She has always thought I am wonderful. I dismissed her admiration of me too often, unwilling to believe I was as accomplished as she said I was. She was also an essential resource and collaborator on this book, and I am awed by the courage she has as I tell our story. Mom, I am grateful for your memories, your companionship, and your unwavering confidence in me.

My sister, Karen, also helped fill a number of memory gaps. She told me that she comes across in this book as almost a superhero.

That's because since we were little kids, she's been a hero to me. Yes, Karen, you've annoyed me sometimes, but you also saved my life. I wouldn't be where I am or who I am today without you. Thank you.

From the first word I wrote of this memoir, I have thought about how I am a mom to Anton and Edward, my beautiful, amazing, intelligent boys. I hope someday parts of this book help you in some small way to decode your own experiences and understand better the choices I made. I am incredibly proud of you and marvel at all you are. I hope you can see that your lives are your own—that they are not about me. I promise that I will keep working to see that too.

And Daddy, thanks for keeping your journals. They helped me write this book with you. I think you would be proud.

About the Author

Jennifer Stolpa Flatt is an educator, writer, and church singer and musician with decades of experience playing the organ, piano, and trumpet. Although baptized and confirmed as a Catholic, Jennifer has been a practicing member of the Evangelical Lutheran Church of America (ELCA) since 2004.

Previously a professor of English and Spanish, Jennifer currently serves as the vice president of student services for a technical college in Wisconsin. Jennifer is also a reader, baseball fan, and mom to two boys, Anton and Edward. She lives in Marinette, Wisconsin, with her husband, Jason, in the Victorian home they are restoring.

Printed in the USA
CPSIA information can be obtained
at www.ICGtesting.com
CBHW031548240724
12123CB00001B/2